D1572922

A HISTORY OF JEWISH LITERATURE
VOLUME I

Israel Zinberg's *History of Jewish Literature*

Israel Zinberg

A HISTORY OF
JEWISH
LITERATURE

TRANSLATED AND EDITED BY BERNARD MARTIN

The Arabic-Spanish Period

THE JEWISH PUBLICATION SOCIETY
OF AMERICA
PHILADELPHIA

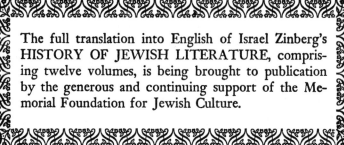
The full translation into English of Israel Zinberg's
HISTORY OF JEWISH LITERATURE, compris-
ing twelve volumes, is being brought to publication
by the generous and continuing support of the Memorial Foundation for Jewish Culture.

Library of Congress Cataloging in Publication Data

Zinberg, Israel, 1873–1938.
  A history of Jewish literature.

  Translation of Di geshikhte fun der literatur bay
Yidn.
  CONTENTS: v. 1. The Arabic-Spanish period.—
  Includes bibliographical references.
v. 2. French and German Jewry in the early Middle
Ages. The Jewish community of medieval Italy.
    1. Jewish literature—History and criticisms.
I. Title.
PJ5008.Z5313   809'.889'24   72–183310
ISBN 0–8295–0228–9 (v. 1)

Contents

The influence of Arabic culture — Midrash and Aggadah as sources of religious poetry — Jannai and Kallir — Ḥasdai Ibn Shaprut as patron and culture-bearer—Menaḥem Ibn Saruk and his *Maḥberet*—Dunash ben Labrat and his polemic—Dunash and Arabic meter—Menaḥem's letter to Shaprut—The controversy between Menaḥem's and Dunash's pupils—Ḥayyuj and Ibn Jannaḥ and their philological work—Joseph Ibn Abitur as liturgical poet—Samuel Ha-Nagid as Talmudist and scholar—Samuel Ha-Nagid as the creator of neo-Hebrew secular poetry.

The cultural-historical significance of Samuel Ha-Nagid — Solomon Ibn Gabirol—His thirst for knowledge in youth—His pride in his poetry—The poet's illness and melancholy—His friendship with Jekutiel ben Isaac—His dirges—The poet's loneliness and hatred of his environment—The poet in exile—Ibn Gabirol's world outlook—His religious poems—National moods in Ibn Gabirol's poetry—Ibn Gabirol as a philosopher—His *Mekor Ḥayyim* — His *Keter Malchut*—Metrical forms in Ibn Gabirol's poems.

Contents

Chapter Three: MOSES IBN EZRA / 65

Moses Ibn Ezra; his carefree youth—Songs of joy—His unhappy love—The poet as wanderer—Poems of despair and hope—The death of the poet's beloved—The poet's life drama—Ibn Ezra as religious poet—The Salḥan.

Chapter Four: JEHUDAH HALEVI THE POET / 83

Jehudah Halevi—His youthful years—His harmonious completeness—Love songs—The poet of national sufferings and hopes—The ideal of Zion as the flower of medieval romanticism—The poet's pilgrimage to Palestine—His odes to Zion—Halevi's ultimate significance.

Chapter Five: RELIGIOUS PHILOSOPHY FROM SAADIAH GAON TO MAIMONIDES / 105

The flowering of natural sciences and philosophy among the Arabs —The Kalam—The Karaites and freethinkers—Ḥiwi Al-Balchi and the "anonymous one"—The influence of Greek philosophy— The allegorical method of Philo—Saadiah Gaon as polemicist and thinker—Baḥya Ibn Pakuda and his *Hovot Ha-Levavot*—Jehudah Halevi as thinker; his *Sefer Ha-Kuzari*—Avicenna and his influence —"The God of Abraham and the God of Aristotle"—Joseph Ibn Zaddik and his *Olam Katan*—Ibn Zaddik as rationalist—Rabbi Abraham Ibn Daud as the first Jewish Aristotelian.

Chapter Six: MAIMONIDES / 133

Rabbi Moses ben Maimon; his youthful years of wandering— Maimonides as court physician, commentator, and religious authority—Maimonides' *Mishneh Torah* and its significance—*A Guide for the Perplexed*; Maimonides as rationalist — Allusions and parables in the Torah—Maimonides' views on God and the immortality of the soul—Maimonides' significance in the Jewish world and in western Europe.

Chapter Seven: ABRAHAM IBN EZRA / 153

Poetic forms of Hebrew literature after Jehudah Halevi—Abraham Ibn Ezra, the wandering scholar—His significance as an enlightener

Translator's Introduction

Among the phenomena whose roots can be traced to the political and social emancipation of the Jews of western and central Europe in the wake of the French Revolution was the emergence in the early decades of the nineteenth century, mainly in Germany but throughout much of the rest of Europe as well, of a new and culturally significant movement called by its participants and followers *die Wissenschaft des Judentums*—"the science of Judaism."

A major purpose of this movement, pursued with single-minded tenacity by a group of Jewish scholars, together with a few non-Jewish colleagues, was to investigate the entire literature created by the Jews over the more than three millennia of their history. The techniques and methods of critical literary, philological, and historical scholarship which had been elaborated at that time, chiefly in German universities, were to be used. Heretofore, with some notable exceptions, Jewish scholars had for centuries confined their studies largely to theological, legal, and moral texts, approaching these with an attitude of religious reverence and with the intention of regulating their lives by the light they found in them. Numerous poetic, philosophical, scientific, historical, and fictional works written by Jews—some published in the first decades after the invention of printing, but many only in manuscript and gathering dust in libraries and archives all over Europe and the Near East—had been completely ignored; their very existence was often unknown to the generality of Jewish students. The proponents of *die Wissenschaft des Judentums* undertook to rectify this situation. They set as their tasks to examine critically all the literary memorials of the Jewish experience they could discover, to publish scientific editions of as many of the documents as possible, and to present the conclusions at which they had arrived through the application of objective scholarly methods.

Among the major fruits of *die Wissenschaft des Judentums* were a number of histories of Jewish literature. Leopold Zunz (1794–1886), the major pioneering figure of the movement and its leader throughout much of the nineteenth century, himself made notable contributions in this area. His early work, *Die gottesdienstlichen*

Vorträge der Juden (1832), traced the rise and development of homiletic literature in the synagogue through the Midrash, Aggadah, and Prayer Book, and provided a classic model for the literary and historical investigation of Jewish writings. Another volume of his, *Zur Geschichte und Literatur* (1845), contained studies in many areas of Jewish literature and life, and was followed by two brilliant surveys of Jewish liturgical poetry, *Die synagogale Poesie des Mittelalters* (1855) and *Die Literaturgeschichte der synagogalen Poesie* (1865). These were based by Zunz on study of rare printed editions and manuscripts in the British Museum, the Bodleian Library at Oxford, the De Rossi Library in Parma, the Bibliothèque Nationale in Paris, and other famous libraries of Europe. Zunz' younger contemporary, Moritz Steinschneider (1816–1907), also achieved renown as a historian of Jewish literature and as the foremost bibliographer of Judaica in his day. His works included catalogues of the Hebrew books at the Bodleian (*Catalogus Librorum Hebraeorum in Bibliotheca Bodleiana*, Berlin, 1852–60) and of the Hebrew manuscripts at Leyden, Munich, Hamburg, and Berlin, as well as studies on Jewish apologetic literature in Arabic, on Judeo-Arabic literature, and on Jewish mathematical and historical writings. One of his most valuable contributions was an exhaustive study of medieval Hebrew translations and the cultural role of the Jews as interpreters, *Die hebräischen Übersetzungen des Mittelalters und die Juden als Dolmetscher: ein Beitrag zur Literaturgeschichte des Mittelalters, meist nach handschriftlichen Quellen* (Berlin, 1893).

Building on the pioneering researches of Zunz and Steinschneider, and largely following their methods, other nineteenth- and twentieth-century scholars—all inspired in significant measure by the program and goal of *die Wissenschaft des Judentums*—undertook the writing of histories of Jewish literature, some confining themselves to limited periods and types of Jewish literature and others attempting to survey the literature in its entirety. Among this galaxy of scholars were Isaac Hirsch Weiss, Joseph G. Klausner, and Simon Bernfeld, who wrote mainly in Hebrew; David Kaufmann and Gustav Karpeles, who employed German in their literary studies; Max Erik, S. Niger, and Max Weinreich, whose work is in Yiddish; and the Russian-born American scholar Meyer Waxman, who wrote his six-volume *History of Jewish Literature* in English.

Within the tradition of *die Wissenschaft des Judentums* is Israel Zinberg, whose monumental *History of Jewish Literature*, dealing with the thousand-year-long European period of Jewish creativity from Ḥasdai Ibn Shaprut in tenth-century Spain to the end of the Haskalah movement in nineteenth-century Russia, is here presented in English translation. Zinberg's *History*, written in Yiddish and probably the foremost scholarly work ever produced in that language, sustains favorable comparison with the work of his predecessors and successors in the study of the history of Jewish literature —and this in all important respects, including comprehensiveness, depth of interpretation of writers and movements, and correlation of literary tendencies with broader social and cultural factors. It is a unique and valuable achievement, rendered all the more remarkable by the unusual circumstances under which it was written.

Israel Zinberg was born in a village near Lanovitz in Volhynia in 1873.* His father, Eliezer, a prosperous lessee of estates in the region, was an ardent proponent of Haskalah, the movement advocating the modernization and secularization of Judaism and the promotion of enlightenment, which in the middle of the nineteenth century gained many adherents among the Jews of eastern Europe, as it had a century earlier among the Jews of Germany. Hoping that his son would become a Jewish scholar and writer, Eliezer Zinberg himself supervised the boy's early education and engaged private tutors for him, including a former teacher at the *yeshivah* or Talmudic academy of Zhitomir. The young man's interests, however, turned to science and he left Russia to study abroad, eventually completing the curriculum in chemical engineering at Karlsruhe and receiving a doctorate at Basel. Returning to Russia in 1898, Zinberg, then barely twenty-five years old, was appointed director of the chemical laboratory at the large Putilov (later Kirov) factory in St. Petersburg. In this position he remained for forty years, until his arrest in 1938.

Shortly after settling in St. Petersburg, Zinberg resumed his interest in the Jewish studies of his boyhood and youth. In 1900 the first significant product of these studies appeared. This was a monograph in Russian on Isaac Ber Levinsohn, the major figure of the Haskalah movement in eastern Europe who was often called "the Russian Moses Mendelssohn." A year later Zinberg became a contributor to the Russian-Jewish journal *Voskhod*, and in the years that followed, valuable articles on Jewish literature and history from his pen, in Yiddish and Hebrew as well as in Russian, were published in the daily newspaper *Der Freind* and in such journals as the Hebrew *Ha-Zeman* and the Russian-Jewish *Yevreyski Mir*, *Novy Voskhod*, and *Yevreyskaya Starina*.

* For biographical details here given I am indebted primarily to Elias Schulman's article "Yisroel Zinberg," *Leksikon fun der Yiddischer Literatur*, VII, 585–95 (New York, 1968).

Zinberg felt a strong personal obligation to disseminate authentic knowledge of Jewish literature and history in popular form among the masses of his fellow Jews in Czarist Russia in their vernacular, Yiddish. To this end he and several associates founded a publishing firm, *Die Neie Bibliotek*, which in the years 1903–5 issued a number of translations from Hebrew and Russian into Yiddish, as well as some original works. In 1912 he collaborated with several other Jewish writers and scholars, including Saul Ginsburg and Simon Dubnow, in the establishment of a new Jewish monthly, *Die Yiddishe Velt*. When the journal was transferred shortly thereafter from St. Petersburg to Vilna, Zinberg continued his association with it and published some important articles in its pages.

In the years before the outbreak of the First World War Zinberg also contributed very extensively to one of the last monuments of Jewish scholarship in Czarist Russia, the sixteen-volume *Yevreyskaya Entsiklopedia* (St. Petersburg, 1908–13). Serving as editor of the section "Neo-Hebrew and Yiddish Literature," he also wrote some three hundred pieces for it, including the articles on such major ancient and modern Jewish writers as Jehudah Halevi, Immanuel of Rome, Moses Mendelssohn, Mendele Mocher Seforim, J. L. Peretz, Sholom Aleichem, and Aḥad Ha-Am. In addition, he contributed to the encyclopedia such specialized articles as those on the Talmudic academy of Volozhin, English missionary societies to the Jews, assimilation, and the censorship of Jewish books in Russia (the last two in collaboration with other scholars).

Working all the while at his post in the Putilov plant, Zinberg, in the turbulent final years of the Romanov dynasty, not only produced a constant stream of scholarly articles, monographs, and books, but participated extensively in the cultural life of the Jewish community of St. Petersburg. He was active in the Jewish Literary Society, the Historical-Ethnographic Society, and the Society for the Dissemination of Enlightenment Among Jews. Before these groups he read numerous papers, always evoking spirited discussion with his challenging and polemical views.

In 1915, at the age of forty-two, Zinberg began the *magnum opus* which was to occupy him for more than twenty years, *Die Geshichte fun Literatur bei Yidn* (History of Jewish Literature). His plan at first was to write the work in Russian, and a considerable part of it was in fact written in that language. Only the first five chapters of the Russian text, however, were published in Kiev in 1919. By that year Zinberg had become convinced that it would be preferable to issue his work in Yiddish. This involved more than a translation of the sections already written in Russian; it required a thorough reworking of the material, for, as Zinberg puts it in his preface to the first volume, "the word is not simply the garment, the vessel of thought; it is also the most important part of thought itself. In Yiddish the literary history of our people must be written in a different style than in a foreign language." By 1927 Zinberg was ready to transmit the first volume of the Yiddish version of his *History of Jewish Literature* to the printer. The work appeared in 1929, not in the Soviet Union but in Poland, under the auspices of the publishing firm of Tomor in Vilna. In the years that followed seven more volumes were published in Vilna, the last in 1937, a year before the author's sudden arrest by the Soviet police.

Zinberg's offense against the state, it appears, was that he had engaged in correspondence with writers and scholars abroad. The efforts of a committee of prominent Jewish writers in New York to save him were of no avail. He was sentenced to exile and confinement in a concentration camp in Siberia. After a long and painful journey from Leningrad on the infamous "prisoners' train," the aged scholar arrived in Vladivostok in December 1938, worn out and fatally ill. He was placed in the concentration camp hospital and died there in the same month.

Zinberg had intended to bring his *History of Jewish Literature* up to the outbreak of the First World War. At the time of his arrest he had completed the first part of the ninth volume entitled *Die Blee-Tekufoh fun der Haskoloh* (Haskalah at Its Zenith). In 1964 the Yiddish manuscript was discovered in Zinberg's archives, which had been removed to the Institute of Asiatic Peoples in Leningrad. After lengthy negotiations Brandeis University obtained a microfilm of the manuscript. It was published in 1966 after being prepared for the press by Dr. Michael Astour.

It requires no special power of imagination to conceive the magnitude of the perseverance, devotion, and energy required on Zinberg's part for the composition of his *History*. Employed all day long in his engineering work at the factory, he could devote only evenings, weekends, and occasional holidays to study and research in the extensive Judaica collections of several of the great libraries of Leningrad and to the processes of reflecting on his materials and writing his chapters. In addition, he was cut off from direct personal intercourse with other Jewish scholars in Russia and abroad with whom he longed to discuss literary and historical problems, and by whom his own thinking might have been enriched. His isolation, his sense of alienation from the spiritual and intellectual climate prevailing in Russia after the Bolshevik revolution, and his anguished feeling that the Jewish world he had known and loved was dying in the soulless atmosphere of the new Soviet order weighed heavily upon his spirit. But he felt compelled to go on with his work and, indeed, found solace in it. In a letter of 1933 to Joseph Opatoshu, the Polish-born author of historical novels in Yiddish who had migrated to America, Zinberg wrote:

As is the way among Jews, mine is an ambivalent existence. I live in two different worlds. Only at night, and very often late at night, am I transformed from an engineer into a Jewish writer, dealing with the God-questings of the Baal Shem Tov and the exotic imaginativeness of the tales of Rabbi Naḥman of Bratzlav. But for this world there is little time. One borrows a bit from sleep, from the hours of rest. But all this does not suffice, and even with a very large capacity for work, one remains a debtor to oneself, for the possibilities and opportunities are too limited in the face of the projected plans.

I have said that Israel Zinberg stands within the tradition of *die Wissenschaft des Judentums*, but this statement requires qualification in view of some of the outstanding features of his *History of Jewish Literature*. The proponents of *Wissenschaft* set as their goal the attainment of an objective and accurate understanding of Jewish history and literature. Their ideal was the removal of all tendentiousness and apologetic, all motives of a theological or other ideological character. Some came close to complete success in attaining this ideal. Steinschneider, for example, who appears to have regarded his task as merely the rendering of an objective report on the literary products of a civilization that was, in his judgment, moribund and required only the opportunity to expire peacefully and be given decent burial, could write with almost total lack of personal concern and allow hardly any personal motivations to intrude upon his work. Zunz, on the other hand, despite his professed goal of scientific objectivity could not prevent himself from presenting, in the preface to his *Die gottesdienstlichen Vorträge der Juden*, an indictment of nineteenth-century German officialdom for withholding justice from the Jews by granting them only special privileges instead of the complete freedom and equality which he felt were rightfully due them. And the content of his work was clearly intended to give support to the demand of the newly emerging Reform movement in Judaism for regular preaching in the synagogue service, an idea of which Zunz was an ardent proponent, by showing that the sermon was in fact native to Judaism and had been an integral part of it for many centuries.

Zinberg shared Steinschneider's and Zunz' ideal of accurate understanding of literary and historical documents and relied heavily on their pioneering work. Indeed, the names and writings of these scholars appear with great frequency in his discussions of secondary sources both in the text and notes of his own work. But he had no illusions about the possibility, or for that matter the desirability, of strictly scientific objectivity in the studies with which he and they were concerned. In another letter to Opatoshu in 1936, Zinberg remarks on the history of the Hasidic movement that had been written by his friend of many years, the eminent historian Simon Dubnow: "Dubnow's work disappointed me greatly. He tried to be strictly, scientifically objective, and so the book was written in a tone that is neither hot nor cold. In cultural history strict objectivity is an impossibility, for when the historical investigator illuminates the facts, his own *Weltanschauung* or philosophy must reveal itself." Zinberg's *History of Jewish Literature* certainly does not manifest the tepid tone he here deplores. On the contrary, it everywhere reflects his love for his people and his admiration for their achievements. And Zinberg himself is not at all reluctant to evaluate and judge, to praise or condemn the writers, books, ideas, and movements he deals with. Moreover, his own *Weltanschauung*, his fundamental personal convictions and values, are clearly evident throughout his work.

The central, existential questions of Zinberg's personal philosophy—more accurately, of his inward spiritual wrestling—were the question of the ultimate meaning of life and that problem which the theologians call theodicy: the reconciliation of the fact of massive suffering, injustice, and evil in the world with faith in an omnipotent, beneficent, and just God. He therefore saw these, not without considerable support from the documents themselves, as fundamental themes pervading the literature he examined. Thus, he wrote:

But no matter how different the periods in the cultural life of the Jewish community in Europe, they are all united by one main problem which runs like a red thread through all aspects of the national creativity. The basic motif, the life nerve of Jewish literature, is the question concerning the purpose of human life. To what end does man live? In what does the goal consist? How can man's great suffering and the endless sorrows of the "chosen" people be justified? How is the tragic mystery of the world to be explained? How can one resolve the great enigma, the profound contradiction: the Creator a God full of compassion, and the world so steeped in evil and corruption?

For Zinberg ethics is the heart and center of Judaism. This leads him to focus on the demands for justice and love of fellowman that are reflected in Jewish literature. It also impels him to give primacy to its expressions of moral and humanistic values. Thus, for example, in the medieval *Sefer Ḥasidim* and *Tanna De-Be Eliahu* it is their universalist ethical teaching that Zinberg finds most admirable, and in the Kabbalist doctrines of the *Zohar* and Rabbi Isaac Luria's theosophy it is the emphasis on the dignity, and indeed the cosmic significance, of the individual, the envisagement of man as a major actor in the drama of world redemption, that he regards as supremely valuable. Zinberg also enthusiastically notes the periodic revival of the ancient Biblical passion for social justice in the later movements of Judaism whose literary expressions he studies. This passion, which finds voice in the protest of the poor and exploited masses against their wealthy oppressors, he sees as a fundamental factor in such important phenomena in the history of Judaism as the rise and spread of Karaism in the Geonic Age, the eruption of the Shabbetai Tzevi messianic movement in the seventeenth century, and the emergence of Hasidism in the eighteenth century, as well as in the literature called forth by these movements.

In associating literary works and tendencies with underlying social and economic movements, Zinberg attempts to fulfill the promise made in the preface to his *History*, where he indicates that "the development of literary forms will here be investigated on the basis of the entire Jewish cultural environment, with its intellectual and social tendencies, strictly connected with the general European civilization of that period." In this he also reflects somewhat his original proclivity for Marxist modes of analysis, for even though he explicitly repudiated his youthful enthusiasm for dialectical materialism (in a letter of 1914 to Samuel Niger he writes: "In my younger years I went for a time to the Marxist synagogue, until I realized that very important prayers are missing from its prayer-book"), its influence in his thinking remained a significant one. Thus, Zinberg seeks to relate the spread of Maimonides' and his followers' rationalism to the social and economic interests of the upper classes in Spanish and Provençal Jewry, and explains the growth in popularity of the mysticism and messianism of the Kabbalah as a result, at least in part, of the destructive effects on the social and economic condition of the Jewish masses in Europe of the Crusades and, later, of the expulsion from Spain. In similar fashion he emphasizes the socio-economic roots of sixteenth- and seventeenth-century Polish rabbinism, of the Hasidic and Mitnagdic movements, and of Haskalah.

Himself a product of Haskalah and heir of the broader European tradition of Enlightenment, Zinberg was naturally attracted to the expressions of independent, rationalist thought in the literature he studied, and his admiration for these is reflected in his work. But with all his enthusiasm for the freely inquiring mind's bold flights of speculation and its rejection of the irrational and the merely traditional, he was not oblivious to the defects of a one-sided rationalism. Thus he scores thinkers like Maimonides and Jacob ben Abba Mari Anatoli for their intellectual "aristocratism" and for the moral callousness manifested in their contempt for the common man. Though not at all a mystic himself, he could respond with genuine appreciation to the mystical aspirations of the Kabbalah and the religious passion of Hasidism and see in these a humanitarian spirit and moral fervor which, he sadly felt, were all too often absent in the rigorously rationalist thinkers and their systems. In Zinberg's view, the spiritual and intellectual history of European Jewry has been largely dominated by two major tendencies which developed along parallel lines but also frequently came into sharp conflict with each other: on the one side, an "aristocratic rationalism," which seeks to widen man's mental horizons and to liberate him from superstition and dogmatism, but which takes little account of the ordinary man's feelings and aspirations and generally lacks any broad social and humanitarian concern; and on the other side, a "democratic religion of the heart," in which the living individual, with his emotions and longing for a fuller and richer life, is primary, and the vision of a more just and equalitarian society is constantly maintained as the goal of human striving. Zinberg's own sympathies, as is clear from his treatment of the authors, books, and movements in which he sees these two tendencies reflected, were mainly on the side of the latter.

The title that Zinberg gave his work, *A History of Jewish Literature,* is not altogether apt, it must be noted, and fails to convey an accurate notion of its scope. Histories of literature generally restrict themselves to belles-lettres; they deal ordinarily only with such genres as poetry, drama, fiction, literary essays, and the like. Zinberg's *History,* however, is far more wide-ranging. It is concerned not only with the belletristic writings produced by Jewish authors in the European period of Jewish history, but with a tremendous variety of other types of literature. Works on theology, philosophy, and ethics; legal codes and books of religious customs; exegetical works and commentaries on the Bible and the Talmud; sermons and apologetic tracts; histories, chronicles, memoirs, and travel accounts; grammatical and philological studies; legends and folk tales; scholarly and popular works on the sciences—all these, and others as well, are discussed in its pages. There are few significant works produced by Jewish authors in Europe from the tenth to the nineteenth centuries—whether written in Hebrew, Aramaic, Arabic, Yiddish, Spanish, German, or some other language—which do not receive a measure of attention from Zinberg. Hence, it would not be much of an exaggeration to say that his *History of Jewish Literature* in fact comes close to being a history of Jewish thought and culture in the thousand-year period with which it deals.

This comprehensiveness is obviously one of the chief merits of Zinberg's *History*, but it may also account, at least to a degree, for some of its flaws and weaknesses. That these are real and substantial can hardly be denied, even by one who has an overall admiration for the work. Zinberg's major defect is undoubtedly his failure to pursue a consistent methodology in dealing with his vast and complex range of materials. Mainly, to be sure, he approaches these—and with generally successful results—from the standpoint of the historian of culture, but this standpoint is occasionally exchanged for that of the literary historian or literary critic. In the latter role Zinberg is less successful; his aesthetic analyses and literary evaluations tend to be somewhat superficial and inadequate. At times, regrettably, Zinberg also becomes little more than a bibliographer, describing briefly the content of various works without illuminating their historical and cultural significance. A rather surprising deficiency in the author's sense of proportion also appears on occasion; certain highly important works are dismissed with only a cursory and superficial discussion, while others of far lesser historical and literary significance are subjected to extended treatment. Furthermore, an unevenness of intellectual quality is clearly evident in the *History* as a whole; many of its pages and chapters are superb, others little more than mediocre. And the author's literary style, apart from its frequent proclivity for rhetorical flourishes and redundant statement, is not always inspired. Perhaps these weaknesses and defects are inevitable in a work of such vast scope, embracing such an enormous diversity of materials, and written over such a long period of time and under such difficult circumstances. In any case, they are more than compensated for by the manifest virtues of Zinberg's *History*, which, competent students agree, remains a unique and invaluable contribution.

What is perhaps most remarkable is that, though Zinberg began writing his *History of Jewish Literature* more than half a century ago and completed it more than thirty years ago, little of his work has been rendered obsolete or invalid by subsequent research and scholarship. To be sure, Zinberg was in error on certain points of fact, and since the time he wrote, new documents have been found and discoveries made which, had they been known to him, would doubtless have led him to reformulate a number of his statements. But these involve matters of relatively minor significance. To be sure, also, other scholars in the field of the history of Jewish thought and literature would dissent strongly from some of Zinberg's interpretations and conclusions, but that is only to be expected in a field in which individual interpretation necessarily plays so great a role. The undiminished and continuing value of Zinberg's monumental study is attested by the fact that the original Yiddish version has recently been completely reissued in a fine edition published in Buenos Aires and that a Hebrew translation (with valuable notes and supplements by Professor A. M. Habermann) has appeared in Israel.

The Yiddish in which Zinberg wrote his *History* is, in comparison with present-day writing in English, a rather ornate and florid language, with a wealth of unique metaphors, similes, and other figures of speech. While attempting to remain faithful in my translation both to the author's style and spirit, I have felt compelled to modify and, in some cases, eliminate a considerable number of his rhetorical flourishes, since the very abundance of these would inevitably strike the contemporary reader as not only tedious but cloying. At the same time, however, I have resisted the temptation to remove all of Zinberg's emotive phrases and figurative expressions and to transform his often sentimental and colorful language entirely into the cool, neutral, and detached style preferred by contemporary academic writers.

One of the characteristics of Zinberg's work is that he very frequently allows the authors with whom he deals to speak for themselves through extensive quotations (in many cases more paraphrastic than literal) from their works. Since the works from which these quotations and paraphrases are taken are in many instances not readily available even to the scholarly reader, I have considered it best not to abbreviate or to omit them; and I have generally preferred to translate Zinberg's paraphrastic version rather than the *ipsissima verba* of the quotation, inasmuch as the former, in most cases, renders the meaning more clearly than the latter.

I have permitted myself only to remove a considerable number of Zinberg's clearly redundant sentences and phrases; to omit the supplements and excursuses at the end of his volumes (since these would be of interest only to the specialist); to curtail and condense some of his lengthier notes and eliminate those that appear superfluous; and, in the case of some medieval poems of which he offers a prose paraphrase in his text, to substitute renderings of the same or similar poems into English by such modern poet-translators as Israel Zangwill, Nina Salaman, and Solomon Solis-Cohen.

I have also supplemented Zinberg's notes to many chapters with a section of bibliographical notes listing a selection of significant books and articles. The works mentioned in these bibliographical notes, which appear at the ends of the volumes, and especially those published since the time Zinberg wrote his *History*, should prove useful to the reader desiring to pursue special topics further.

Israel Zinberg's *History of Jewish Literature* is one of the last and greatest monuments of European Jewish scholarship. The world that nurtured it is, as a result of the Nazi holocaust, irrevocably gone. It is hoped that the present translation will help keep the memory of that world alive and lead to a deeper appreciation of the priceless literary treasures created by European Jewry during its millennial history.

BERNARD MARTIN

Case Western Reserve University
Cleveland, Ohio

Acknowledgments

The generous support of the Memorial Foundation for Jewish Culture, New York City, and of Mr. Leonard Ratner and the Ratner family, Cleveland, is gratefully acknowledged by publisher and translator alike. Without this generosity it would not have been possible for Israel Zinberg's monumental work to reach the new audience that it is hoped a translation into English will afford. The editor and translator wishes to express his appreciation to his friend Dr. Arthur J. Lelyveld, Rabbi of the Fairmount Temple of Cleveland and President (1966–72) of the American Jewish Congress, for his aid in securing a grant from the Memorial Foundation for Jewish Culture for the publication of this work. The cooperation of the Jewish Publication Society of America in granting permission to reprint materials for which it holds the copyright is also acknowledged. Finally, the editor and translator desires to acknowledge his gratitude to the staff of the Press of Case Western Reserve University for their kind helpfulness at every stage in the publication of this work.

From the Author

Not without reason are Jews called the "people of the book." The book occupies such an important place in its life that for many scholars the history of the Jewish people is transformed into the history of Jewish literature. Cultural life, the work of intellect— this was the only field in which the Jewish people could reveal its independent powers and the unique capacities of its spirit. This was the sole realm that remained to the eternally wandering people which, for many centuries, had no political life of its own but always lived in exile.

Its frequent banishments and migrations, its persecutions and troubles, each time disrupted anew the social foundations of the Jewish community and threw it into the depths of distress. But the people took along its cultural treasures; over these its enemies had little power. To be sure, cultural creativity was, in highly significant measure, dependent on the external environment, on the social conditions under which the Jews lived. The more the economic foundations of Jewish life were restricted, the stronger the lack of rights in the Jewish quarter became, and the more persecutions increased, the narrower and more one-sided did Jewish spiritual life, and above all its outstanding phenomenon, literary creativity, also become.

Precisely for this reason, in the history of Jewish literature the periods of growth and decline, of flowering and decay, occurred in an altogether different order than among the other peoples of Europe. Jewish cultural history has its own character; it developed in its own peculiar fashion and went through unique stages. In the cultural history of western Europe, for example, the end of the fifteenth century, when European thought began to free itself from the iron chains which had weighed so heavily upon it for many generations, is considered the boundary dividing the Middle Ages from modern times. The discovery of America and of new ocean passages to the distant lands of Africa and Asia; Gutenberg's great invention, printing, which became the instrument of culture and science; the religious Reformation which shattered the solid walls of Catholic Christendom—these major events brought a spiritual revolution to Europe and ended the dark night of the Middle Ages. The same date, the end of the fifteenth century, has however a completely different significance in Jewish history. It knows of no proclamation of a new world; no new spiritual and intellectual powers are then born. This is a period of national destruction, marked by the tragic end of the Spanish-Jewish community, the most magnificent bearer of Jewish culture for centuries. It was not dawn that then broke over the Jewish ghetto but twilight that descended on it.

The same phenomenon is evident in a later period. In the middle of the seventeenth century the European world was deeply impressed with the idea which the great philosopher of that era, René Descartes, expressed in three brief words, *Cogito ergo sum*—the fact that I *think* is the clearest proof that I live and exist. And precisely at that time, when the intellectually free human personality, which thinks and creates and builds on its own account, had just attempted to liberate itself from the dominance of the medieval heritage, the Jewish world became truly dark, and the real Middle Ages began. This was the result of the catastrophe which befell the largest part of the Jewish people in that era. The Thirty Years' War brought spiritual and economic havoc to German Jewry, and Chmielnitzki's hordes scourged the Polish communities with fire and sword, and drowned them in blood and shame.

On the other hand, in the completely dark period of the Middle Ages, from the tenth to the thirteenth centuries, at a time when all of Europe was still largely sunk in intellectual slumber, the Spanish Jews, together with the Arabs, were bearers of culture and learning, of art and science.

But no matter how different the periods in the cultural life of the Jewish community in Europe, they are all united by one main problem which runs like a red thread through all aspects of the national creativity. The basic motif, the life nerve of Jewish literature, is the question concerning the purpose of human life. To what end does man live? In what does the goal consist? How can man's great suffering and the endless sorrows of the "chosen" people be justified? How is the tragic mystery of the world to be explained? How can one resolve the great enigma, the profound contradiction: the Creator a God full of compassion, and the world so steeped in evil and corruption? And the contradiction must be resolved, the order of the world must be *justified*—in order for man not to lose the courage and power to carry on in the face of the suffering of life and not abandon hope and faith.

The fundamental motif of the profoundest poetic work which the centuries have bequeathed to us, the Book of Job, with its passionate revolt against the unjust order of the world and its shattering protest against the undeserved sufferings of men and the tears shed in vain, resounds also in the melancholy pages of medieval Jewish literature. To this problem the deepest thinkers and most important personalities of Jewry in the Middle Ages devoted their powers. Some of them sought a solution in the lofty tower of free philosophic thought; others, in the narrow paths, veiled in mystery, of mysticism and esoteric wisdom. For ages the entire foreground of Jewish cultural life was occupied by the struggle between these two tendencies.

I speak here only of *European* culture and the *European* period in Jewish literature, because only these will be dealt with in the present work. To write a scientific, independent work on the basis of primary sources and personal investigation, which would include the *entire* literary creativity of the Jewish people during the long period of its cultural life, is virtually beyond the capacity of one scholar. This is something that no one in fact has yet done. We have in certain areas some compiled works, but we, the "people of the book," to this day have no true history of our literature. I have therefore set myself a more limited task: to deal only with the later period of the history of Jewish literature, which occupies a time span of over a thousand years, the so-called European period, beginning at the moment when European Jewry, i.e., the Jewish communities settled in European lands, stepped forth for the first time as an independent cultural factor and began to participate in the development of the national literature. This moment is closely bound up with one of the most important events in the general history of Jewish civilization: cultural hegemony and intellectual dominance over the entire Jewish people passes from the Asiatic East to the southern corner of western Europe. With the beginning of the Second Millennium, according to the Christian reckoning, the European period of general Jewish culture is inaugurated.

We set ourselves the task of presenting the fullest possible portrait of Jewish intellectual and cultural creativity throughout this period. We will therefore not content ourselves with a history only of so-called belletristic literature. The development of literary forms will here be investigated on the basis of the entire Jewish cultural environment, with its intellectual and social tendencies, strictly connected with the general European civilization of that period.

It is true that this is in contradiction to the tendency which has recently appeared in increasingly prominent fashion among many historians of literature: to make their discipline self-subsistent and independent, and furthermore, to separate it from cultural history.

From the Author

Followers of the so-called formal method will promptly point out that, with the tasks we set ourselves, our work might be considered more a history of social and intellectual movements than a history of literature. We shall not here permit ourselves to be led into the question whether those scholars who insist that by the history of literature should be understood exclusively the historical development of purely literary art forms are really justified. One thing, however, is clear: as far as the literature of the Jewish people is concerned, one can accomplish little with this system. The whole cultural and social life of the Jews in the Middle Ages could have developed only in the word. The written word was the only form in which the will-energy and creative power of the Jewish community, its uniqueness and way of life, could be embodied for future generations. Among other peoples, leading an independent life, the taste, the consciousness, the ideas, and the whole organically growing particularity of the people are incorporated in the most varied forms—not only in literature and art, but also in political and social institutions, in communal organizations, in architecture, in the style of cities and streets and houses. But among the Jews, those homeless wanderers, all this could be clearly reflected only in their literary creativity. And indeed, being closely connected with their life of exile, this creativity had to be organically interwoven with their intimate world of sorrows and hopes, their search for the great mystery that lies hidden in the tragedy of life, the purpose and justification of their suffering, of their innocently shed blood and tears. It is therefore, in general, no accident that the most important Jewish poets, from Solomon Ibn Gabirol to Moses Ḥayyim Luzzatto, were not only artists but thinkers, preachers, and moralists as well. Aesthetics was frequently bound up with ethics, logical thought and investigation with intuitive creation. We do not here raise the question whether this association was deliberate. We have before us a real fact and must reckon with it. And anyone familiar with the unique development of Jewish literature will have to admit that here it is harder than in the case of any other literature to carry through a strict distinction between literary history (*histoire littéraire*) and the history of literature (*histoire de la littérature*).

We must also emphasize that we intend by no means to present here a kind of "catch-all" in which no Jewish author will be missing. Our task is to deal only with the significant and major phenomena in the realm of Jewish creativity. We will therefore dwell only on the Jewish writers and thinkers who actually had some influence, at least for their own generation, on the development of Jewish civilization and thought.

From the Author

We have been writing this work since 1915. During this time, in the historic years of world judgment and chaos, we have succeeded, despite poverty and distress, despite moral and economic destruction, in completing the first four volumes, to the Haskalah period. These volumes we first wrote in Russian and are now *reworking* into Yiddish. We emphasize the term "reworking," because this is not a question of mere translation. The word is not simply the garment, the vessel of thought; it is also the most important part of thought itself. In Yiddish the literary history of our people must be written in a different style than in a foreign language. We are publishing the first parts of our work in Yiddish earlier than in Russian.* The later parts will appear presently, provided our history finds favor with the reader.

—Israel Zinberg
December 1927

* Only the first five chapters of the Russian text appeared in Kiev in 1919.

Transliteration of Hebrew Terms

א is not transliterated   ו = v (where not a vowel)   ל = l   פ = f

מ = m

ב = b   ז = z   נ = n   צ = tz

ב = v   ח = ḥ   ס = s   ק = k

ג ,ג = g   ט = t   ר = r

ד ,ד = d   י = y   ע is not transliterated   שׁ = sh

ה = h   כ = k   שׂ = s

פ = p   ת ,ת = t

כ = ch

◌ָ = a   ◌ֱ = e

◌ַ = a   ◌ִ = i

◌ֳ ,וֹ = o   ◌ֵ = ei

◌ֻ ,וּ = u   ◌ֶ = e

short ◌ָ = o   ◌ָ: = o

י◌ֵ = ei   ◌ֲ = a

vocal *sheva* = e

silent *sheva* is not transliterated

Abbreviations

JQR	*Jewish Quarterly Review*
JQR, n.s.	*Jewish Quarterly Review,* new series
MGWJ	*Monatsschrift für die Geschichte und Wissenschaft des Judentums*
PAAJR	*Proceedings of the American Academy for Jewish Research*
REJ	*Revue des Études Juives*
ZHB	*Zeitschrift für hebräische Bibliographie*

THE ARABIC-SPANISH PERIOD

Introduction

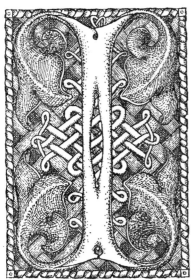I N the beginning was the word." Not only did God, according to ancient legend, create the world through His word, but man also creates his own world with the aid of the word. As long as an entity has no name, is not yet inscribed with the mark of the word in man's memory, it does not exist for him nor live in his consciousness, for only through the word does man arrive at self-awareness and recognition of the world. There is a profound truth in the Biblical legend which tells how the Creator brought before Adam all the creatures that swarm on the land, in the air, and in the seas, so that Adam might give them *names;* and precisely with the name that the first man gave it does each creature *live.*

This powerful instrument, through which man created his civilization and comprehended the whole world, did not, however, come easily to him. Only with great effort and struggle did man obtain it. For untold centuries he molded and polished this implement, and yet did not succeed in so completely mastering it that it would faithfully and fully execute his will. Man still feels that he is "heavy of speech" and crude in word. To magnify the power of the word, to make it clearer and stronger, it was accompanied by mime and expressive movement. This is noticeable not only in every individual but in the poetic creativity of every primitive community as well.

When we study the cultural history of any people, we always observe the same phenomenon. At the primitive stages of culture, spiritual chaos still reigns. This is a state in which everything is jumbled together and there is yet no notion of specific boundaries, of clear and definitely articulated forms. The songs, for example, which the community creates still contain the most varied types of poetry and literature—lyric, drama, epic, and history as well—for these folk songs recount how the ancestors lived and how they carried on wars with other tribes and foreign gods. Furthermore, these poems are still associated with song, play, dance, and worship. Speech is accompanied by mime and gesture. The poem is not read or declaimed; it is sung, accompanied by musical instruments and rhythmic bodily motions. And all this is mingled together in a prayer in which the soul of the community expresses its sentiments regarding the unknown powers and spirits that rule over it and the world.

This confusion of boundaries, this blending of various cultural elements, is called syncretism. In time, as the community rises to a higher level of cultural development, syncretism is weakened. Out of the chaos, boundaries which distinguish various realms of creativity from each other gradually begin to appear. Poetry—the essence of the human spirit and of its creativity, which is incorporated in the word—slowly emerges from alien hegemony and becomes increasingly independent. Great changes also occur in it: the various elements which in the beginning were intimately bound together eventually separate into independent and discrete forms—lyric, epic, drama, etc.

Even after syncretism has been weakened, however, the poetic creativity of a people long continues to bear a collective character, i.e., the impress of the entire community, not of the individual and his personality. Poetry remains anonymous, knowing nothing of individual names; everything produced in the poetic realm belongs not to this or that singer but to the community as a whole. The individual is so powerfully under the influence and spiritual domination of the environment that he is swallowed up by it. In primitive and little-developed cultures the community is monochromatic; its members are very little differentiated from one another. Their strivings, ideas, and opinions, their entire world outlook, are identical.

When the individual in such a monochromatic and homogeneous society produces a poem, it never occurs to the composer or anyone else that the poem belongs to him and not to the entire community. Because, in fact, such a poem reveals not the personality of the poet in question, not his individual "I," but the collective "I," in which the personality of the composer is lost, like a drop of water in a river.

Only gradually, as cultural life becomes richer and more highly developed, does the self-perception of the individual begin to grow.

Personalities appear who are to a certain degree able to free themselves from the boundless sovereignty of the collective. Such a highly endowed personality rises above the environment; it is spiritually more mature than the masses; in it perceptions and ideals to which the majority has not yet arrived are disclosed; in it problems and demands of which the community still has no awareness arise. And when such a personality produces a poetic work, it expresses not only the consciousness and world outlook of the community but of its own soul, with its unique dreams, hopes, sorrows, and pains.

Naturally, such a great change does not occur all at once. Independent national poets are the result of a long process of evolution. Often they are preceded by poets who are for the time being unable to become independent creators, who are still too much under the domination of the collective creativity, the spiritual heritage of the community. These popular poets can only collect the treasures, the diamonds and pearls in the depths of the folk creativity. They can only polish them and unite them into a harmonious whole. Such, for example, was the author of the famous ancient Greek epics, the *Iliad* and the *Odyssey*—the brilliant blind poet Homer.

It was only after him, when Greek civilization attained a still higher level, that such great poets as Sophocles, Euripides, Aeschylus, and others who produced their own masterworks that made their names immortal arose. These geniuses also drew their nourishment from their environment; they too were under the constant influence of the conditions of life, world outlook, and ideals of their people, but all these they refined in the depths of their souls and created new poetic forms saturated with their own spirits. The plays of Sophocles or Euripides were held sacred by the people of Greece. To stage one of their dramas, in which the profound tragedy of life is unfolded with such magnificent simplicity, was considered by the Greeks an act of piety. It was actually likened to worship, to a paean to the mighty gods who ruled the world. In the case of these masterworks, however, the people rightly considered that they had been produced not by the community, but by the individual, the poet blessed by God—or by the Muses, as was then believed.

Such was also the case in other branches of literature. The primitive lyric, in which the entire community expressed its feelings of joy and sorrow, was transformed into the effusion of the soul of the individual, of the gifted, noble, and deeply sensitive poet. Sappho, the famous lyrical poetess who lived in Greece in the days of the prophet Isaiah, declares in one of her songs: "The Muses have crowned me with immortality; my name and memory will remain for all generations." Here the personal feeling of the poet is clearly expressed; it is the *individual* that the Muses have made famous; the songs which he has created are *his* possession, something that belongs to him and no one else.

We have indicated that in the beginning, on the lower levels of culture, the memories concerning the past, the legends about the lives and deeds of the fathers, were the substance and chief element of popular poetry. As civilization advanced, however, there developed by degrees a new branch of literature, historiography. In Greece, for example, there arose prominent historians, such as Thucydides, Herodotus, and others, who collected for future generations the memories of former times and wrote down the important events of their own day, which they had witnessed with their own eyes.

Thus, the primitive and anonymous folk creativity is gradually transformed into national literature. Out of simple popular songs and legends created by the community, there develop in the course of centuries entire branches of art and literature. The community, the only producer of spiritual treasures in ancient times, bows before the personality of the gifted individual who rises above the mass. This individual becomes the creator of the national treasures; he places his stamp upon them, unites them with his spirit and his name. Naturally, the national literature does not entirely suppress the collective folk creativity. While talented poets and writers build and create, the collective, the common people, also spins its dreams and legends. This folk creativity undoubtedly has an extremely significant influence on the national literature. The poets frequently draw sustenance from it. But it no longer has by itself any solid existence. It lives only in the mouth and memory of the people. One generation transmits it orally to another, but much is thereby lost, much is forgotten or worked over, much in time is resurrected, but in a completely different shape and form.

When we turn to a consideration of the development of Jewish literature, we soon realize that in this particular the Jews are different from other peoples of the world. The history of ancient Hebrew literature presents us with a phenomenon unparalleled in any other nation or language. To be sure, the cultural history of the Jewish people also tells how the simple folk singer of ancient times is eventually transformed into the artist-poet, the master and creator. Ancient Jewish civilization also produced historians, thinkers, writers of great talent, but everything remains as before; the literature continues to be anonymous for centuries. The community does not bow before the individual; on the contrary, the individual, the divinely endowed artist, bows before the community. He is actually submerged in it; everything that he creates, everything about which he dreams and hopes, and for which his soul yearns, belongs finally to the people. The folk creativity remains strictly bound to the national literature. All the spiritual treasures that are produced among the people belong to the *entire* community; they bear only its name, they know of only one creator, and that is the community of Israel.

In many places in the Bible, especially in the Pentateuch, remnants of syncretism are still clearly discernible. Miriam the prophetess, for example, praises God for His great salvation with song, dance, and play, all together. But there is also in the Pentateuch a great epic, occupying the whole book of Genesis and the first chapters of Exodus up to the departure of the Israelites from Egypt. So ingeniously to polish ancient legends and stories that lived in the memory of the people, to harmonize them and to construct such a superb epic work—this only a poet of great literary power could achieve. But we do not know the name of our Jewish Homer. The collective swallowed him up, and this work of genius belongs not to the individual but to the entire people.

So, too, the names of our equivalents of Thucydides and Herodotus, the gifted authors of the ancient historical books—Judges, Samuel, Kings—remain unknown to us. Such a beautifully modest idyll as the Book of Ruth could have been produced only by a genuine artist who knew the magic "secret of condensation" and understood how simple words are transformed into vivid colors, into plastic forms and images. But the poet did not think of his personal glory, of immortalizing his own name; his only desire was to celebrate for future generations the modest beauty and perfect grace of Ruth, the daughter of Moab, who was privileged to be the ancestress of the most beloved of Jewish kings, David the son of Jesse.

The Song of Songs, the magnificent "song above all songs," the immortal poem of love which is "strong as death," made famous the beautiful shepherdess Shulamith, King Solomon's beloved, but not the poet who created the masterpiece. The same phenomenon recurs in the case of the Book of Psalms, which is so dear to the hearts of all the peoples of the world, to the souls of all the oppressed and afflicted. Among the spiritual treasures of all the ancient civilized peoples these prayer-poems, in which are revealed with such tenderness and simplicity the hidden depths of the human soul, with its humble longing for God, have no parallel; yet even such a personal effusion of the soul, the exalted religious mood of a man when he pours out his heart in prayer to the Almighty, does not bear the name of him who with trembling lips brought it into the world. The poet of the Psalms, with his rich and colorful world of feelings and yearnings, is submerged in the community; his profound experiences, the sweet sorrow of his soul which dreams and longs for God's beauty and glory, are mingled with the prayer of the congregation of Israel. The most intimate lyric of the individual is stamped with the seal of the community; the prayers of the Psalter, odorous of spices and incense, are associated with the name of the national hero, the darling of the people, David the son of Jesse, the progenitor of the Messiah. It is him, the great king, the pride and hope of the nation, that the people crowned with the title "sweet singer of Israel."

Among the twenty-four books of the Bible are two profound poetic-philosophic works, Job and Ecclesiastes. Those who created these masterpieces stood high above their environment; with their philosophic vision and poetic soul they posed problems and revealed contradictions which remained veiled for the majority of their generation and also for later times. And even these profound thinkers and poets never thought that the works, which they brought into the world with so much pain and doubt from the depths of their tortured souls, were their own property and ought to bear their names. These books, too, belong not to the individual but to the entire people, and the people attached to them the names of their beloved heroes, Moses, the greatest prophet, and Solomon, the wisest king.

To be sure, the Bible also contains books that do bear the names of their authors; these are the books of the prophets. But not as authors, as creators of poetic works, are their names inscribed in the memory of the people, but rather as God's chosen, the bearers of His word and emissaries of His punishment. With reverence and humility later generations inscribed on tablets the fiery words of doom of these divine messengers. But here also there was very little interest in the author himself and his name. Frequently the prophecies and sermons of different prophets, separated from each other by centuries, were combined in one book under one name.

This boundless dominion of the community over the individual, this blending of popular creativity with the national literature, extends throughout the length of the entire Biblical era and for centuries afterwards. Ezra, Nehemiah, and their successors firmly established the basic motif of later Judaism: "God, the Torah, and Israel are one." The people prized and preserved for future generations only that which was suited to strengthening this sacred triple bond, everything bound up with the community of Israel; but what belonged to the individual, even to the individual of genius, the people calmly erased from the book of life, snuffed out from their memory, and let perish. For example, the Book of Proverbs, which absorbed the wisdom and insight of the people, was considered sacred and included in the greatest national treasure, the Bible; but the Proverbs of Ben Sira, since they are associated with the name of an individual, were banned and became "books forbidden to be read." In time they were entirely lost, and it was only relatively recently, at the end of the nineteenth century, that a Jewish scholar had the good fortune accidentally to discover, in some half-rotted *genizah* pages, the ancient, long-lost Hebrew text of Ben Sira and revealed it anew to the world.

It was in Ben Sira's age that an event of immense cultural-historical significance occurred. In North Africa, in the city of Alexandria in Egypt, two different worlds, the two major civilizations of that time, the Hebraic and the Hellenistic, encountered each other. The Jewish spirit here adopted Greek forms. The control of the Jewish community over the individual here, in a foreign land, was weakened. And here there emerged within the Jewish community scholars and poets in the Greek fashion, such as Philo, Aristeas, Ezekiel, and others, who created on their own account and wrote works under their own names. These works, however, have no relationship to the Jewish popular creativity or to the Jewish national literature. They are Greek works, infused only to a limited degree with the Jewish national spirit.

In that same period there occurred within the Jewish community of Palestine a major transformation which had the greatest significance for Jewish cultural life: the people ceased speaking Hebrew. In the times of the prophet Isaiah and King Hezekiah the Aramaic language, which was then the vernacular of all of eastern Asia, was very little known among the Jewish people; only the wealthy and the ruling classes were familiar with it. The great masses understood only their own vernacular, Hebrew. But by the time of the teachers of the Mishnah the Aramaic dialect, interspersed with a number of Hebrew as well as Greek and Latin words, had already become the vernacular of the Jewish community, and the teachers of the Mishnah called it *lashon hedyot,* the language of the plain people. It was in this dialect that the Torah was expounded to the common folk in the synagogue and at assemblies, and it was also the language of instruction in the Jewish school. Aramaic became the cultural factor that aroused national sentiment in the masses and strengthened the bond uniting the people, God, and the Torah. It was interwoven with the language of the Bible; Hebrew and Aramaic became twin sisters. Both were sacred in the consciousness of the people; both developed the national culture further, even in later ages, when the Aramaic dialect also died as a spoken language and became, together with Hebrew, exclusively a literary language. The Torah is still read in both throughout the Jewish world (twice in the original and once in the Targum). Prayers were composed in both. In the Aramaic dialect were created national treasures which are revered by the people, not only the Talmud but even the *Zohar* of the Middle Ages. Even the prayer with which the living bid farewell to the dead, the Kaddish, is in Aramaic, as are some of the hymns of the greatest religious poet of modern times, Israel Najara.

In the Haskalah period of the nineteenth century the *maskilim*, or "enlighteners," constantly underscored the fact that the Talmud was very poorly edited. They complained that in it are mixed together, without any order, profoundly wise elements, laws and sacred instruction, with foolish stories, bizarre exaggerations, and childish superstitions. But precisely what the *maskil*, with his common sense, considered a defect is in the eyes of the cultural historian the greatest virtue. Because the Talmud is the result of many generations of collective effort, because the entire community built this mighty structure, there had to be in it all types of folk creativity—religious laws, philosophic ideas, and speculative doubts, together with popular stories, legends, magical incantations, proverbs, jokes, dancing songs, and the like. The Talmud also is, by its very nature, an anonymous work: its author is the entire people of Israel, from the greatest scholar to the meanest ignoramus. This great anthology is a monument of popular creativity as well as of national literature. The folkloristic and the national, the personal and the communal, the individual and the collective—all are fraternally braided together in it.

This is also true of the old Midrashim, those unique collections of homilies in which the wisdom of the most skillful of preachers is associated with simple folk stories and legends. The Midrashim, too, have no specific creator. The people laid down building stones, and from these the individual preacher constructed an edifice. Beloved legends out of which the people wove garlands for their heroes were explained by the learned preacher in his own way, veiled in a mantle of *pilpul* and adorned with verses from the Bible.

After the conclusion of the Talmud, the Jewish community became, as it were, intellectually somnolent. There was a temporary standstill in its cultural creativity. Then the Jewish spirit was suddenly awakened from its somnolence by a world-historic event which had a tremendous effect on the subsequent development of all of Jewish civilization. This reawakening was connected with the new faith, Islam, that Mohammed founded and that the Arab tribes quickly spread by means of the sword throughout the world. We shall have opportunity later to consider more fully the great revolution that Islamic civilization provoked in the spiritual life of the Jewish community in general and in its literature in particular. In the meantime we note only two extremely important particulars. First, the majority of the Jewish community once more lost its language. The largest part of the Jewish population lived in the lands over which the Arabs established their hegemony, and in a short time these Jews exchanged their vernacular, Aramaic, for the language of the new world empire, Arabic.

This new vernacular of the Jewish community, however, could not, as we shall see presently, take the place in the national Jewish culture that the Aramaic dialect had occupied in its time. It did not become the twin sister of the Biblical tongue but rather its rival. For centuries the Arabic language became, for the major part of the Jewish people, the most significant factor of general culture but not of national creativity. This called forth an entirely new era in the development of Jewish national literature. The individual overcame the collective; Jewish literature ceased to be anonymous, and stopped bearing the exclusive impress of the community. The individual—the poet, the thinker, the seeker who stands *above* the community—now began to create on his own account and assemble national treasures under his own name. The specific character by which the old Hebrew-Aramaic literature so sharply differentiated itself from its sisters was lost. From the Arabic period on, national literature among Jews was also sundered from popular literature, but with a very significant distinction: among most of the peoples of the world, both branches of cultural creativity develop in the same language, but among Jews they developed in different languages. The two golden threads were no longer woven together in one skein; each was spun separately. The national literature was produced by individuals who stood above the people, and the people created separately for themselves. One generation transmitted to another whole treasures of legends, stories, songs, and parables, but always orally. Not in books were these inscribed; they remained only in the memory of the living generation. Much was thereby lost, much eventually received a different vesture and sustained numerous transformations. Part, though, was improved; it was utilized by superior individuals, the creators of the national treasures.

At the same time, under the influence of Arabic civilization, another change of greatest significance in the cultural history of the Jewish people occurred: the victorious Arabs carried the green flag of their prophet Mohammed from anterior Asia to North Africa, and from there swept into southern Europe and established a powerful kingdom in Spain. On the Iberian peninsula Arabic civilization reached its zenith and, under the brilliant rays of this civilization, the Spanish Jewish community, which soon became the spiritual center of world Jewry, also burgeoned.

A new page in the history of Judaism was opened. Anterior Asia ceased to be the center of spiritual hegemony, and its place was taken by Europe. The Asiatic period of Jewish cultural history came to an end; a new era, the European, began. To consider this period, lasting over a thousand years, in the history of Jewish culture in general and of literature in particular is the purpose of the present work.

CHAPTER ONE

From Ibn Shaprut to Ibn Gabirol

EFORE the Arabs settled on the Iberian peninsula, the Jews there lived in a degraded, depressed condition. The fanatical Visigoths who ruled Spain persecuted them severely and held them in captivity.[1] Under such difficult circumstances the Spanish Jews were in a state of spiritual decline, and had little knowledge even of Judaism. In religious matters they were accustomed to apply to the major source of Jewish learning, the community in Babylonia, with its celebrated Talmudic academies, exilarchs, and Geonim.

The Arabs who, at the eighth century, shattered the power of the Visigoths in Spain brought genuine liberation to the Jews living there. The Arabs not only freed the Jews from slavery but also spread light and knowledge. In a few generations these Spanish Jews, no longer spiritually impoverished, became the most important bearers of culture, both general and Jewish, and for this they were indebted mainly to their liberators and teachers, the Arabs. These were blessed with something not to be found at that time among any people of Christian Europe: their intellectual and spiritual life was harmoniously

1. One of the last of the Visigoth kings, Egica, persecuted the Spanish Jews with special cruelty. He suspected that they carried on dealings with their brethren in North Africa, where the Arabs already ruled. In the year 694 a decree was issued that all the Jews were handed over as slaves to the nobility of the land, who might do with them whatever they wished, except release them.

integral, and their culture unitary and seamless. The Arabs knew nothing of the division under which the Christian civilization of Europe in the Middle Ages suffered. The peoples of Christian Europe had received their religion, then the sole bearer of culture, from an external source. The only cultural language of medieval Europe was also a foreign one, the dead Latin language. The tongues and dialects which the European peoples then spoke served only as vernaculars and were not employed for cultural purposes. Under such circumstances the vernaculars did not have the possibility of developing normally and attaining the status of cultural languages. Religion and science, in their alien Latin garments, were separated as by a solid wall from the people and its language. Given such a partition, there could be no question either of normal development of religion and science or of genuine national culture. The Arabs, however, did not know of this contradiction and division. The Koran, the sacred book of Islam, grew out of Arabic soil and was created out of the living vernacular of the people. The religious enthusiasm and cultural reawakening of the Arabs in that period, when Islam revealed itself to the world, had a remarkably powerful influence on the development of the popular language, for a whole universe of new concepts and ideas was required to embrace it. The living speech of the people, when it became a sacred language, was also raised to the level of a flourishing cultural language, the language of science and literature.

This rich Arabic civilization had an effect also on the other peoples in its orbit, especially the Jews. The Christian tribes in Spain regarded the Arabs as their worst enemies and had little desire to benefit from their unwished-for neighbors, with whom they carried on bitter warfare. The Jews, however, adopted a different attitude. For them the Arabs were true liberators. Arabic, which has considerable similarity to Hebrew and Aramaic, was already at that time the vernacular of the largest Jewish community. About two hundred years after the appearance of Mohammed the entire Jewish population of anterior Asia had exchanged its old vernacular, Aramaic, for Arabic.[2] The same thing happened among the Spanish Jews. Under the government of the highly cultured caliphs, the two related civilizations, the Jewish and the Arabic, established fraternal bonds. They influenced each other, and this influence produced magnificent results. One cannot here speak of assimilation or of self-annihilation, but only of stimulus, of spiritual and in-

2. See Zunz, *Gesammelte Schriften*, I, 45.

tellectual influence. Arabic culture worked on the somnolent Jewish powers like a catalyst, eliciting the strongest life processes, and the material deeply sunk in sleep was thereby transformed into energy and spirit that could not rest but strove ever upward.

Arabic, the sacred tongue of Islam, did not become the natural language of the Jewish community, but the efflorescence of this language and its literature motivated the Jews to bring Hebrew to the same high state. Under the influence of the rich and beautiful Arabic, refined taste developed among the Spanish Jews, and the feeling for beauty produced an interest in the poetic treasures of the Bible and the language in which it was written. As Arabic poetry flowered in Spain, the Jews became envious, and among them the desire arose to create not only religious but secular poetry in Hebrew, employing Arabic forms and principles of meter.

Religious or liturgical poetry had developed among the Jews only after the Talmudic era. Even in the days of the Second Temple, the public religious cult was no longer restricted merely to the sanctuary and the altar. Outside the Temple, houses of prayer or synagogues began to appear. In addition to sacrifices there were sermons and prayers. The custom, established by Ezra, of translating and interpreting to the people in its vernacular the weekly portions of the Torah eventually became very popular. Out of these "explanations" of the Torah sermons filled with moral instruction and ethical content gradually developed. Such homilies were given by the teachers of the people on Sabbaths and festivals in the synagogues and houses of study. The famous heads of the Sanhedrin, Shemaiah and Avtalyon (first century B.C.E.), already bore the name *darshanim* (preachers) because they were accustomed to speak to the people, teach them, comfort them in distress, and strengthen their trust in God's speedy salvation. Such sermons were always inaugurated with a verse from the weekly portion of the Torah, but the preacher was not concerned with expounding the plain meaning of the given verse. This was only a matter of form; the verse was the introduction, the framework, on which the preacher would weave his artful texture of heartfelt instruction, earnest words of reproof, and the lovely legends and parables out of which both the Aggadic part of the Talmud and the ancient Midrashim were later constructed. After the destruction of the Temple, when sacrifices ceased, their place was taken by prayers and, most importantly, by sermons and homilies. Almost all the men of the Mishnah and of the Talmud were also preachers, creators of the Aggadic Midrash. They would preach to the people, pour salve on their grieved hearts, comfort them in the troubles and misfortunes which befell them, awaken in them hopes of speedy redemption, and strengthen them with imaginative tales about the beloved national heroes of former ages.[3]

After the Talmud and the ancient Midrashim were written down, the well of Aggadah was not stopped up. The stories and legends of the people occupied a very honored place in the public religious cult in the later period as well. They merely changed their outer garment. The preacher was transformed into the *paytan*, or liturgical poet, and the material of the sermons was changed into poetry. Under the influence of Christian liturgical poetry among the Syrians, Greeks, and others, Jewish poetry was created. The *paytan*, who in most cases was also the *ḥazzan*, or precentor of the congregation,[4] performed the same role that the preacher had in the earlier period. He also employed the ancient material of the Aggadah in his poetry. The substance remained the same; only the form, the outer vestment, was changed.[5]

The first Jewish *piyyutim*, i.e., prayers in the form of poems, were composed in the seventh century. Their creators, however, still had no conception either of meter or of rhyme. The first to introduce rhyme into Jewish religious poetry was the *paytan* Jannai,[6] the teacher of the celebrated Eleazar Kallir. Kallir's poems are familiar throughout the Jewish world, but Kallir himself, his life and personality, are altogether unknown. We do not even know precisely the country and period in which he lived. In general, scholars are inclined toward the view that he flourished in southern Palestine in the seventh century. (In any case, a philologist of the tenth century, Jehudah bar Sheshet, speaks of him as of an ancient *paytan*.) Kallir undoubtedly had a spark of the genuine poet in him, but he did not know the "secret of concentration." The knowledge of Hebrew grammar was at that time still in its infancy (something that always operates negatively on the development of a language that is no longer spoken), and Kallir, furthermore, had no instinctive feeling for the inner rhythm and harmony of the Hebrew language. Its material refused to respond to his stiff fingers, though

3. For details regarding the history of Jewish preaching, see Zunz, *Die gottesdienstlichen Vorträge der Juden*, and Maybaum, *Jüdische Homiletik* (1890).

4. It is very possible that even the word *ḥazzan* is derived from *ḥarzan*, meaning "versifier." See *Literaturblatt des Orients*, 1844, p. 686.

5. See Michael Sachs, *Die religiöse Poesie der Juden in Spanien*, p. 179; Zunz, *Die synagogale Poesie des Mittelalters*, pp. 59–60; also his *Die Literaturgeschichte der synagogalen Poesie*, pp. 23–26.

6. See S. D. Luzzatto, *Mavo Le-Maḥzor Benei Roma*, p. 8; L. Landshuth, *Ammudei Ha-Avodah*, pp. 102–4. According to more recent investigations, Jannai was not the first in this realm. See H. Brody, *Studien*, p. 9.

he sought to force it with violence. He created new words, bizarre and clumsily formed, like stones piled up and thrown together one on top of the other without any semblance of order. Not only the common mortal but even the expert scholar cannot find his way here; he does not always succeed, even after great effort, in getting at the plain meaning. Only in places, among these unpolished and stony forms, does the flame of feeling and poetic inspiration suddenly break through, and the astonished reader feels that he has really to do with a poet, not with a simple rhyme-maker.

Jannai introduced into Hebrew poetry the form of acrostic, but neither he nor Kallir knew of meter and rhythm. Their rhymed lines and verses are of various lengths and dissimilar constructions. Hebrew poetry became familiar with the principles of meter only in Arabic Spain, where secular poems first appeared. But before the Spanish Jews introduced into their literature Arabic poetic forms, they laid the foundations of Hebrew linguistic science or philology. This also occurred under the influence of the Arabs, who produced a great deal in the realm of philology, especially during the tenth century when Arabic civilization in Spain reached its highest level.

The beginning of Hebrew linguistic science and of secular poetry constructed according to Arabic forms is associated with the name of Ḥasdai ben Isaac Ibn Shaprut, who was adviser and chief physician to the Arabic caliph Abd er-Raḥman III in Cordova. The Jewish officer (born in 915 in Jaen, died after 970) is also known in general history because of his letter to the king of the Chazars, Joseph II, and the latter's reply, both of great significance for the history of the kingdom of the Chazars in the last years of its existence.[7]

Ḥasdai's importance consists, first of all, in the fact that he liberated the Spanish Jews from Babylonian hegemony, for until his time they were dependent in spiritual matters on the Jewish cultural center in Babylonia. His wealth gave Ḥasdai the means to recruit rabbis and Talmudic teachers from Babylonia and North Africa; he settled these in Andalusia, and under their supervision established Talmudic academies. He also provided the new academies with books. The home of the philanthropist became a meeting place for various scholars and writers who received support from him.

The famous thirteenth-century poet Jehudah Alḥarizi tells in his flowery rhetorical style of the cultural-historical role of the Jewish minister:

7. Several years later the Russian tribes, led by Prince Oleg, destroyed the kingdom of the Chazars on the Volga. The upper strata of the kingdom, together with the king's family, had converted to Judaism in the eighth century.

And it came to pass in the year 4700 after creation that a spirit of strength and song descended into Spain. Then the Hebrews undertook to adapt their tongue to the form of song. . . . But their linguistic artistry at that time was inferior and the language of their poems limped, until the eighth century arrived and they began to play on the eight-stringed harp. . . . At that time the sun of glory rose over the land of Spain, the great prince, Rav Ḥasdai Ibn Shaprut, may he rest under the wings of the *Shechinah,* for he fulfilled the needs of all. And in his time the waves of wisdom began to rise. . . . For this prince with his grace revived everyone, and with his generous hand attracted the faint hearts of all the children of exile. He proclaimed from land to land: "Let whoever wishes to lend a hand come to me, and I will take upon myself all his needs." And around him gathered every scholar and rabbi from east and west, from the lands of Edom and Arabia, and he prepared for them the table of his kindness and spread over them the clouds of his glory. And the fiery pillar of his glory attracted and shone before their eyes. And the wise men of that generation assembled around him and shone like the brilliant stars. A divine spirit was poured over him, and wisdom and understanding and art and knowledge, to stimulate minds and to arouse hearts with fire. And since then all the arts in Spain have wakened with joy and spread over the entire world. . . . In the wisdom of song eyes were opened and divine visions drew the heart. In his time wisdom appeared among the Jews.[8]

Among the scholars maintained at Ḥasdai's court was the first Hebrew philologist in Europe, Menaḥem Jacob Ibn Saruk (born in Tortosa c. 910, died c. 970). He was Ḥasdai's secretary and court poet. According to his own account, he used to write for his patron "tablets of laudation, letters of praise, books of glory, words of benediction, and poems of mourning." Scholars long ago demonstrated that the famous letter to the king of the Chazars was not composed by Ḥasdai himself but by his learned secretary (in order that future generations might know who the true author was, Menaḥem ingeniously wove his name into the letter in an acrostic). His position with the Jewish prince gave Menaḥem the opportunity to devote himself to scholarly work. What made him famous was his *Maḥberet,* the first Bible dictionary in Hebrew, which, for a long time, was the major source of linguistic knowledge for the Jewish community in Christian Europe, a community which could not make use of the later works in Hebrew philology because these were written in Arabic. But this work, which made its author renowned in later generations, brought him much grief in his own lifetime. A short while before Menaḥem's work appeared, Shaprut invited to his court a learned young philologist from Fez, Dunash

8. *Taḥkemoni,* Gate 18.

ben Labrat (c. 920–c. 990), a pupil of the famous Saadiah Gaon.[9] When Dunash read the work of Menaḥem which had just appeared, he immediately perceived, with the keen sensitivity of the true scholar, that this work with all its virtues also had not a few defects that required correction. But doubtless Dunash had, in addition, some partisan and purely personal motives. He was jealous of Menaḥem, who had gained a considerable reputation through his book and had become greatly elevated in the eyes of Ḥasdai Ibn Shaprut. Dunash, who, it appears, also wished to play a prominent role at Ḥasdai's court, decided to attack his rival. First he issued a sharp polemic against Menaḥem's work. That in this he was not concerned with purely scientific matters is easily discernible in the passionate, palpably insolent tone in which the critique is written.[10] Above all he was zealous to point out Menaḥem's errors to his patron, so that the latter might become unfavorably disposed toward the poor scholar.

As an introduction to his polemic work Dunash wrote a poem of praise to "the great prince, the brilliance of the world and the pride of the people," Rabbi Ḥasdai ben Isaac. This poem has a definite cultural-historical value, for Dunash ben Labrat here appears as an innovator; this is the first poetic work in Hebrew written strictly according to the principles of Arabic meter. The author himself considers it necessary to emphasize this point, and adds proudly that his measured and weighted verses are "like dew on the hearts of the wise men of Spain and will remain in the memory of all future generations."

After the poem of praise comes the introduction to the work itself, also in the form of a poem consisting of one hundred and fifty four-line verses constructed according to the same meter and style as the poem of praise.[11] But the tone here is entirely different. This introduction, as well as the whole book, which Dunash pre-

9. Formerly it was assumed in the scholarly world that Dunash ben Labrat (his Hebrew name was Adonim Ha-Levi) later wrote a critique of his teacher's Arabic translation of the Bible (*Sefer Teshuvot Dunash ben Labrat al R. Saadiah Gaon*); in more recent times, however, it has been doubted whether Dunash wrote this work. See Porges, *Über die Echtheit der dem Dunash ben Labrat zugeschriebenen Kritik gegen Saadjah;* Kaufmann, *Denkschrift*, pp. 245–56; *MGWJ*, 1902, pp. 66 and 141. On Dunash as a religious poet, see Landshuth, *Ammudei Ha-Avodah*, p. 161; *Maḥzor Vitry*, II, 178.

10. Dunash's critique, together with Rabbenu Tam's countercritique (*Sefer Ha-Hachraot*), was published by Herschell Filipowski in 1855.

11. Both poems were published by Filipowski in 1855 and reprinted with a long introduction by David Kahana in 1894. A third poem by Dunash, written in the same meter as the first two, was discovered in the Cairo *genizah*. It was published by Jacob Mann in *The Jews in Egypt and Palestine under the Fatimid Caliphs* (1922), II, 21–23.

sented as a gift to Hasdai, has more the character of a sharp, malicious lampoon than of a scientific, critical work. Dunash is not content with insulting Menahem and calling him ignoramus, simpleton, etc.; he also indulges in gossip, accuses Menahem of heresy, and declares that the latter is favorably disposed toward the Karaites, with whom the rabbinic Jews at that time carried on a bitter quarrel ("And this evil opinion is the opinion of Anan, the chief of the heretics who opposed the disciples of our master").[12]

It appears that Menahem had at the prince's court others as well who hated and envied him. These understood how to exploit Dunash's tract and also, on their side, endeavored to rouse Hasdai against the scholar. The end of the affair was a very sorry one for Menahem. With Shaprut's knowledge, some of his associates fell upon Menahem's house on a holy day and destroyed everything, even tearing out the windows and doors and carrying them away. Menahem himself was beaten and driven out of the city. The scholar then addressed to his former protector a letter from abroad and humbly inquired why the latter had poured out his wrath on him. Shaprut gave a brief reply, and not by accident has this reply remained in the memory of future generations—so characteristic is it of court personalities with their puffed-up pride and smugness. "If you are really guilty," was Shaprut's response, "I have punished you according to your deserts; but if you are not guilty, I have thereby brought you eternal life." Even the calm and modest Menahem could not remain silent at such an answer. The injured feeling of self-respect, the pride of the scholar who knows the worth of honoring Torah and cannot forgive the desecration of a person's spirit and soul, awoke in him. He sent Hasdai a letter which, of itself, has earned him a place in the history of Jewish literature.

Menahem appreciates quite well how dangerous it is for him, a poor scholar, to set himself against the powerful minister. The letter, therefore, begins in a sedate, humble tone, but the feeling of pain and anger quickly prevails, and he sharply demands from the man who has offended him reckoning and account for the sufferings and insults he has so innocently sustained. "My prayer reaches to God," writes Menahem.

To Him, the protector of the oppressed and innocent, I raise my cry, and as long as I live my angry voice will not be silenced . . . I who am hunted and oppressed, I who, through you, have been hurled into the abyss of deprivation and distress turn to you, my former lord and protector. Or have you forgotten that you are only a common mortal

12. *Teshuvot Dunash*, p. 75.

like myself, that both of us are no more than ashes and dust? The mightiest kings and princes and the poor and needy—does not an identical fate await them: to return to the earth that gave birth to all?

Deeply pained is my heart, for in all the world there are no sufferings like mine. My sole consolation is the thought that there is a judge in the world, the Judge who lives eternally. He will demand recompense for all the insults and shame I have suffered. I believe and am certain that my Protector lives! He will demand account and reckoning, He will judge my cause. It may be that *here* there is "no justice and no judge." I know, however, of a certainty that the God of justice exists, and that the day will come when all of us will have to stand before His judgment seat. It will come—this great day of judgment—when the homeless will no longer be compelled to go wandering and the great and powerful will no longer be protected by gold and silver. The day will come when all will be equal, the prince and the pauper, the rich man and the wage-earner. . . . That day will come, and everything will be weighed and measured, and the mighty and great will no longer have the power to oppress and dominate. . . .

"I demand of you account and reckoning"—Menaḥem turns to Shaprut—

for I am righteous and innocent. You have answered me: "If you are really guilty, I have punished you according to your deserts; but if you are not guilty, I have thereby brought you eternal life." Do you think that this is a righteous answer, that this is the way of justice? Or do you believe that with mockery and laughter you will close my mouth and with frivolous words bring me to silence? Listen, mortal! You are, after all, a scholar in Israel, and so you must have some notion of what justice and right are. You say, "*If* I am guilty . . ." Does one judge on the basis of "if" or "perhaps"? Can one carry out a verdict on the basis of conjectures? Not on the ground of solid proofs, but on the basis of thoughts deeply hidden in one's heart? "If you are not guilty," you write, "I have thereby brought you eternal life." Well, then, what of the unjust judge, what will become of him? With what will he come before the true Judge . . . ?"

"Even among savage tribes," Menaḥem further writes, "such a judgment has not been heard of. Even among idolaters there is more respect for right and justice. This cannot be silenced! Even after my death this great wrong will not be forgotten. I shall crumble into dust, but even then my cry will split the heavens."[13]

13. Menaḥem's letter was first published by S. D. Luzzatto in *Bet Ha-Otzar* in 1847, afterward by H. Graetz in *Leket Shoshanim* (1862), and by Z. Stern in the introduction to *Teshuvot Talmidei Menaḥem*, xxii–xxxiii.

Dunash's critique of Menaḥem Ibn Saruk was also not left without response. Between the disciples of the two scholars a literary quarrel began which has a certain cultural-historical value because, to a degree, it brought fresh life, as well as new forms, into the Hebrew language and its literature. The cause of the offended Menaḥem was taken up by three disciples, the learned Isaac Gikatilla, Isaac Ibn Kapron, and the young Jehudah ben David Ḥayyuj, who later achieved fame in the realm of philology. These attacked Dunash with a counter-critique, *Teshuvot Talmidei Menaḥem.*[14] They also deemed it necessary to present, in the form of an introduction to the *Teshuvot*, a long poem of praise to the prince Shaprut. This poem is written in the same style and meter as Dunash's two poems, in order to prove—and, indeed, they underscore this—that they also are capable of writing Hebrew poems according to the principles of Arabic meter. At the same time they sharply criticize Dunash's accomplishment and endeavor to show that Arabic meter is not at all suitable to the Hebrew language. "Our own inheritance," they complain, "he destroys and makes waste, and confines the holy tongue in strange bonds." This opinion they substantiate at length in the book itself,[15] referring Dunash to his own teacher, Saadiah Gaon, who avoided Arabic meter in his poems.

It must be admitted that there is considerable truth in the charges of Menaḥem's disciples. The greatest Jewish poet of the Middle Ages, Jehudah Halevi,[16] later came to the same conclusion in his old age. But the opposition of Menaḥem's disciples had no effect, and from the time of Dunash on, Arabic meter completely dominated Hebrew poetry for ages.

The *Teshuvot* of Menaḥem's disciples are written in the same sharp, lampooning tone as Dunash's critique.[17] But all of them are surpassed in this respect by Dunash's pupil, Jehudah Ibn Sheshet, who undertook to defend the honor of his teacher and wrote a reply to the complaints of Menaḥem's disciples. Ibn Sheshet bestows on his adversaries such epithets as donkeys, dogs, swine-eaters, simpletons, fools, wild asses, apes, ignoramuses, etc. On the other hand, he is not at all parsimonious in eulogies of his teacher. Dunash is for him the "great scholar of the West" who has no peer. His wisdom is wide as the sea and quenches the thirst of all who are

---

14. Published by Z. Stern in 1870.
15. *Teshuvot Talmidei Menaḥem*, pp. 21–30; see also S. Pinsker, *Likkutei Kadmoniot*, pp. 62–65.
16. *Kuzari*, II, 78–80.
17. See pp. 15, 24, 25, 33, 40, and 41.

eager for knowledge. His poems are engraved for eternity, and in all future generations they will delight the hearts of men.[18]

In fact, these rivals, Menaḥem as well as Dunash, were no more than beginners. Their significance consists principally in the fact that they were the *first*, the courageous pioneers. With their work they undoubtedly awakened interest in scientific philology. But the true father of Hebrew grammar, the "chief of the grammarians" as Abraham Ibn Ezra in his *Safah Berurah* called him, was Menaḥem's disciple, the aforementioned Jehudah ben David Ḥayyuj (born in Fez in the middle of the tenth century, died at the end of the century).

Just at that time there lived and worked in Cordova, then the major center of Arabic civilization in Europe, some renowned Arabic grammarians who raised the scientific study of language to a magnificent height. Even the masses began to take interest in philological matters.[19] Under the influence of these scientific endeavors Ḥayyuj grew up and approached his work, with which an entirely new era in the study of the Hebrew language begins. Where utter chaos once reigned, he, with his keen eye and the sensitivity of a first-rate scholar, created order and disclosed strictly valid principles and rules. He was the discoverer of the famous principle which became the foundation of all of Hebrew grammar, namely, that in Hebrew there is no verb whose root consists of less than three letters. He substantiated his theory in two scientific Arabic works, *Kitab al-Af'al Dhawat Huruf al-Lin* (The Book of Verbs Containing Weak Letters) and *Kitab al-Af'al Dhawat al-Mathalain* (The Book of Verbs Containing Double Letters), which were twice translated into Hebrew, first by Moses Gikatilla and later by Abraham Ibn Ezra.

The Jewish "chief of grammarians" undoubtedly deserves an honored place in the history of general European philology.[20] Yet, great as his merit was, he was excelled by his brilliant follower and pupil Jonah Ibn Jannaḥ (990–c. 1050), one of the most important philologists of the European Middle Ages.[21] His masterwork, *Kitab al Tankiḥ* (Book of Minute Research), on Hebrew grammar,

18. See pp. 6, 15, and especially 44.
19. See P. Kokowzoff, *Novie Materiali* (1916), p. 5 (Russian).
20. See Kokowzoff, *op. cit.*, p. 73.
21. In Arabic he was called Abu Al-Walid Merwan Ibn Jannaḥ. Born in Cordova in the year 990, at the time of the upheavals of 1012 he left his native city and, after a long period as a wanderer, finally settled in Saragossa, where he practiced medicine. He died in the middle of the eleventh century. For more about him, see W. Bacher's monograph and also his introduction to *Sefer Ha-Shorashim* (1892); also Ewald, *Literaturblatt des Orients*, 1844, pp. 675–78.

is the richest product of Hebrew linguistic science, a veritable treasury of information about philology and Biblical exegesis. This work had the profoundest influence not only on all later Jewish grammarians but also on Biblical scholars and exegetes. All of them drew from this rich and deep well.

The first Jewish grammarians, Menaḥem and Dunash, wrote their works in Hebrew, but the great philologists who came after them, Ḥayyuj and Jannaḥ, employed the Arabic language, and with their work laid the foundations of the rich Arabic-Jewish scientific literature that quickly blossomed in Spain. What we have already observed must, however, again be emphasized: these scholars were under the powerful influence of Arabic civilization, constructed Hebrew grammar according to the categories of Arabic grammar, and, incidentally, also employed Arabic terminology. But all this was only a means to a strictly defined goal—to investigate the language of their own national sanctuary, the Holy Scriptures, and better to understand and expound the meaning of the Bible. This is expressed quite clearly by the greatest of them, Ibn Jannaḥ. He explains that the chief aim of his life is to arrive at the true meaning of the Bible and that, in order better to attain this aim, he has undertaken to investigate the Hebrew language.

"The Holy Scriptures revealed by God," writes Jannaḥ in the introduction to his major work,

can be properly understood only on condition that one has solid knowledge of the language in which they are written. This becomes all the clearer to us the more we strive to understand the content of Scripture and the more our mind grasps the greatness of Him who revealed these books to us through the holy spirit.

This is a very characteristic feature of the whole era in general. The pious Jews of Spain did not at all abdicate before Arabic culture. To be sure, they were under its powerful influence, but they endeavored—and, indeed, with great success—to bring the alien treasures of knowledge under the dominance of Jewish religious thought, to connect them organically with their own national-cultural creativity.

Ibn Jannaḥ and his predecessors, however, not only promoted a better understanding of the meaning of the "Holy Scriptures revealed by God"; with their classic, scientific philology, they also laid the foundation and prepared the soil for the brilliant period of efflorescence of Hebrew poetry and belles-lettres.

Dunash ben Labrat first introduced the principles of Arabic meter into Hebrew poetry. He also introduced a unique style of polemic literature—the lampoon in the form of a poem, with sharply pointed rhymes. In addition, he composed liturgical hymns.[22] Nevertheless, he was not an authentic poet, and it was not with him that the dawn of Hebrew poetry came in Spain. Nor were the three *paytanim* who appeared shortly after him genuine poets. All three bore the same name, Isaac. They were the previously mentioned pupil of Menaḥem, Isaac ben Gikatilla; the teacher of Jannaḥ, Isaac ben Mar Saul; and Isaac Ibn Ḥalfon. The last of these was the first itinerant poet among the Jews and earned a livelihood by honoring men of wealth and patrons with his songs of praise.[23]

The first genuine poetic notes appeared in the religious hymns of another scholar of that generation, Joseph bar Isaac (Ibn Stans) Ibn Abitur. This scholar spent a restless life of wandering. He was esteemed at the court of the cultured Caliph Al-Ḥakim of Cordova and, at his wish, wrote a commentary in Arabic on the Talmud. After the death of the famous rabbi of Cordova, Rabbi Moses ben Enoch, a controversy broke out between his son, Rabbi Enoch ben Moses, and his pupil Ibn Abitur over the rabbinic office in Cordova.[24] The conclusion of the matter was that Ibn Abitur left Spain, roamed about all his days, and died around the year 1000 in Damascus. Ibn Abitur still belongs to the old school. He wrote in the style of Eleazar Kallir, with difficult, strange words that do not conform to grammatical principles and rules. Ibn Abitur was also strictly a liturgical poet; he wrote *maamadot* for Yom Kippur and other religious hymns and did not concern himself with secular matters.

The real initiator of the new era, the father of secular poetry among the Jews in the Middle Ages, was the celebrated Samuel Ha-Levi ben Joseph Ha-Nagid, or Ibn Nagdela, one of the most remarkable and interesting personalities of the Spanish Middle Ages.

Samuel Ha-Nagid (born in 993 in Cordova, died in 1055 in Granada) was educated in one of the Talmudic academies which Ḥasdai Ibn Shaprut established in Spain under the supervision of the scholars Rabbi Moses and his son Rabbi Enoch, who came from Babylonia and laid the foundations of Talmudic and Judaic study in

22. See Landshuth, *Ammudei Ha-Avodah*, p. 61; *Maḥzor Vitry*, II, 178.
23. A few of the poems of praise that he sent to Samuel Ha-Nagid are printed in Samuel's collection of poems (*Zikkaron La-Rishonim*, 1, 91, 94, and 98).
24. This controversy over the rabbinate is very rich in details that are of considerable significance for the cultural situation of that time; these are described in the *Sefer Ha-Kabbalah* of Rabbi Abraham Ibn Daud. Concerning the name Stans (from the two words *shut enosh*) see *MGWJ*, 1923, pp. i–iii and 59.

Spain. Samuel was the first significant product of these academies. He was the first expert in the Talmud, the first Jewish scholar who grew up on Spanish soil. In the year 1027 Samuel was recognized as the chief rabbi,[25] the spiritual head of Spanish Jewry; and when, about ten years later, the last great Gaon in Babylonia, Rav Hai, died, he, the chief rabbi and head of the Spanish academies,[26] became in fact the spiritual heir of the Geonim of Babylonia. When, following Rav Hai's death, the well of Talmudic knowledge in Babylonia dried up (the academy in Sura was closed in 1034 and the one in Pumbeditha in 1040), the academies in the West under the supervision of Rabbi Samuel became the new, living spring that watered the field of Jewish knowledge. His *Mevo Ha-Talmud* (Introduction to the Talmud), in which he tried to bring the massive material assembled in the Talmud into some order, was accepted throughout the Jewish world, and to this day the Talmudic text is printed together with the scholarly notes of the celebrated Spanish rabbi. Samuel also wrote novellae to the Talmud under the title *Hilkata Gibbarwa*.

Samuel, however, did not devote himself exclusively to the laws of the Talmud. "Occupy yourself diligently with secular books," he used to say; "they will be useful guides in social life." And he practiced what he preached. This rabbi was a first-rate scholar of literally encyclopedic knowledge, a brilliant philologist who, with full right, had the courage to enter into a long learned controversy with the great Hebrew grammarian Ibn Jannaḥ.[27] This was a controversy between two giants equal in power and importance, and experts agree that Rabbi Samuel's major work, his Bible dictionary *Kitab al-Istighna* (*Sefer Ha-Osher*),[28] does not rank lower in importance and scientific value than Jannaḥ's masterwork, *Kitab al-Tankiḥ*.

This great Bible dictionary, which consists of twenty-two parts, was compiled by a man who did not spend all his days in study of Torah. Samuel was not only a professional scholar interested in scientific questions but also a statesman, politician, and general who was as much at home on the battlefield as in the academy. He inscribed his name not only in the history of Jewish science but also

25. Saadiah Ibn Danan in *Ḥemdah Genuzah*, 29; Rabbi Abraham Ibn Daud, *Sefer Ha-Kabbalah*.
26. Solomon Ibn Gabirol calls Rabbi Samuel in one of his poems (which we have published) *rosh yeshivah*, "head of the academy."
27. For details concerning this, see W. Bacher in his introduction to *Sefer Ha-Shorashim*, pp. xv–xvii, and Kokowzoff, *op. cit.*, pp. 77–87.
28. For details concerning this monumental work and, in general, concerning Samuel as philologist, see Kokowzoff, *op. cit.*, and S. Poznanski, *RÉJ*, LXVIII, 183 and 188.

in the history of Moslem Spain.[29] In his youth Samuel had been a simple shopkeeper, but because of his brilliant capacities reached the highest levels of political power. As prime minister (vizier) of the caliphs of Granada, Habus and his son Badis, he was in fact for many years head of the government of Granada.

This rabbi and statesman, diplomat and philologist, was also the founder of secular Hebrew poetry. The historical writer Ravad (Rabbi Abraham Ibn Daud), who recounts in his *Sefer Ha-Kabbalah* interesting details about Samuel Ha-Nagid's life, adds: "In the days of Hasdai the Jewish poets had barely begun to chirp, but in Samuel's time their voice already resounded loudly." The poet Moses Ibn Ezra speaks in his Arabic work on poetry and meter *Kitab al-Muhadarah wal-Mudhakarah* (in Hebrew, *Shirat Yisrael*) with great enthusiasm about Samuel Ha-Nagid as the author of three poetic collections, *Ben Tehillim, Ben Mishlei,* and *Ben Kohelet.* Until modern times only a few fragments of Samuel's *Ben Mishlei* were known. These could not give a true conception of his poetic talent, and reliance was therefore placed on a single phrase which Moses Ibn Ezra incidentally quoted in Solomon Ibn Gabirol's name: "cold as the snows of Hermon or as a song of Samuel the Levite."[30]

In the 1870's, however, Abraham Elijah Harkavy found, among old manuscripts in the St. Petersburg Library, a number of poems of Samuel's *Ben Tehillim.*[31] Only then did it become evident that scholars had been in error when they accepted the verdict of one phrase, torn out of an entire poem which was itself lost and whose true meaning was therefore difficult to establish.[32]

29. Dozy, in his great work *Histoire des musulmans d'Espagne,* was the first to demonstrate the important role of Samuel Ha-Nagid as a Spanish statesman.

30. In one of the fragments of Ibn Gabirol's *Diwan* this phrase is found with a slight change, "and its waters are like the snows of Shanir or like a song of Samuel the Levite." See our article in *Yevreyskaya Misl,* I, 18.

31. Harkavy published these poems, together with those previously known, in a work entitled *Zikkaron La-Rishonim* (1879). As time went on, Harkavy and other scholars discovered several other previously unknown poems of Samuel Ha-Nagid, and in 1910 they were printed anew under the editorship of H. Brody. Not long ago David Yellin announced (*Maddaei Ha-Yahadut,* I [1926], 153) that his relative David Sassoon in London possesses a manuscript of Samuel's complete poetic works, among them also *Ben Kohelet,* which until recently had been believed entirely lost.

32. Recently Brody and the author of these lines discovered in ancient manuscripts a long poem of praise by Solomon Ibn Gabirol, in which he speaks with great enthusiasm of Samuel Ha-Nagid's poetic talent. See also Kaufmann, *MGWJ,* 1899, p. 310.

Ben Mishlei is written in separate two-line verses. In each verse Samuel expresses a specific thought or a maxim about ethics and proper conduct.[33] He, who had risen to the highest level of power through hard work, says in his *Ben Mishlei,* "Do not say, my brother, that rest is the best thing in the world. Remember that this is the way leading to subservience. To the throne of dominion and power only the steps of hard labor and effort bring man." "Not infrequently," says Samuel, "we see blind people whose heart is full of sight, and people with sound eyes who are as if blind. Hence, there are eyes that do not see, but the heart senses and reveals the most hidden secrets." "There are three to whom you should always speak softly even when they answer you heatedly and contemptuously: the king who rules over you, a seriously ill person, and a woman." "Rain gives life to the earth, but if there is too much of it, it kills what it endowed with life; only the well of wisdom and knowledge need not always be measured and weighed—it is ever the bearer of life."

The clever but cold and pedantic verses of *Ben Mishlei* cannot, of course, give a true conception of Samuel Ha-Nagid's poetic talent. This is revealed only in those of his poems which Harkavy published. In Spain, a land blessed by nature, Arabic poetry, as we have indicated, blossomed richly. Joyous wine poems and yearning songs of passionate love resounded freely and excitedly. The Arab poets, dazzled by the rich, sparkling colors of the Orient, tried to outdo each other in the songs of praise with which they celebrated their patrons, the rulers and princes. At the festive table, where men were drunk with spices and strong wine, polished jests, clever riddles, and biting epigrams flew like sharp arrows. The Jewish vizier, the great scholar and lover of the Hebrew language, endeavored to represent all the multicolored, exciting tones of life in the ancient, sacred language of the Psalter and the Song of Songs, of Amos and Isaiah. He himself sings wine songs, invites his friends to "drink from pitchers, both by day and night." He also dispatches poems of praise to his friends and associates, and writes elegies on the deaths of distinguished figures, such as Rav Hai Gaon and others. But the best and most original elements of Samuel Ha-Nagid's literary legacy are the triumphant war poems that he wrote on the battlefield.

The state of Granada in general, and its Jewish vizier in particular, had numerous enemies in the neighboring Arabic states. The army of Granada, under the command of Samuel, often car-

33. For more precise details concerning the plan of the entire book, see D. Yellin, *MGWJ,* 1912, pp. 721–28.

ried on warfare. Not infrequently Samuel's army was surrounded on all sides, but the ingenious and calm warrior always succeeded in delivering his army from danger and bringing it to brilliant victory. These triumphs were celebrated by the heroic vizier in Hebrew poems. After a hiatus of many centuries, Jewish battle poems, expressing praise and gratitude to the God of war, the mighty helper on the battlefield, were again heard. Samuel's wine songs are awkward and crude, but his songs of praise and battle poems are saturated with fiery enthusiasm, with the flame of powerful feeling. At times the odor of blood is to be smelled in them. The fervor of ancient Biblical days, the victorious cry of the era of King David and his heroes, echo in them.

Characteristic is the song of praise in which Samuel celebrates his triumph over the army of his enemy Ibn Abbas. The paean begins with glory to the "God of might, the God of vengeance, the God who is above all praises and laudations." Soon, however, the song of praise passes over into a quiet mood of prayer, in which a confident plea to the God of mercy, who takes up the cause of innocently shed blood and is the sure helper of those who hold the sacred Torah precious, is heard. Immediately after the heartfelt prayer the tone again changes. In the God-fearing man is awakened the warrior who has just conquered his enemy. Intoxicated with victory, he recounts the bloody details of the battle:

Their strong men lay on the battlefield, puffed up like bellows and pregnant women. All together they lay, slaves and lords, princes and servants together. With their king, the new Agag, they all lay around like dung on the field and were not brought to burial. Only one out of a thousand was saved, like single grapes in an abandoned vineyard. Blotted out is Amalek's memorial from the Spanish land, his army scattered, his kingdom destroyed . . .

The slain we left for the jackals, for the leopards and wild boars; their flesh we gave as a gift to the wolves of the field and the birds of heaven. And great was the banquet, all were satiated. Over thorns and thistles were their limbs dragged; the lionesses stilled their young with them. . . . Great and rich was the banquet prepared, and all were filled, drunk on blood without measure. The hyenas made their rounds, and the night was deafened with the cries of the ostriches . . .

And we conquered their land, destroyed the fortresses and towers, subjugated villages and towns, and overwhelmed the capital city with violence.

Several years later a new enemy, the caliph of Seville, arose, and Samuel and his army were surrounded. The pious rabbi and warrior at this critical moment offered a brief but heartfelt prayer to God:

Thou seest that I am in great need, hearken to my plea! . . . I am sunk in a deep abyss, the waters have reached above my head. Stretch out Thy helping hand! Flaming fire burns under my feet. Rescue Thou me! . . . My tongue is silenced before the great danger, and my lips are closed. But all hearts are open before Thee. Hasten Thou to my help.

Samuel was victorious in this war also. The chief of the enemy's army, Ibn Abbad, was killed and his army defeated. Intoxicated with victory, Samuel then sang "a great and splendid hymn of praise to a God splendid and great":

. . . to Thee, my Rock, to Thee praise is seemly.
Thou art my God and from Thy hand cometh power.
. . . .
I will tell of Thy glory in the gates,
And give thanks to Thy name amidst the congregations.
. . . .
About a year ago, on a day of terror like this,
Thou didst save me and made the wicked my ransom.
After the death of Ben Abbas,
At the approach of Ben Abbad, fear took hold of me.
. . . .
Between my king and him, there is strife and jealousy
And each rules his land far from the other.
. . . .
Then he went out and prepared for battle,
And stood with his armies on the frontiers.
And he conquered a city and a kingdom on his path,
And there was none to prevent him and none to protest.
. . . .
Then we passed over into his land in strength
To take vengeance for the despoiled princes.
. . . .

. . . .
And when I saw warriors afraid
And mighty and strong men trembling
. . . .
And when I saw death's first-born before me,
and soldiers dying in battle,

I raised my hand in the name of God,
the Honored, the Mighty, acclaimed by the voice of seventy armies.

. . . .

And mine is the Lord who said, "Trust in Me
and I shall make thy lines fall in pleasant places.
I shall smash for thee the teeth of the lions.
I shall strike down the giants before thee."
Then He put on the garment of wrath and went forth,
As on the day of Pharaoh and his drowned army.
And He revealed Himself, not by a window or in secret,
And He looked down, and not from behind walls,
And He exalted Himself above mine enemies.
And they were like chaff from a threshing floor,
And rotted there like leaves.
And He brought confusion among them and made them skip
Like the young of an ox, like a kid, like calves.
And He made them forget their strength
And they were in their battle like women and young children.

. . . .

. . . .

And I was wearied of seeing the smiting and the smitten
Bespattered, dipped in life's blood

. . . .

And warriors stricken, pierced,
And cast aside, corpses of the heathen.

. . . .

And they were like filth on the face of the earth.
And their heads in the dust like dung.

. . . .

And we captured our captors,
and those who thought to eat us up were themselves eaten.

. . . .

They put their trust in bows and in lances
But I was saved by the name of the Mightiest among the gods.

. . . .

. . . .

Sons of my people, sing with me this song of praise,
Let it be placed at the head of all paeans.

. . . .

A song of praise to the God who saved His friend,
who composed it for the redeemed to sing.

··◦[*31*]◦··

It is a song of praise, great and glorious,
to the God who is glorious and whose deeds are great.

A short while thereafter (in 1042), a strong, united army of two neighboring kingdoms set out against Granada. Before the battle, Samuel Ha-Nagid sent as a memorial a lovely parting song to his only son, Joseph. After he had prevailed in this battle also, he immediately reported the happy news to his son through a carrier pigeon:

> Send a carrier pigeon,
> Though she cannot speak,
> With a tiny letter
> Attached to her wings,
> Sweetened with saffron water
> And perfumed with frankincense.
> And when she rises to fly away,
> Send with her another,
> So that if she meets a hawk,
> Or falls into a net,
> Or delays and does not make haste,
> The second will speed away.
> And when she reaches Joseph's house,
> She will coo on the rooftop.
> And when she comes down to his hands,
> He will rejoice in her like a songbird.
> And he will spread her wings,
> And there will read a letter:
> "My son, know that
> The cursed band of rebels had already fled,
> Scattered on the hills
> Like chaff from a windswept field"
> . . . .
>
> "My son, put your heart
> In the glorious hand of my God,
> And rise and sing my song of praise
> In the assembly of my people.
> And make it an amulet
> Bound on your hand,
> And let it be written on your heart
> With a pen of iron."

CHAPTER TWO

Solomon Ibn Gabirol

AMUEL HA-NAGID, with his unusually versatile personality, made a very powerful impression on his generation. The poets of that period celebrated in numerous compositions the remarkable Jewish prince, who was at one and the same time the head of a Talmudic academy and a military leader, a poet and a scholar. One poet, Joseph Ibn Ḥasdai, acquired his reputation and has a place in the history of Jewish literature solely because of his "Shirah Yetomah," a song of praise in honor of the vizier of Granada. The poet proclaims that Samuel has attained all the secrets of wisdom. Great as the sea is his understanding, the breadth of his heart surpasses the distance from East to West. All kings draw from his light and knowledge. In comparison with him, all counselors and statesmen are like sheep and oxen. Another poet declares that "Samuel Ha-Nagid shines over our land as did, in his day, the prophet Samuel in Ramah and in Mizpah."[1] In addition to having extensive rabbinic knowledge, Samuel was also proficient in the secular sciences of that era. His authority greatly strengthened the influence of Arabic culture on the Jewish community. In his own lifetime Spanish Jewry produced a brilliant personality whom the nourishment of Arabic civilization provided with the potentiality of developing his powers and becoming the creator of marvelous treasures, not only for his day but for future ages. This genius, the first great poet and thinker

1. Solomon Ibn Gabirol, in his poem "Mi Zot Kemo Shaḥar": "Go to Samuel, who has risen in our land as Samuel rose in Ramah and Mizpah." For other poems of praise which we have discovered and published in which Samuel Ha-Nagid is compared to a "divine form," see our work in *Yevreyskaya Misl*, I, 18 (reprinted in *Shirei Shelomo ben Yehudah Ibn Gabirol* [1924], I, 188).

to whom European Jewry gave birth, was Solomon ben Jehudah Ibn Gabirol.

A sorrowful poet was Solomon Ibn Gabirol, the first European author who carried in his heart the deep "pain of the world," *Weltschmerz* as it is called in German literature. And sorrowful and dark was his life as well. Misfortune pursued him not only in his lifetime but even after his death. His famous philosophical work, as we shall see later, wandered for centuries over the European world of thought under a stranger's name. Even sadder was the fate of his poetic legacy. The poem collections (*diwans*) of all the other major Jewish writers of that period, such as Jehudah Halevi, Moses and Abraham Ibn Ezra, Jehudah Alḥarizi, and others, have come down to us in full, but it was Ibn Gabirol's fate that his collection was not preserved and eventually disappeared. For a long time it was even doubted whether, in fact, such a *diwan* of his poems ever existed. Until the end of the nineteenth century only a few score of Ibn Gabirol's secular poems were known, poems that were found by accident in old manuscripts, mostly written by inexperienced scribes and copyists who, out of ignorance and lack of proficiency, made numerous mistakes so that it was often literally impossible to discover the meaning. Only in recent decades has it been established that in the Middle Ages Solomon Ibn Gabirol's *diwan* did exist in several versions. Some remnants of such versions have been discovered in modern times by various scholars (Harkavy, Davidson, Brody, and others). The writer of these lines also had the good fortune to discover some previously unknown remnants of Solomon Ibn Gabirol's legacy. He found in old, half-rotted pages a few score hitherto unknown poems of the great singer.

Our poet's literary works are the only source from which we can obtain some knowledge of his life. The few details found in other sources are mostly false and cannot be relied on.[2] From several of his poems it has been established that he was born around the year 1021 in the city of Malaga.[3] When he was still a child he

2. For example, Saadiah Ibn Danan recounts (*Ḥemdah Genuzah*, p. 25) that Solomon Ibn Gabirol was a pupil of the famous Gaon R. Nissim. The latter, however, lived in Africa and spent only a short time in Granada. But Ibn Gabirol came to Granada when he was already twenty-four years old and had a reputation as a great scholar. At that time he did actually become acquainted with R. Nissim, and in his honor composed the poem "Sh'eltem al Levavi" (published in H. Brody's *Shaar Ha-Shir* and reprinted in *Shirei Shelomo ben Yehudah Ibn Gabirol* [1924], p. 81).
3. Because of this, some of his religious hymns are signed Shelomo Malako (so the city of Malaga was called among Jews in former times). S. Sachs' suggestion that Gabirol also used to sign himself Shelomo Malk is a simple error, as we have already shown in our Russian edition, p. 22.

settled in Saragossa and there spent his adolescence. The only thing we know of his youthful years is his immense, literally insatiable, thirst for knowledge. "And I wearied myself with wisdom from my youth"; "and she [wisdom] was my sister from my youth"; "and, lo, understanding was a mother to my soul, and wisdom and knowledge were my sister"—so the poet often speaks.[4] In a poem that Ibn Gabirol wrote in the seventeenth year of his life, he relates how a close friend reproved him:

Do not ask for too much, my friend. Not everything can be attained. Human life is very brief. You plant a vineyard, but are you certain that you will enjoy its fruit before you depart from the world? And are you striving to reach the summit of wisdom? Do you hasten up mountains swiftly as a deer? Do you run fast like a rider across the valley into the lowland? Are you striving toward the height of the heavens where no eagle with mighty wings has yet attained and no human foot has ever trod? You wish to be like the free birds of the wilderness, while your fate is to be only the scapegoat of the desert! Withdraw from the paths of wisdom, do not strive for that which you cannot reach. . . .

Proudly the poet answers:

The most precious thing in the world is searching and knowledge. How I should despise myself if I were to forget wisdom and, like an insignificant worm, crawl after earthly desires and slavishly enjoy life. No, my friend! As the moon accompanies the light-giving sun in the heavens, so will I remain by the side of wisdom, its constant and faithful companion. But, oh, do not think, my friend, that we purchase wisdom for small change in the noisy regions of life! Do not think that he who has enjoyed the well of wisdom will also crawl in the dust and scrabble after a greedy morsel. Wisdom is the goal and final purpose of all divine ways. It is the mirror and reflection of the eternal source of life. God himself in His omnipotence created it.[5]

Ibn Gabirol's poetic talent matured extremely early. When he was only sixteen years old, the fame of the poet already resounded in distant lands. When the Gaon Rav Hai died (in the year 1038),

4. One of the still unpublished poems of his youth ends with the verse: "And I wear the garment of wisdom and instruction, and knowledge has adorned me with its veil."
5. In the poem "Beḥar Mehaḥali," first published by S. Sachs in *R. Shelomoh ben Gabirol U-ketzat Mi-Benei Doro*, pp. 16–23. A better and more accurate text of this poem was found by us in an old manuscript in the Leningrad Library (see also the Bialik-Ravnitzki edition of Ibn Gabirol's poems [1924], I, 45).

men from Babylonia and Egypt asked Ibn Gabirol to write an elegy.[6]

The poet himself understood that he was one of the elect, one of the preciously unique, and proudly declared:

> I am the master, and song is a slave to me;
> The harp of all poets and minstrels am I.
> My song is a crown to all kings of the earth,
> And a mitre on the heads of the noble and high.
> Though my body treads on the earth here below,
> My spirit soars to the clouds in the sky.
> Sixteen though I am, yet my wisdom excels
> The wisdom of one who is eighty well-nigh.

In another poem Ibn Gabirol declares,

I am still very young. I have enjoyed the world for only sixteen years, and yet I am the pride and joy of all hearts that yearn after the source of wisdom and its hidden secrets. . . . My song can split rocks and create a fresh spring out of hard stones. The gates of wisdom which are closed for my people stand wide open before me. My way strives upward to the heavens, and among the stars have I spread my tent. My word will be inscribed in the memory of all future generations, and eternally will my song be the rod of punishment for all dark minds.[7]

In still another poem the seventeen-year-old Ibn Gabirol relates with pride that "Babylonia and Egypt acclaim him and Hanes wishes to be acquainted with him." "The world has revealed to me its deep secret," he declares, and he emphasizes, incidentally, that he is proficient in all the sciences of his time and that "his soul is intimate with the stars in heaven."

But from this soul that was "intimate with the stars in heaven," the plain, sinful earth, with its pleasures and joys, very early took away its charm. The youthful poet paid dearly for his early maturity. The powerful thirst for knowledge worked very injuriously on the still undeveloped body. Ibn Gabirol had even in his adolescent years to suffer intense physical pain. The poems that he

6. Ibn Gabirol lamented Rav Hai's death in four poems. One, "Bechu Imi," has long been known. Two others, "Mi Yaḥavosh Nezer Beno Yishai" and "Ha-Lo Tivkun," were published by Harkavy, and the poem "Nigdeah Keren Adinah" was found by us in an old manuscript in the Leningrad Library and published in *Yevreyskaya Misl.*

7. We first found these verses in an old manuscript in the Leningrad Imperial Library (see our article in *Yevreyskaya Misl,* I, 126). Cf. the poem in the Bialik-Ravnitzki edition, III, 1.

wrote as a sixteen- and seventeen-year-old youth are already filled
with heartbreaking cries: "Sickness has wasted my body"; "I toss
on my bed the whole night through, as on thorns and piercing
reeds"; "cursed be the sickness that has wasted my flesh."[8] "In
insatiable thirst for knowledge," he complains, "I have lost my
health, as others have in the passion of love."[9] "My body is emaci-
ated, a weak fly can carry it away on its wings."[10]

Melancholy and doubt awakened extremely early in the heart
of the poet. "From my youth on has my heart punished me," he
laments. "A sixteen-year-old and already so ancient," he says of
himself. And he turns in pain to his dead mother: "Ah, woe is me
that you brought me into the world. How well it would have been
had you remained barren."

Even in his youthful years the smile died on the poet's lips, and
his song veiled itself in sadness. Unknown to him was the song of
love; great sorrow drove it away.[11] "My soul," he laments, "opened
wide for me the doors of sorrow and closed behind me the gates
of youth."[12]

Ibn Gabirol's keen speculative mind very soon became familiar
with the sharp knife of doubt and merciless negation. The singer
who, with great pride, had declared, "the roll of the heavens is
locked up in my heart,"[13] was even in his youth disgusted with
the vanity of the world and the pettiness of life. Furthermore—
and this is especially important to emphasize in a poet of the Middle Ages—his sentiment has a purely secular character, without
the slightest religious trace. This brings the young Ibn Gabirol's
poetry close to the modern world outlook, and the contemporary
European feels, in the despairing verses of the poet of Malaga of
the eleventh century, echoes of his own pain and sorrow.[14]

8. *Ha-Shiloaḥ*, XXV, 558; reprinted in the Bialik-Ravnitzki edition, I, 51.
   Some scholars conjecture that Ibn Gabirol suffered from tuberculosis.
9. Leopold Dukes, *Shirei Shelomoh*, p. 38; Bialik-Ravnitzki edition, I, 25.
10. Bialik-Ravnitzki edition, I, 125.
11. In Ibn Gabirol's poetic legacy there is not a single love poem. We did,
    indeed, discover in an old manuscript in the Leningrad Imperial Library
    a short love poem which bears his name, but we are very doubtful
    whether this poem actually is his. (See our article cited in Note 7.)
12. In the poem "Lu Haitah Nafshi."
13. In the poem "Shemesh Meromim," first published by us (see the Bialik-
    Ravnitzki edition, I, 187).
14. The vanity of the world and of human life is, to be sure, a very com-
    mon motif in old Hebrew poetry. But among all the other older poets,
    aside from Ibn Gabirol, this motif bears a purely religious character
    and draws sustenance from the pious sentiment of "repentance." These
    are really not poems, but *seliḥot* (penitential poems), ethical instruction
    worked over into verse.

"Life," Ibn Gabirol laments, "has, like a snake, bitten my heels.
. . . So that eagles should not fly to the heavens, life cuts down
their wings. I am such an eagle, I also lie with broken wings."[15]
Full of despair is the song of the sixteen-year-old poet:

My melody is veiled in sorrow, my song permeated with sighs. When
I hear of joy and laughter, I weep with bitter tears. . . . My friend
said to me: "Is it right for a sixteen-year-old to lament the hatefulness
of life? And in youth sorrowfully to bow his head like the pale lily
under the burning rays?" — Ah, from childhood on, sadness has
haunted my heart, and my soul is despondent. I wished to understand
the mystery of life, but my striving was in vain. My spirit remained
disquieted and sad. . . . My friend says to me again: "Can anything
be helped with lamentation? Not through tears can pain be assuaged,
and weeping can heal no wound. Better remain silent, my friend, and
do not surrender hope!" — But what help can hope bring? And can
one hope ceaselessly? He who carries a mortal wound in his heart,
whose spirit is broken, can no longer find healing.[16]

A single ray of light illuminated the poet's youth. This was his
friendship with a distinguished personality, the astronomer Jekutiel
ben Isaac (Ibn Hassan in Arabic). This friendship was celebrated
by Ibn Gabirol in many lovely poems. "In our heavens," he declares, "a luminous star has risen. Jekutiel is his name. And all the
other stars in heaven pale before him."

Ibn Gabirol turns to the holy spirit, to the goddess of song who
hovers over him:

O dove, lily of Sharon! Come hither in your golden clothing adorned
with bells that dazzles no less than did the mantle of Aaron the priest.
When I see you, it seems that the bright sun is risen in all its glory.
Sit by me, my beloved. Reveal to your friend the fragrant flowers of
beauty. Take in hand the harp, the cithara, and all the musical instruments that man has fashioned, and sing your song of praise, sing of the
beloved, the chosen, the best of all lords and nobles, sing of Jekutiel,
the light of the world, the pride and hope of our generation.

Soon, however, the poet's only joy was also destroyed in the
most tragic way. In the year 1039 Jekutiel perished. Enemies
slandered him, and he was punished with death. His friend's tragic
fate had a profound effect on the young poet. "If Jekutiel's days

15. From the poem "Keshoresh Etz."
16. The poem "Melitzati Bedaagati Hadufah" has been printed many times.
The most accurate text is Davidson's in *JQR*, n.s., IV (1913), 68; reprinted in the Bialik-Ravnitzki edition, I, 3.

have come to an end, the stars in heaven will also not shine eternally." Thus begins Ibn Gabirol's poem of two hundred verses, in which he mourns the death of his unfortunate friend. Full of quiet sadness also is his brief elegiac poem "Re'eh Shemesh":

> Behold, the sun reddening in the evening,
> As if she had clothed herself with a scarlet robe.
> She strips the north and south of color
> And covers the west with purple.
> And the earth she leaves naked,
> Hidden in the shadow of night.
> The sky then grows dark, as if
> In mourning for the death of Jekutiel.

After Jekutiel's death, Ibn Gabirol's melancholy became even more intense. "Life," he complains, "has handed me a cup filled with sorrow, and commanded me to quaff it to the last drop."[17] Filled with despair is his heartbreaking poem "Ahi Tevel":

Oh, child of earth, how cruel is your mother! — She devours her own children before they have enjoyed anything of the world! If the sons of earth had their eyes opened, they would change the earth into a blasted wilderness! If men understood what my heart has understood, they would spit on the earth with mockery and gall! . . . How hateful to me is the earth, I am disgusted with its shame and corruption! . . . We, children of earth, all tremble in its accursed net; we all carry its sinner's stamp on our brow; we all reflect its fearful image. Why, then, do we tremble so before death, and why does it fill us with such terror? Why is man so afraid? Why does he keep himself in bondage? Death is surely our redeemer, and yet we quake before his cup! With thankfulness should we drink the blessed liquid.[18]

Under the burning sun of Arabic Spain, where life welled up like a mighty spring, the Jews also drank freely from the joyous fountain. The Jewish youth of the wealthier classes imitated the Arabic youth, whiled away their time pleasantly in vineyards, gathered in companies around beakers of wine, sang happy songs throughout the nights, jested and laughed, and treated each other to cheerful witticisms. Even our melancholy poet, it seems, occasionally, in his younger years, participated in such a happy company. There has even come down to us a wine song of his (to be sure, it is the only example), which he composed when he spent

17. In the poem "Keshoresh Etz."
18. Bialik-Ravnitzki edition, I, 137.

an evening with a group at the home of a certain Moses. The host, it appears, was a miser and gave his merry guests wine in scanty measure. At the end, the group had to fill their empty glasses with plain water. Then Ibn Gabirol sang a caustic song to the stingy host:[19]

> The Feast's begun
> And the Wine is done,
> So my sad tears run
> Like streams of Water, streams of Water.
>
> Three score and ten were Wine's bold braves.
> But a full score more were Water's knaves,
> And silent are our watery graves.
> For—whence tuneful note?
> When the minstrel's throat
> Tastes naught but Water, Water, Water!
>
> Around the board you see no smile;
> Untasted dishes rest in file,
> How can I touch these dainties while
> There stands my cup
> To the brim filled up
> With hated Water, Water, Water!
>
> Old Moses chid the Red Sea tide,
> And Egypt's dusky streams he dried,
> Till Pharaoh's fools for Water cried!
> But Moses dear,
> Why dost thou here
> Turn all to Water, hated Water?
>
> Can I myself to aught compare?
> To the frog who, damp in watery lair,
> With dismal croakings fills the air.
> So frog and I

19. Every verse of this poem ends with a refrain which, translated literally from the Hebrew, reads: "When the wine is done, my eyes run with streams of water." Unfortunately, this ingenious poem has not come down to us in its entirety. At least two verses are missing from it. This can easily be seen from the acrostic. The letters at the beginning of each verse ought to form, when taken together, *Shelomoh Katan*. The two penultimate verses are, however, missing, and the initial letters of the verses form only *Shelomoh* ——*n*. [The translation given here is by the Anglo-Jewish scholar Israel Abrahams. Zinberg presents an inferior seventeenth-century Yiddish translation of the Hebrew text. —B.M.]

Will sing or cry,
The song of Water, the dirge of Water.

The man whom Water can delight
For aught I care may turn Nazirite;
Total abstention shall be his plight!
And all his days
To his lips shall raise
Cups of Water, always Water!

The Feast is done,
And Wine there's none;
So my sad tears run
Like streams of Water, streams of Water.

In time, as the sorrowful mood of the poet grew, he became isolated from other people and began to withdraw from the friends of his youth. In one of his poems Ibn Gabirol describes how astonished his comrades were at first. They tried to console him with conversation, to drive away his melancholy, and to awaken in him desire for life:

Your rivers of tears can flood mountains. Why do you not sing of wine? Why do you not greet the foaming cup? Before it your sorrow would flee, like the frightened enemy before the sword! — Yes, true, I answered them, sadness is drowned in the cup, sorrow and pain are forgotten. Wine creates wings that free one from the daily lament and lift him to the heavens of joy and laughter. . . . But *me* the cup cannot help! Even if it were as large as the Red Sea, it would not become the abyss that could swallow my sorrow! Constantly greater grows my sadness; it can cover the world. It tears my heart to pieces, devours my blood and marrow like flaming fire. . . . I cry in the darkness out of pain and sorrow, and the dark night veils me in its mantle, and my cry is silenced, my sobs are choked. . . .[20]

Saturated with even deeper despair is another poem of Ibn Gabirol's which has, unfortunately, come down to us in such a corrupt condition that it is, in places, virtually impossible to obtain the meaning. This poem begins with Oriental images and similes:

The stream of tears would change my cheeks into a fruitful field, if fresh tear-springs did not drive away the first. No sooner do the bitter tears stop for a moment in their rushing stream than terrible sobs frighten them away, and swiftly they run further, driven by terror. . . . The night is the watcher over my weeping, the stillness

20. The poem is entitled "Ulai Demaot."

guards my sighs, and the stars look down from the heavens, listen to my heart-cries, and whisper to each other. . . . In the long nights golden youth with its bright days, beautiful and many-colored like a necklace of opals and rubies, revive in memory. Now my day is darkened like the night; then even the nights were bright. . . . No sooner would sadness awaken than I immediately hurried to friends, who pressed grapes and shed their blood . . . hands in blood, and yet no murder. They created new life, carved out the spring of fresh divine powers. In my heart, too, they kindled the sweet rush of burning desire, and when the sun bowed its head before Queen Night, they, intoxicated, kissed cheeks more beautiful than the bright sun. . . . And suddenly in my heart a thought full of sadness and despair awakens: Beauty is a delusion! How vain and petty are joy and desire! And even those who laugh and dance, drunk with enjoyment and pleasure, cry out of pain and weep bitterly when alone at home. . . .[21]

This thought, "How vain and petty are joy and desire," obtains all the greater power with the poet, the more his proud self-consciousness grows. Less and less can the profaneness of daily life, with its petty interests, satisfy him. This mood is clearly expressed in the lovely song "Haforas Lailah":[22]

Night has spread its wings and made a rush to capture the sun. . . . Already it has covered the light of day with its robe; the moon has decked herself in her green crown and disappeared under the cloud, which lovingly embraces her. Everything is as if congealed; almost imperceptibly has the myrtle trembled in its light, sweet sleep. Long did I look into the night, and its lights in heaven, astonished, asked: What, oh man, have you to do here? . . .

My friends are gentle with sweet words; they wish to assuage the pain of my heart. Vain is their effort! The pain is not to be alleviated, the wound not to be healed. Even the fire of Nebuchadnezzar's ovens can not burn out the spring of my tears. I do not hope for the morning; every new day is a fresh test, a new touchstone for my suffering. . . . They all say to me, "Seize the moment and enjoy the riches of life." But the vineyard of life is only for petty, vain men who scrabble and with greedy hands wrest the still unripened fruits. And the proud lion can not still its hunger with dried grass and chaff carried away by the wind. . . . For exalted spaciousness, for the free heavens, yearns my soul; the flat, sandy islet can not satisfy me. I am not of those who bend under the yoke of life, I will not bow my head, I wish to be the master of my own fate. No matter that my lot is sorrowful, no matter that the blessed dew does not refresh the garden of my life, no matter that

21. The poem "Revivei Dimacha." The text of the four lines that follow is heavily corrupted, and the poet's thought is interrupted in the middle.
22. Regrettably, the text of this poem is also strongly corrupted in places.

my path is full of stones; my pride will not be subjugated, the insignificant gifts of life will not dazzle me. . . .

The more spiritually and intellectually mature the poet became, the more the feeling of alienation and loneliness grew in him. "The world was once beautiful, but I have come into it too late," he laments. The separation between him and his environment grew ever greater, and finally there occurred with Ibn Gabirol what happens not infrequently with the great figures of an era who stand significantly above their surroundings: the separation and alienation were transformed into cold contempt and genuine hatred. "My eye embraces the whole world and fathoms the depths of human hearts," proudly declares Ibn Gabirol. And to this eye the vanity of daily life, with its petty joys and concerns, with its spiritual emptiness, ridiculous pride and arrogance, sharply revealed itself. The poet observed how many of his former friends were trying to imitate the then-fashionable mode—singing songs, writing odes and love songs, playing the role of patrons of science and art, of which they had very little knowledge. In this he saw an insult to what was for him so precious and beloved; hence, his song became an instrument of reproof with which he condemned the desecration of sanctities. With hatred and contempt he branded his generation and environment for their wrongs.

When Ibn Gabirol was asked why he had long been silent, he responded with indignation and scorn:

How should I sing when in our day every simpleton and fool stretches out his hand to the poet's crown? Poetry has been stripped of its royal mantle and wrapped in beggar's rags. The proud queen has been dragged from the throne and her purity sullied by filthy hands. The divine, prophetic word has become a pastime, the holy fire has been degraded into a plaything. . . . Men of knowledge have disappeared; they have been driven away with pride and arrogance by ignoramuses and spiritual eunuchs. . . . No wisdom, no knowledge is dear to these. All they care for is that their name should resound, glitter with praise and glory. . . . These rhymsters think they are poets, they call the grating crow's cry song! Oh, when will the new Phinehas ben Eleazar[23] come who, with powerful hand, will spear through the arrogant Zimris who rape the daughter of song, the princess of poetry? . . . My generation will I reprove with my poetry. It hates my song, but it will never forget it . . .[24]

23. It is related in the Pentateuch that when the children of Israel openly whored with the daughters of Midian, the priest Phinehas ben Eleazar struck one of the sinners, Zimri, through with his spear.
24. In the poem "Azai Beseif Halom." Unfortunately, this poem is also strongly corrupted, and we give here the content of only a few verses.

The consciousness that he was one of the unique, one of the elect, together with his growing feeling of hatred and contempt for the pettiness and vanity of his environment, became the major motifs of many of Ibn Gabirol's poems. "My friend tells me," begins the poem "Ateh Hod,"

"Forget your sorrow, suppress your tears, and with closed lips go proudly on your way. Do not abandon hope—for your fate is so beautiful; you are the brilliant star that shines over our generation, and lovelier than the richest necklace of pearls are your measured words and divine song." — "Ah, no," was my answer, "I cannot and may not be silent! I can find no rest, like the foaming waves of the seething sea. I am the target of sorrow's arrows, I am the chariot of suffering and pain, and over me misfortune with its black wings flies." . . . I am the man who is young in years only, rich in knowledge alone, like the wisest elders. My body wanders in the depths, but my spirit rises higher than the clouds . . . I cannot look on calmly and see how petty and vain minds pass for pillars of wisdom, and clumsy versifiers wish to shame me with their songs. I am repelled by the shameful tribe! They wish to compare themselves with me, but how can they, the blind, appreciate my true worth? I am the master of song, the guardian of the well of wisdom. I am the seeker of pearls who gathers treasures from the profoundest depths. From melodies, words, and sounds, I create, as if through magic, divine songs. I am the man who freely penetrates into the most hidden sanctuaries. The sharpest peaks of the mountains of wisdom, the distant heavens of the kingdom of thought, spread themselves before my feet like a colorful carpet of flowers . . . I sing, and my song rejoices all longing souls and liberates all languishing hearts from sadness!

But suddenly these proud verses are interrupted by chords of despair: "Woe is me! How crude and ignorant is my generation, a generation of shameful men and traitors! Over this I grieve my whole life long, and my heart weeps bitterly."

The poet does not weary of hurling arrows at the "bands of dull-witted persons" with "empty hearts and minds." Sadly he addresses his contemporaries: "Oh, when will you finally fulfill the wishes of my heart? They still remain strange to your heart. How long will I reprove, and you remain deaf to my words? How long will I spread light before your eyes, and they still not become seeing?"

These words were undoubtedly extremely displeasing to many of Ibn Gabirol's townsmen in Saragossa. They considered themselves highly insulted and, it appears, an appeal was made to the poet no longer to attack his society so sharply. "No," was the poet's answer, "I am not of those who find favor with their soft, sweet words. I am not of those who bend the knee before the mighty and powerful. I belong to those who proudly set themselves against the world, like the rebellious priest who destroys his former idols." And he turns with scorn to his townsmen:

Your foolish demand will not be fulfilled. I will not seal my lips because of the baying of aroused dogs. Not the black raven but the white dove[25] is the emissary that fulfills the will of its sender. Try to stop the circuit of the planets, command the stars to leave their places—so will you succeed in silencing me before I inscribe my song for eternity in the hearts of the world. . . . See, oh man, black clouds are here buffeted by the wind, and they remain as deeply black as before. Now consider the rays of the sun. These are ever the source of light, the joy and consolation of human hearts. And just as the black cloud is not to be compared to the luminous ray, so can a vile Kehoth not liken himself to Phinehas the priest.[26]

At this time, it appears, Ibn Gabirol composed his poem "Nefesh Asher Alu Sheonehah," which is very typical of his eternally restless, eternally searching spirit that strives toward the heights on the wings of speculative thought. Deep inspiration and exalted feeling permeate every verse of the poem; our prose paraphrase can, unfortunately, not convey the remarkable beauty of the original:

How restless you are, my soul! You strive upward, and your thoughts fly and hover like sparks over the flaming fire. You are like the heavenly spheres that constantly hasten on their way far above the earth and its multitude. Your thoughts are as deep as the seas that hide in their abysses the foundations of the world. . . .
They all say to me: "Only abandon your constant quest, and the world will bestow upon you its richest treasures." They consider this a consolation, but from such comfort my sorrow grows even greater. I thirst and I seek, like the redemption, the free man with eagle eyes. But my searching is in vain. Our generation is not worthy of giving birth to such men. . . . Hear, oh earth! If my demand remains unfulfilled, I will spatter you with gall; if your eyes will not see my light, you are worthy of the blind mole's dark fate. . . . I have desired so greatly and lovingly to lend beauty to the world! I would forgive her all her sins, if only she would knock at the doors of repentance. But my demand is in vain. O sinful earth, turn aside your face, shatter your foundations, you are covered with filth! You have scorned proud cedars for dwarfish thornbushes. Stupid men, the chaff

25. A reference to the raven and the dove that Noah sent out after the flood.
26. Dukes, *Shirei Shelomoh*, p. 22.

and refuse of the generation, hold their heads high and arrogantly
forget what justice, truth, and understanding mean. If justice ruled the
world, how would those flecked with shame dominate everything
beautiful? To give birth to this foolish arrogance, they violate the
bright daughters of the sun.

Again the poet turns to those who are so odious to him:

You thorns and wild growths of the forest, you declare war against me
because I hold aloft the light of knowledge and am the guardian of
the wisdom so despised by you. Because you are blind, do you wish
those with open eyes also to grope in darkness? No, I will not part
from wisdom. God's word has sealed an eternal bond between me and
herself. How can I forget you, my faithful mother? How can I stretch
forth my hand and remove from your head the brilliant crown, you
comfort and pride of my soul? I remain your son forever! How great
is my pleasure and the joy of my soul when I rest by the fragrant
banks of your refreshing streams of balsam. . . . Strive further upward, my spirit! Rise above the clouds that cover the rays of the sun.
— I have taken an oath: I must not and may not rest until I shall have
uncovered the hidden grounds of wisdom!

Many of Ibn Gabirol's poems are permeated with this unquench-
able thirst for wisdom. Especially characteristic is the poem "Ani
Ha-Ish," which begins with the verse: "I am the man who has
girded up his loins and will not turn back until he has fulfilled his
oath. . . . I am the man who himself destroys what he has built
with his own hands, tears up the roots that he has himself planted,
and breaks the fences that he has himself erected."

In the meantime, the relationships between the poet and the
people in his environment became increasingly hostile. Powerful
persons in the community, who felt themselves offended by his
reproving verses, decided to take revenge on the annoying critic,
and the twenty-four-year-old Ibn Gabirol had to flee from Saragossa, in which he had spent his youth, and settle in Granada, where
he obtained support from Samuel Ha-Nagid.[27] Before leaving
Saragossa he poured out his scorn for his opponents in the long
poem "Niḥar Bekori Geroni"[28]: "I must live among a wild people,
I am buried alive, my dwelling is my coffin! I am all alone in the

27. There are a large number of poems of praise in which Ibn Gabirol
 celebrates the famous Jewish philanthropist and scholar. Some of these
 were first discovered by the author of the present work.
28. Printed several times. See the Bialik-Ravnitzki edition, I, 4. In another
 poem that Ibn Gabirol wrote at the same time, "Mah-loch Yeḥidah,"
 he expresses his desire to leave Spain.

world, a sick man without mother and father[29] and brother. My only friend is my thought. . . . My words of reproof have brought them to fierce anger, they have declared war against me, but my weapon, the arrow-tipped word, will destroy them. . . ." And, again, above the proud verses a heartrending cry of woe breaks through:

Woe to me and woe to my understanding! I find myself among men who exchange God's holy word for the foolish incantations of spell-makers and magicians. . . . In vain do my eyes seek somewhere in the world a point of light where my hope may again flower! . . . The earth has become hateful to me! I wait for death as for a liberator. Despicable to me is the earth with all its splendor; I do not desire its joys, eternal sorrow do I carry in my heart. . . . Why do I bear the yoke of life, why do I crawl here like a blind man? Oh, how disgusted I am with life and with my own sick body. How happy my soul would be if death set it free.

But the despairing poet had one thing that always remained precious to him. He mentions this in the last verses of his poem: "On me lies the obligation to fulfill grandfather Solomon's[30] command: to search constantly and uninterruptedly, to delve into the secrets of wisdom. Perhaps they will enlighten my eyes. This command is my sole consolation, my only portion in the world."

"Grandfather Solomon's command" in fact became the major goal and final purpose of Ibn Gabirol's life and creativity. This first great European poet of *Weltschmerz* conquered his sorrow, choked back his tears, and overcame his anger and hatred. In the later period of his life Ibn Gabirol rose to such a spiritual and moral height that no enmity or scorn could reach it. The petty and accidental vanished, swallowed up in the great and immortal. "The higher man raises himself," the poet proclaims, "the smaller the earthly and corporeal appear. They vanish like a bird in the heavens or a ship on the great sea."[31]

In the later period of his creativity Ibn Gabirol was imbued with the idea that the immortal and eternal rule with boundless power over everything that exists. The idea of immortality, however, was not for him an abstract philosophical concept that can be grasped only by the mind. It filled the poet's entire being; he felt it with

29. Davidson, *op. cit.*, has discovered a poem of Ibn Gabirol's in which he laments the death of his father.
30. King Solomon, as the author of the philosophical book of the Bible, Ecclesiastes.
31. Shemtov Falaquera, *Likkutim*, III, Section 87. See also *Mekor Ḥayyim* (1926), p. 137.

all his soul, in every corner of his great heart. For Ibn Gabirol was not only a bold thinker, a free investigator with a keen and critical eye. His was also a deeply and ardently believing nature, imbued with the mystic fire of religious enthusiasm. He strove ceaselessly to the eternal light, but believed that everywhere, even in the petty and vain, some sparks of this light are scattered, and all of them yearn to return to their source. "Do not marvel," says the poet, "that man strives to fathom the hidden ways of wisdom. The very spirit that rules over his body is also the power that brings everything into motion."

Ibn Gabirol rarely describes nature in and for itself,[32] but he does so constantly in connection with his soul-world, his moods and experiences. His restless, constantly probing spirit sought in nature powerful images in which it might incorporate and express its feelings and thoughts. When he describes a dark, stormy night that lightning has pierced like an arrow,[33] his own stormy and restless soul is reflected. When he portrays the splendor of the starry southern night, he considers it necessary to declare that the stars, "the brilliant, gleaming diamonds scattered over dark blue Atlas," are the speechless messengers revealing to the deaf the great mystery of eternal wisdom that rules the world.[34]

On the highest levels to which Ibn Gabirol's spirit rose, his solitude came to an end. As his personality felt itself interwoven with the world spirit, he conquered the restlessness of his soul and overcame his painful doubts. He no longer set himself against his insignificant generation and the pettiness of life, but fused himself with all of humanity, and his "I" became submerged in the great "I" of the whole world. Mystical enthusiasm, the flame of profound religious experience, displaced *Weltschmerz*. The poet was inspired by the consciousness that man is not an insignificant grain of sand carried along by blind chance, not a poor-souled worm crawling in the darkness, but a link in the great chain of being, a major element in the mighty cosmic structure, a significant part of the vestment in which divine wisdom discloses itself. "The infinite breadth of the universe," he cries out enthusiastically, "is too small to serve as Thy dwelling place, yet Thou residest in my thought."[35]

With this idea, which occupies, as we shall see, the most important place in Ibn Gabirol's philosophic system, the poet's re-

---

32. Dukes gives in his *Shirei Shelomoh* two short poems of Ibn Gabirol's, in the first of which spring is celebrated (pp. 7–8), and in the second, autumn (p. 38). It is, however, very probable that these are only fragments of larger poems.
33. In the poem "Ani Ha-Ish Asher Shines Azoro."
34. Bialik-Ravnitzki edition, I, 12–13.
35. *Ibid.*, II, 47.

ligious lyrics are saturated. Characteristic in this respect are the
following lines:

Three things conspire together in mine eyes
To bring the remembrance of Thee ever before me,
And I possess them as faithful witnesses:
Thy heavens, for whose sake I recall Thy name,
The earth I live on, that rouseth my thought
With its expanse which recalleth the expander of my pedestal,
And the music of my heart when I look within the depths of myself.
Bless the Lord, O my soul, forever and aye.[36]

The proud poet, who "carries the whole universe locked in his
heart," bows humbly before God the Creator with heartfelt prayer-
poems on his lips. In Ibn Gabirol's religious poetry, deep feeling
with exalted thought, a religious-philosophical world outlook with
noble inspiration and lyrical pathos, are harmoniously blended. Like
the spire of a medieval Gothic cathedral, Ibn Gabirol's religious
song strives upward toward the heavens.

At the dawn I seek Thee
Rock and Refuge tried,
In due service speak Thee
Morn and even-tide.
'Neath Thy greatness shrinking
Stand I sore afraid,
All my secret thinking
Bare before Thee laid.
Little to Thy glory
Heart or tongue can do;
Small remains the story,
Add we spirit too.
Yet since man's praise ringing
May seem good to Thee,
I will praise Thee singing
While Thy breath's in me.[37]

The God before whom the medieval Jewish poet pours out his
soul is not, however, merely the omnipotent Creator of the world.
He is also the God of Israel, the God of the chosen people, the God

36. From *Selected Religious Poems of Solomon Ibn Gabirol*, translated
    into English verse by Israel Zangwill, from a critical text edited by
    Israel Davidson (Philadelphia: The Jewish Publication Society of
    America, 1923), p. 8.
37. *Ibid.*, p. 2. This hymn is printed in many Jewish prayer books.

of Abraham, Isaac, and Jacob, who revealed himself on Mount Sinai in the sight of all Israel.

When one considers the inner world of our poet, a very important point, namely, the melody of deep national sorrow that echoes strongly in many of his religious poems, must also be touched upon. We have already noted the great influence on the development of Hebrew exercised by the flowering of Arabic literature. The living vernacular of the Arabs, when raised to the level of a holy language, that of the Koran, began to be scientifically explored. Within a relatively short time it became the language of high culture and science. Philological investigations into Arabic elicited, as we have observed, a powerful echo in Jewish circles. There also men began to explore with great enthusiasm the beauty of their own sacred language. It is therefore quite understandable that Ibn Gabirol, who drew nourishment from Arabic culture, looked upon himself as the guardian and redeemer of the holy language, sent by Providence to awaken love for it in the hearts of his brethren. As a nineteen-year-old youth, Ibn Gabirol attempted to expound briefly, in the form of a poem, the rules and principles of Hebrew grammar. This work, entitled *Anak*, consisted of four hundred verses, but only the first one hundred have come down to us, and for these we owe thanks to the twelfth-century scholar Solomon Parhon, who quotes them in the introduction to his *Mahberet He-Aruch*.[38] Of special interest are the first fifty verses, which are only the introduction to the work itself. In this introduction the poet laments that the eye of his people has become blind, that they have forgotten their holy book and that its language is strange to them; "they can no longer even read the script." Ibn Gabirol hears a divine voice calling to him: "Arise! You have been elected by God to be the spokesman for the dumb with their locked lips. Arise. Do not say, I am too young. The old are too weak to be the support of the holy crown." "I am ready," answers the poet; "I know that God has so commanded."

In the style of the ancient Hebrew prophets Ibn Gabirol turns indignantly to his people:

God has declared war against you, O remnant of Jacob! You have forsaken the unique and chosen language. See, when your forefathers

38. In *Mahberet He-Aruch*, however, the text of these verses is very much corrupted. They are reprinted in corrected form in the *Zunz-Jubelschrift*, II, 191–92. We have also found a very good text of these verses of Ibn Gabirol's in an old manuscript in the Harkavy Collection in the Library of the Society for the Dissemination of Enlightenment, in Leningrad. Our quotations here follow this manuscript.

became rebellious and entered blindly upon strange ways, the prophet Isaiah reproved them with his wrathful word. With such a people one will have to speak in a strange, mixed language, with stammering tongue.

Angrily the poet cries out: "The mistress has forgotten the word, and the concubine preserves it. Woe to the people which tends strange vineyards and has neglected its own."

Ibn Gabirol, however, not only reproved his people but also comforted them and poured unguent on their wounds. He, whose own soul from childhood on was veiled in sorrow, sensed with special keenness the fate of the eternally wandering people. The great, historic national tragedy, the sufferings and pain of Israel, found a powerful echo in the poet's heart. He laments,

Our years pass away in poverty and scorn. We hope for light, but shame and slavery are our fate. Contemptible slaves rule over us, and we still languish in exile.

Unfortunate captive, driven into a strange land, as a maidservant, an Egyptian maidservant, have you been sold. . . . From the day, O God, that You forsook her, she has been waiting constantly for You. Redeem her from captivity, O Almighty! . . . Everything has an end, but my misery has none! Generation follows generation, and my wound is still not healed. In captivity I become faint, I am drowned in the abyss, and no one takes hold of the rudder to save the ship and steer it to shore. . . . Behold, we are hunted and oppressed, brought to shame and scorn. They rob and oppress us. We are crushed into dust. We perish under the heavy yoke. How long, O God, will our enslavement last, how long will strangers rule over us? Ishmael[39] is like a lion, Esau[40] like a bird of prey; the remnant that the one leaves of us, the other devours.[41]

Suddenly there breaks through the sorrowful, elegiac melody a bright, joyous chord. The poet describes how a divine voice is heard proclaiming the tidings that the day of redemption is near; and from the top of the mountain the sounds of the long-awaited trumpet are heard. The messenger with white wings proclaims: "The redeemer of Zion is at hand!" It is with this hopeful chord that many of Ibn Gabirol's national-religious poems that are written in the form of a dialogue between God and the community of Israel end:

39. The Mohammedan peoples.
40. The Christian peoples.
41. This prayer is read in the synagogue service on the first Sabbath after Passover.

O forsaken and persecuted one, why do you weep and mourn? Have you despaired of Him for whom you have been waiting so long?" — "My redemption is again postponed and my darkness is lengthened." — "Wait, O suffering one! It will not be long. Soon I shall send My messenger. He will prepare the way, and on Mount Zion I will anoint My king.

These dialogue poems form a transitional stage to an extraordinary group of poems that Ibn Gabirol composed in the classic style of the Song of Songs. The melancholy poet, who never wrote a single erotic poem, created a whole series of songs of praise in which the flaming speech of earthly love is transfused into mystical religious fervor. These celebrate in colorful, unveiled images the eternal and sacred bond of love between the beautiful bride, the congregation of Israel, and its royal and incomparable Beloved. To give some notion of the unique style in which these poems are written, we here present three of them in a translation which naturally cannot convey the Biblical beauty of the original.

You who wander over the fields with the tents of Cushan,
Stand on the peak of Carmel,
Lift up your eyes to the mountains of Bashan.
Look there, O beloved, to the forbidden garden;
See, your beds are already filled with flowers.
Why, my beloved hart,[42] have you left my garden
To feed in the garden of Jakshan
Under the trees of Dishan?
Come, return to the garden, and there we shall eat choice fruits,
And in the bosom of the beautiful-eyed one
You will lie and sleep.[43]

Arise, open the locked gate
And send back to me the hart that has fled.
On the day you return to me
You will rest between my breasts,
There you will place upon me your sweet odor.
— Tell me, O lovely bride,
How does your beloved look,
The beloved whom you bid me send back to you?

42. In medieval Hebrew poetry a beloved man is very often called a hart (*tzevi*) and a beloved woman a doe (*tzeviah*). The word has an additional significance here because *tzevi* also means "beauty" in Hebrew.
43. The poem "Shochant Ba-Sadeh," which is read, according to the Sephardic Rite, on Simhat Torah.

Is he beautiful-eyed, ruddy, and lovely to look upon?
— My friend and my beloved is this,
Arise now, anoint him.[44]

I welcome you, my friend, bright and ruddy,
Greetings to you from one,
The temple of whose head is like a pomegranate.
Run to your friend,
Come out to save her,
Like the son of Jesse,
Her who is surrounded by the armies
Of the children of Ammon.
— What ails you, O beautiful one,
Who awakens love and whose voice sounds
Lovelier than the silver bells on Aaron's robe?
The time that you delight in,
The time of love, I will hasten,
And descend upon you like the dew of Hermon.[45]

At first glance it might seem that this mystical language, with its imaginative religious symbolism and passionate longing characteristic of the later Kabbalah, harmonizes only slightly with the bold flight of critical speculative thought. In the later parts of our work we shall, indeed, note how from the thirteenth century on there become increasingly prominent in Judaism two antithetical tendencies which carry on constant and relentless warfare: on the one side, free, polished, but ice-cold philosophical thought, which comes forth under the banner of the followers of Maimonides, and on the other side, mystical feeling, the "Torah of the heart," wrapped in the mantle of romanticism and revealed through the "hidden wisdom," the medieval Kabbalah. In Ibn Gabirol these two tendencies are still harmoniously blended. In him the passionate mystic still lives in peace with the rationalist thinker for whom the loftiest goal and greatest happiness consist in thought itself, in attaining pure truth. For him the process of inquiry is the sure way leading man from the earthly and finite to the heavenly and infinite. But exploring and understanding the nature of God are, in Ibn Gabirol, bound up with constant striving for the highest ideal,

44. The poem "Shaar Asher Nisgar" is also read on Simḥat Torah.
45. The poem "Shalom Lecha Dodi." Still other poems of Ibn Gabirol's are read on Simḥat Torah. Three similar poems were printed by Dukes in his *Zur Kenntnis der neu-hebräischen religiösen Poesie,* pp. 157–59; also in *Literaturblatt des Orients,* 1843, p. 307. Several similar poems are published in the Bialik-Ravnitzki edition, III, 43, 46, and 64.

with longing for God, the eternal source of light and life. In his philosophic thought we find not the cold rationalism of Aristotle but the idea world of Plato, veiled in poetic images.

In this respect, the most remarkable fruit of Ibn Gabirol's religious poetry, his famous moral-didactic poem *Keter Malchut*, is typical. But this work is so intimately connected with his philosophical system that we must first become familiar with that system properly to appreciate its value.

As a man who commanded the highest levels of the culture of his era, Ibn Gabirol manifested his creative power in various realms of knowledge. He himself mentions twenty writings of his.[46] He had not only an insatiable thirst for knowledge but a powerful drive toward creation; he wrote not because he wished to write but because he *had* to. The thoughts and images born in his tempestuous spirit gave him no rest; they followed him like shadows and demanded *tikkun*, "repair" or "improvement." To free himself of them, he had to bring them into the world, dress them in a garment, give them form and life. Thus he produced one work after another, if only to be liberated from the shades born in hosts in his creative spirit.

Of all Ibn Gabirol's scholarly works, however, only three have been preserved, one in the Arabic original and two in Hebrew translation.[47] Two of the three, *Tikkun Middot Ha-Nefesh*[48] and *Mivhar Ha-Peninim*, were very popular among Jews, but have no particularly great value. The first is a book of ethical instruction prescribing how man is to govern his spirit and liberate himself from all kinds of desires, so that he may attain the high degree of God-seeking. The unique quality of this brief work is the following: when the author sets forth his moral demands, he does not base them on any religious laws and principles; ethics for him is independent of religion. The second work is a collection of wise sayings, moral maxims, and proverbs, gathered from various sources, mainly Arabic. Several proverbs are typical of our poet. His spirit, constantly engaged in striving and seeking, is antagonistic

46. In the well-known poem "Keshoresh Etz," line 48. See also S. Sachs' *R. Shelomoh ben Gabirol U-Ketzat Mi-Benei Doro*, pp. 46–48. The medieval philosophical writer Moses of Salerno mentions a work of Ibn Gabirol's called *Shaar Ha-Shamayim*. From the first chapters of the *Mekor Hayyim* it is easy to conjecture that Ibn Gabirol also wrote a work called *Torat Ha-Nefesh*. Munk confirms this theory.

47. S. Munk, *Mélanges de philosophie juive et arabe* (Paris, 1859), believes that a Latin translation of a fourth work of Ibn Gabirol, *Torat Ha-Nefesh* (*Traite de l'âme*), has remained.

48. The poet composed this work in Saragossa in the year 1045. The Arabic text, which is in the library of Oxford University, was published with an English translation by Stephen S. Wise in 1901 under the title *The Improvement of the Moral Qualities*.

to the arrested and the static. "Wise is a man," notes *Mivḥar Ha-Peninim*, "as long as he seeks wisdom; but as soon as he thinks he has already attained the goal, he becomes foolish."[49]

Only in his third work does our poet show himself to be a profound thinker who posed in all its breadth the problem of the cosmic, universal spirit that knows nothing of manifoldness and diversity. This work, entitled *Mekor Ḥayyim,* is undoubtedly one of the most remarkable philosophic works the Middle Ages have bequeathed to us.[50]

Ibn Gabirol here struck out on an entirely new path. He was the first among the European thinkers of the medieval era who had the courage to place philosophic investigation above accepted authorities. He, the author of mystical-religious hymns and ardent national poems, as a thinker striving to attain the truth and fathom the eternal mystery of life and being, refused to recognize any religious boundaries or the restraints that faith sets before the freely inquiring mind. Religion relies upon the authority of the past, on the tradition of the fathers; it assumes that it already possesses the truth, which it has received in the form of a legacy from earlier generations. The free investigator, however, wishes to attain the truth by himself, with his own mind, following his own search.

"Why was man created?" This is the first question the disciple poses to his master[51] in *Mekor Ḥayyim*. The reply: Knowledge, the exploration of the mystery of the world, is the goal for the sake of which man's soul was brought into being.[52] In this lie its supreme delight and happiness,[53] which liberate it from death and unite it with the source of eternal life.[54]

According to Ibn Gabirol's philosophy, the essence of God is complete unity and indivisibility. "Unity rules over everything,

49. Steinschneider expresses certain doubts as to whether *Mivḥar Ha-Peninim* was composed by Ibn Gabirol. See his *Hebräischen Übersetzungen,* pp. 382–83. J. Guttmann denies this notion in his *Die Philosophie des Solomon Ibn Gabirol,* pp. 18–20.
50. The Arabic original was almost entirely lost (only a few brief fragments survived). There is only the Latin translation, *Fons Vitae,* and the Hebrew extract, *Likkutei Sefer Mekor Ḥayyim,* which was composed in the thirteenth century by Shemtov Falaquera and published with a French translation by Munk. In 1926 the Latin *Fons Vitae* appeared in a Hebrew translation by Jacob Bluwstein under the title *Mekor Ḥayyim Le-Rabbi Shelomoh ben Gabirol.* At the end of the Hebrew edition (pp. 225–65), Falaquera's *Likkutim* are reprinted.
51. Ibn Gabirol wrote his *Mekor Ḥayyim* in the form of a conversation between a philosopher and his disciple, following the pattern of Plato's dialogues.
52. *Mekor Ḥayyim,* p. 4.
53. *Ibid.,* p. 137.
54. *Ibid.,* p. 221.

and everything is in it and through it."[55] God is the source and origin, the primordial being beyond all time. Everything in the universe, everything that exists and endures, is created through the union of matter (*yesod* or *homer*) and form (*tzurah*) in various proportions and degrees.[56] Outside of matter and form there is nothing else.[57]

Through the terms "matter" and "form" Ibn Gabirol expresses, in his own way, the idea that had already been put forward by the sages of the Talmud concerning the dual character of divinity. Matter is the *passive* part which receives influence, form the *active* part which exercises influence.[58] But Ibn Gabirol, as an authentic Jewish thinker imbued with the concept of unity, with the foundation principle that "He [God] is one and His name is one," insists that form and matter are inseparable; they are twins incapable of existing without each other.[59] There is no matter without form and no form without matter. Even purely spiritual entities, intelligences without any trace of corporeal stuff, even the human mind and the angels as well, consist of form and matter together.[60] The whole endless and varied chain of phenomena, all the innumerable products of the two basic elements, are considered by Ibn Gabirol as a constant emanation from the first and only source. Out of it streams everything that is, just as a river streams out of a living spring (hence, the name of the work, *Mekor Hayyim*, the Fountain of Life).[61]

The link uniting the absolute-infinite with the finite, the eternal Creator with the creatures born out of the working together of form and matter, is, according to Ibn Gabirol, the will of God,[62] which is also the power of God.[63] This concept of God's will is central in his system. The Creator and His will are inseparable.

55. *Ibid.*, p. 208.
56. Falaquera's *Likkutim*, IV, Section 11; *Mekor Hayyim*, p. 141.
57. *Mekor Hayyim*, p. 16; cf. *ibid.*, p. 149.
58. *Ibid.*, pp. 180, 196, and 200.
59. *Ibid.*, p. 154; *Likkutim*, IV, Section 17; cf. *ibid.*, V, Sections 42 and 43.
60. *Likkutim*, II, Section 31; cf. *ibid.*, IV, Sections 6, 8; *Mekor Hayyim*, pp. 144, 146, and 147; cf. *ibid.*, p. 170.
61. *Likkutim*, V, Section 71. Cf. Falaquera, *Moreh Ha-Moreh*, p. 94. See also *Mekor Hayyim*, p. 216.
62. In Hebrew, *hafetz* and also *ratzon*. See Falaquera, *Moreh Ha-Moreh*, p. 93.
63. *Likkutim*, I, Section 2; *Moreh Ha-Moreh*, p. 93. See also *Likkutim*, V, Sections 42, 56, 59, 60, 62, 64, and 72, and III, Section 39; cf. *Moreh Ha-Moreh*, p. 50. In places in Ibn Gabirol, God's will is also called God's *word*, e.g., in *Likkutim*, V, Section 56. Ibn Gabirol once calls God's will by the name *Kavod* (Glory). This name, as we shall later see, came to play an especially prominent role among the Jewish mystics.

God's will is the universal creative power, which produces everything, both form and matter.[64] He and He alone is the cause of
every motion, of the striving and desire to come into motion, i.e.,
to live and to seek. God permeates everything that exists and endows everything with spirit and life. There are not two separated
worlds, the world of pure matter and the world of pure spirituality.
The body is not the prison of the soul, for everything bears the
image of God, everything is in God and God's reflection is on
everything.[65] All things without exception are illuminated and
permeated by the divine light, both common matter and noble
form. All draw nourishment from God, and this nourishment, the
divine influence which is called in philosophy "emanation" (in
Hebrew, *atzilut*), passes through various stages, through ten
sefirot.[66] These *sefirot* are all a reflection of the primal source. The
first *sefirah* directly reflects the Fountain of Life, the source of all
that lives and exists. The second is a reflection of the first, the third
of the second, and so on. The further the distance between the reflection and the original source, the paler is the image and the more
matter and corporeality are joined in it.[67] The lower the degree of
the form, the larger it is in measure and bulk. The last *sefirah* is the
terrestrial world which we grasp with our senses. Thus the universe passes gradually from pure spirituality into common matter
and corporeality. Even here, however, the divine influence is still
at work. Matter, too, is permeated with the eternal light, bears the
reflection of its rays, draws nourishment from the source of life.
For everything that is, is necessarily connected with this source.
All worlds, all degrees, all levels of forms and creatures continue

64. *Mekor Ḥayyim*, p. 214; *ibid.*, p. 213. In the Latin translation of
Mekor Ḥayyim (Fons Vitae) it is indicated that Ibn Gabirol wrote a
special work on the concept of "God's will." In Latin it was called
Origo largitatis et causa essendi. The Hebrew name is *Mekor Ha-
Hatavah Ve-Ilat Ha-Metziut.* See Munk, *op. cit.*, p. 223; Hebrew trans-
lation of *Mekor Ḥayyim*, p. 216.
65. Ibn Gabirol also expresses this thought in his poem "Ahavticha Ke-
Ahavat Av Yeḥido."
66. Here the influence that the well-known mystical work *Sefer Yetzirah*
exerted on Ibn Gabirol is discernible. The influence of this work is
also noticeable in Ibn Gabirol's religious poems, "Sheloshim U-Shtaim
Netivot" and especially "Shochen Ad" (published in *Otzar Neḥmad*,
II, 77–79, and in *Siftei Renanot*, p. 54). The great influence of the
Sefer Yetzirah on Ibn Gabirol's system is further noticeable in the fact
that the author of *Mekor Ḥayyim* compares the creation of the
world to the *word* spoken by man and in the great value that he places
on the concept of number. "Number is the foundation of all that exists"
(*Mekor Ḥayyim*, p. 156; cf. *ibid.*, p. 45).
67. *Likkutim*, V, Section 26; cf. *ibid.*, III, Sections 32 and 33, and *Moreh
Ha-Moreh*, p. 11.

to strive with great love for the one divine source of light,[68] which is also the source of joy, the seal of graciousness and goodness.[69] Man reflects in himself the whole world. He is an *olam katan*, a microcosm, fully reflecting the image of the *olam gadol*, the macrocosm.[70]

We have observed that Ibn Gabirol grounded the imperatives of morality without reference to the principles of religion. The same phenomenon is visible in his *Mekor Ḥayyim*, or *Fons Vitae*. His conception of the world, his philosophical ideas of God and creation, are not based at all on the authority of faith. The majority of medieval thinkers proceeded from the idea that philosophy is only a "maidservant" of the "mistress," which is faith; philosophy can only explicate and make more comprehensible the truth revealed by faith. But Ibn Gabirol, the poet and thinker whose striving for truth was so closely associated with ardent love and yearning for God, went his own way. To investigate philosophical truth freely and without hindrance, he relied exclusively on reason and on human sentiments and perceptions, not on faith or the tradition of the fathers. In his entire work, therefore, not a single verse of the Bible, not a single quotation from the Talmud, is given.[71] On the other hand, the influence of the Greek philosophers, especially those who came from the school of the neo-Platonists,[72] is considerable. Not by accident is Plato the only thinker mentioned by name in *Mekor Ḥayyim*.[73]

It is very possible that this is what was responsible for the strange fate of Ibn Gabirol's *Mekor Ḥayyim*. This work played a major role in medieval Christian philosophy. The name of its author, however, was transformed into the Arabic Avicebron (also Avicebrol). In the first half of the twelfth century (around 1130–50), a Christian cleric of the Spanish city of Segovia, Dominicus Gundisalvi, with the help of a converted Jew, John Hispanus (Ibn Daud, corrupted into Avendehut), translated *Mekor Ḥayyim* into Latin under the title *Fons Vitae*.[74] This translation made a

68. *Likkutim*, V, Sections 47 and 48; cf. *ibid.*, V, Section 52.
69. *Mekor Ḥayyim*, p. 205.
70. *Likkutim*, III, Section 6; see also *Moreh Ha-Moreh*, p. 55. This idea derives from Plato.
71. Because of this, many Jewish scholars complained about the author of *Mekor Ḥayyim*. See, e.g., Rabbi Abraham Ibn Daud's *Emunah Ramah*, Introduction.
72. For details, especially on Plotinus' influence on Gabirol, see M. Joel, *Ibn Gabirols Bedeutung für die Geschichte der Philosophie*. On other thinkers who had an influence on Ibn Gabirol, see Munk, *op. cit.*, pp. 233–61, and the Russian edition of our history (1920), p. 43.
73. *Mekor Ḥayyim*, pp. 151, 169, and 190.
74. Ibn Daud first translated the *Mekor Ḥayyim* into Spanish and Gundisalvi then rendered it into Latin from the Spanish translation.

great impression on the learned Christian world. The French scholar Jourdain believes that it is impossible rightly to understand and appreciate the scholastic philosophy of the thirteenth century without a familiarity with Ibn Gabirol's work.[75] The foremost philosophers of medieval Christian Europe, such as Albertus Magnus and Thomas Aquinas, studied *Fons Vitae* diligently, and Aquinas' opponent, Duns Scotus, adopted the central principles of Ibn Gabirol's system.[76] Even scholars of a later period, such as Giordano Bruno, spoke with great respect of *Fons Vitae*. Its author, however, was thought to have been a Christian or Moslem. Some medieval Christian scholars even believed that Avicebron was an Arabic thinker who had adopted the Christian faith, for in *Fons Vitae* certain neo-Platonic ideas that are very close to the Christian world of ideas of that period are very prominent.[77] About a hundred years after the Latin translation appeared, the Jewish scholar Shemtov Falaquera made a Hebrew extract of the Arabic original.[78] This extract (*Likkutim*) was found in the Bibliothèque Nationale in Paris by the Jewish scholar Solomon Munk and published in 1846. Along with this, Munk made an unexpected discovery; when he compared Shemtov's *Likkutim* with the Latin *Fons Vitae*, he became convinced that the scholastic Avicebron and the famous Jewish poet Solomon Ibn Gabirol were one and the same person.[79]

A twin to *Mekor Ḥayyim* is Ibn Gabirol's *Keter Malchut*. The poet himself calls this poem the "crown" of all his religious songs. His philosophic outlook, his conceptions of God the Creator and His will, the source of all that lives, receive here a poetic vestment and are permeated with the enthusiasm of a profoundly religious nature.

Wonderful are thy works, as my soul overwhelmingly knoweth.
Thine, O Lord, are the greatness and the might, the beauty, the triumph, and the splendour.
Thine, O Lord, is the Kingdom, and Thou art exalted as head over all.
Thine are all riches and honour: Thine the creatures of the heights and depths.
They bear witness that they perish, while Thou endurest.

75. See also Munk, *op. cit.*, p. 151; M. Joel, *op. cit.*, p. 3.
76. See Munk, *op. cit.*, pp. 297, 300; Guttmann, *Die Beziehungen des Johannes Duns Scotus zum Judentum, MGWJ*, 1894.
77. In fact, however, Ibn Gabirol was quite hostile to Christianity.
78. In the introduction to his *Likkutim*, Falaquera says, "I have gathered extracts from his works, and in these extracts all his thought is contained."
79. *Literaturblatt des Orients*, 1846, p. 721.

Thine is the might in whose mystery our thoughts can find no stay,
  so far art Thou beyond us.
In Thee is the veiled retreat of power, the secret and the founda-
  tion.
Thine is the name concealed from the sages,
The force that sustaineth the world on naught,
And that can bring to light every hidden thing.
Thine is the lovingkindness that ruleth over all Thy creatures,
And the good treasured up for those who fear Thee.
Thine are the mysteries that transcend understanding and thought.
Thine is the life over which extinction holdeth no sway,
And thy throne is exalted above every sovereignty,
And Thy habitation hidden in the shrouded height.
Thine is the existence from the shadow of whose light every being
  was created.
Of which we say, in His shadow we live.
Thine are the two worlds between which Thou hast set a boundary,
The first for deeds and the second for reward.
Thine is the reward which Thou for the righteous hast stored
  up and hidden,
Yea, Thou sawest it was goodly and didst hide it.
. . . .
Thou art One, the first of every number, and the foundation of
  every structure,
Thou art One, and at the mystery of Thy Oneness the wise of heart
  are struck dumb,
For they know not what it is.
Thou art One, and Thy Oneness can neither be increased nor less-
  ened,
It lacketh naught, nor doth aught remain over.
Thou art One, but not like a unit to be grasped or counted,
For number and change cannot reach Thee.
Thou art not to be visioned, nor to be figured thus or thus.
Thou art One, but to put to Thee bound or circumference my
  imagination would fail me.
Therefore I have said I will guard my ways lest I sin with the
  tongue.
Thou art One, Thou art high and exalted beyond abasement or
  falling,
"For how should the One fall?"[80]

80. From *Selected Religious Poems of Solomon Ibn Gabirol*, translated into
  English verse by Israel Zangwill, p. 82 ff. [Somewhat more of *Keter*
  Malchut is here given than in Zinberg's Yiddish text. —B.M.]

The entire medieval universe, with all its heavens, "spheres," and *sefirot*, finds an echo in Ibn Gabirol's *Keter Malchut*. And high above in the highest (the tenth) *sefirah* is the sanctuary of man's crown, reason or intelligence. And even higher, above the sphere of intelligence, under the Throne of Glory, near the source of eternal light, rest the righteous and pure souls who are illuminated by the rays of immortal light:

Who can approach Thy seat?
For beyond the sphere of Intelligence hast Thou established
 the throne of Thy glory;
There standeth the splendour of Thy veiled habitation,
And the mystery and the foundation.
Thus far reacheth Intelligence, but cometh here to a standstill,
For higher still hast Thou mounted, and ascended Thy mighty
 throne,
"And no man may go up with Thee."

O Lord, who shall do deeds like unto Thine?
For Thou hast established under the throne of Thy glory
A standing place for the souls of Thy saints,
And there is the abode of the pure souls
That are bound up in the bundle of life.
They who were weary and faint here await new strength,
And those who failed of strength may here find repose;
For these are the children of rest,
And here is delight without end or limit,
For it is The-World-To-Come.
And here are stations and seeing-places for the standing souls,
Whence, in "mirrors of the serving women,"
They can behold and be seen of the Lord.
In the palaces of the King do they dwell,
And glory in the sweetness of the fruit of Intelligence,
For He giveth them of the dainties of the King.
This is the rest and the heritage
Whose goodness and beauty are endless,
Such is "the land which floweth with milk and honey and
 such the fruit thereof."[81]

In this masterwork are united the thinker and the poet, the free, proud flight of philosophic thought and the humble, pious heart. The beginning of the work is harmoniously blended with the end.

81. *Ibid.*, pp. 102–3. [Here also more of Ibn Gabirol's poem is given than in Zinberg's text. —B.M.]

Keter Malchut begins with noble sentiment and inspiration: this, says the poet, is an exalted paean in honor of the boundless wisdom of the Creator. And at the conclusion of the poem come quiet, humble prayer chords; here the poet's broken heart confesses before his Lord, the "God full of mercy."

The Jewish people know very few details of the life of their great poet. But popular legend spun its imaginative web around Ibn Gabirol's name, and later generations recounted wonderful tales about the sorrowful poet of Malaga. The author of *Shalshelet Ha-Kabbalah*, Gedaliah Ibn Yaḥya (sixteenth century), relates the following legend about the death of Ibn Gabirol. An Arabic poet in Valencia became very jealous of his Jewish colleague's talent. Out of envy he killed Ibn Gabirol and buried his body in a garden under a fig tree. From then on, this tree began to bear wondrously beautiful and unusually sweet fruit, at which all the inhabitants of the city marvelled. The report of the extraordinary tree reached the caliph himself, who summoned the owner of the garden. Finally the Arab confessed his crime and, at the command of the caliph, was hanged from the same tree.[82] The only kernel of truth in this legend is the place where Ibn Gabirol died. In the old cemetery in Valencia part of the poet's tombstone has actually been found.[83] But the legend of the tree with the lovely fruits which used to ripen earlier than all others is a symbol of the poet himself, whose creative spirit matured so early and called forth so much amazement with its incomparable fruits.

Ibn Gabirol's speculative power and poetic talent simultaneously raised to a high level both Jewish philosophic thought and Hebrew poetry. He was also a master in the realm of poetic meter. On the foundations laid by Dunash ben Labrat, Ibn Gabirol constructed a marvelous structure, and Abraham Ibn Ezra rightly calls him "the father of metrical songs."[84]

82. The same legend, but in another form, is also told by Joseph Zambri (see Neubauer, *MGWJ*, 1887, pp. 500–501). There is also a legend that Ibn Gabirol created a *golem* in the form of a woman.

83. The year of Ibn Gabirol's death has not been definitely established. On the authority of the poet Moses Ibn Ezra, who relates that Ibn Gabirol died before he was thirty years old, it was long believed that his death occurred around the middle of the eleventh century. More recently scholars have shown that Ibn Gabirol was still living in 1068 and have come to the conclusion that he died around 1070, when he was close to fifty. An indication that this view is correct is to be found in one of Ibn Gabirol's religious poems where he says of himself, "I am already gray" (in the *tocheḥah* "Ad Matai Yitzri").

84. See Ibn Ezra's commentary on Genesis 3:1. Also his *Sefer Tzaḥot* (1827), pp. 10–11.

The meter of Ibn Gabirol's poems is based on the combination of two major elements, the *yated* with the *tenuah*. *Yated* is a syllable which has under it a *sheva na* or a *hataf*, e.g., *shema, be'et, asher, adei, emet*, etc.; *tenuah* is a syllable that consists of one vocal, e.g., *mah, li, bo, het*. The *yated*, which corresponds to the iamb of European meter, is expressed by the symbols ‿ ⁻. The *tenuah*, which corresponds to half of a spondee in European meter, is expressed by the sign ⁻; a *yated* together with a *tenuah* correspond to the European bacchius (‿ ⁻ ⁻); a *tenuah* and after it a *yated* correspond to the amphimacer (⁻ ‿ ⁻).[85] Through combining *yated* with *tenuah* in various ways, Ibn Gabirol and his followers created all possible forms and the rich meter of their poems. Every line of verse, which carries in Arabic-Hebrew meter the name *bayyit*, is divided into two parts. The first is called *delet* (door, entrance), the second *sugar* (closing). Most of Ibn Gabirol's secular poems and some of his religious hymns are maintained in one rhyme, i.e., all the lines (*battim*) in the poem end with the same syllable. Ibn Gabirol often attains remarkably beautiful effects by using words that sound alike but have different meanings, or different words with the same syllable at the end. Many of his religious hymns are written in the form of four-line verses. The first three lines have their own separate rhyme, but the last line of every verse in the poem has the same rhyme. In some poems not only the last words of each line but also the next to the last have an identical rhyme.

In many of his religious poems the name of the poet, mostly with the humble addition "Ha-Katan" (the Little), is woven into the beginning letters of the lines in the form of an acrostic. Because of this, Ibn Gabirol is often called in medieval literature "Shelomo Ha-Katan." The poet of the thirteenth century, Jehudah Alharizi, in characterizing Ibn Gabirol, therefore says of him:

He called himself "little," but, in relation to him, giants look like dwarfs; he has no peer among all the Jewish poets of earlier and later generations. The "little one" rules over all! God anointed him king over all the Jewish poets! He is unique, incomparable. His song is— Solomon's song above all other songs.

85. For more details concerning Judeo-Arabic meter, see, among the older sources, Abraham Ibn Ezra in the places mentioned above; Saadiah Ibn Danan in his *Perek Be-Haruz* (Neubauer's *Melechet Ha-Shir*, pp. 4–18); the supplement to Moses Kimhi's *Mahalach Shevilei Ha-Daat*, with Elijah Levita's commentary; the anonymous *Shekel Ha-Kodesh*, printed at the end of David Ibn Yahya's *Leshon Limmudim*. Among the modern sources see Franz Delitzch, *Zur Geschichte der jüdischen Poesie* (1836); B. Halper, *JQR*, n.s., 1913, pp. 153–224; H. Brody, *Über die Metra und Versgedichte* (1895).

CHAPTER THREE

Moses Ibn Ezra

ORMED like a Gothic cathedral, rising to the heavens, is Hebrew poetry in the work of Solomon Ibn Gabirol; here, profane songs are unknown. Shortly thereafter, however, a young poet bubbling with love of life and childlike joy burst into this noble cathedral with loud laughter. Beneath its melancholy vaults resounded his cries for the pleasures of life. The name of this poet was Moses ben Jacob Ibn Ezra. He was born into a rich and prominent family of Granada around 1070. He received an excellent education and studied Jewish subjects with a scholar and poet of that period, Isaac ben Jehudah Ibn Ghayyat,[1] who after the tragic death of Samuel Ha-Nagid's son in the year 1066 assumed his office as head of the Talmudic academy in Lucena. Educated also in Arabic culture, Ibn Ezra was well versed in all the sciences and philosophies of his time. In addition, he was familiar with the classical languages, Latin and Greek.

Highly gifted and brought up in wealth, the young poet imbibed freely of the joys of life. He was in love with nature and feminine beauty and enthusiastically celebrated in his poems the colors of

1. Ibn Ghayyat achieved his reputation mainly as a liturgical poet. Of his many *piyyutim* (Landshuth, *Ammudei Ha-Avodah*, pp. 111–16, lists 116 of them), especially well known is the earnest prayer "Yonah Hipsah Bintot Ha-Yom," which is read at the Neilah service of Yom Kippur. The rest of the poems in his *Maamad Yom Ha-Kippurim* are overly burdened with philosophic and astronomical concepts of that era, and their poetic value is very slight.

the Spanish fields and vineyards and the charm of the Spanish women.

> The garden dons a coat of many hues;
> The mead a broidered carpet hath unrolled;
> The woods are brave in chequered mantles—Now
> A wondrous scene may every eye behold:
>
> The newborn flowers acclaim the newborn Spring,
> And forth to meet his coming, gaily throng;
> High, at their head, on sovereign throne is borne
> The rose—the flowrets' queen—queen of my song.
>
> From prisoning leaves she bursts, and casts aside
> Her captive garb, in royal robes to shine.
> I drink to her! Nor heaven forgive the wretch—
> If such there be—who spares his choicest wine![2]

Ibn Ezra's bond with nature, the feeling of joy that filled his heart, find an especially strong echo in his long poem *Tarshish:*[3]

> Why should I grieve? The purling of the brook,
> The throstle's song, I hear. On couch of blooms,
> More brilliant than the weave of Persia's looms,
> I lie beneath the myrtle's shade, and look
> On the bright necklace of the turtle dove—
> And dream—and dream, ah me, of my lost love![4]
>
> Dwell beside the beds of roses
> Abide in the shade of the myrtles;
> And behold the dew of night upon their leaves,
> Like drop of bdellium and tiny pearls.[5]
>
> Beside the flower-beds thy lodging make,
> Nor hut nor palace for thy dwelling take;
> The dove, the throstle, all the woodland choir
> Shall sing thee music passing harp or lyre.[6]

2. From *Selected Poems of Moses Ibn Ezra*, translated by Solomon Solis-Cohen, from a text edited and annotated by Heinrich Brody (Philadelphia: The Jewish Publication Society of America, 1934), p. 45.
3. Published in 1886 by Baron David Günzburg. [We here include, in Solomon Solis-Cohen's translation, more and different verses of the *Tarshish* than Zinberg gives in paraphrase in his text. —B.M.]
4. *Selected Poems of Moses Ibn Ezra*, p. 76.
5. *Ibid.*
6. *Ibid.*, p. 77.

I went out into the garden in the morning dusk,
When sorrow enveloped me like a cloud;
And the breeze brought to my nostril the odor of spices,
As balm of healing for a sick soul—
Then a sudden dawn flamed in the sky, like lightning,
And its thunder surged like the cry of a woman that gives birth![7]

The poet rejoices that the clouds have watered the garden beds.
Happy are the flower beds when the heavens weep tears. All the
grasses and buds sing their wordless song of praise to the rain for
its graciousness in bringing them out of dark slumber into the bright
world.

The young Ibn Ezra celebrates not only the grace and splendor
of the Spanish fields but also the power of the vineyards:

Drink! Whilst the rain-drenched earth for summer yearns,
And shivering forests dream that spring returns,
The ruby wine glows in its crystal cup
Like flame of God, within the hail that burns.[8]

All they that live on earth are niggardly
Beside the vintner's gracious alchemy;
He takes your bits of silver—speaks—Behold,
Your cups are running o'er with liquid gold![9]

Summers and Winters have I seen and sung,
And Spring and Autumn praised with pen and tongue—
All are glad seasons when the wine-skin's full,
And all are drear when the last drop is wrung.[10]

My soul will I give in ransom
For the child of the vine,
The grandchild of the vineyard—
She makes the poor bold as princes,
And the lowly equal to the exalted.[11]

Our poet was in love not only with the "daughters of the vine"
but also with the daughters of Eve. After the great verses of the
Biblical Song of Songs were written, poems of earthly love and

7. *Ibid.*
8. *Ibid.*, p. 70.
9. *Ibid.*, p. 72.
10. *Ibid.*
11. *Ibid.*, p. 73.

passion disappeared from Hebrew literature. The Song of Songs, the "song above all songs," the poem of "love that is strong as death," was stripped of its garment of corporeality and became pure spirituality, filled with sacred and esoteric mysteries.[12] The love story of the beautiful shepherdess Shulamith was transformed into a mystical dialogue between God and the congregation of Israel. But under the blue sky of Arabic Spain, where the Jews found a second home and once more enjoyed the sap of the earth,[13] earthly songs again resounded in the ancient language of the Bible. Moses Ibn Ezra was the first Jewish poet who brought into the tents of Israel, together with the odors of fields and flowering meadows, the flame of erotic love, the enchantment of feminine beauty.

"My soul," the poet confesses, "has been taken captive by the charm of the lovely one, whose tresses are black as night and whose face is bright and mild like the silvery ray of the moon."[14] "The full breasts of my beloved have pierced my heart like an arrow." "The days I am separated from my beloved are black as her locks, the nights with her beautiful as her cheeks." Ibn Ezra's loved one is a typical frivolous daughter of the hot Southland. Dance and song—these are her existence, and she bubbles with love of life and joy, with half impudent, half wicked laughter. "I asked my lovely one," the poet relates, "why can you not endure old men?" — "Why," was her answer, "do you love not old women but young girls?"[15]

The charm of his beloved is portrayed by the poet in the following verses:

> Beautiful are the fingers of the loved one;
> When she plays upon the harp or lute,
> They fly over the strings swiftly as arrows,
> And smoothly as the pen of a ready writer.
> When she lets the music of her voice be heard,
> Throstle and robin upon the branches
> Hush their song.[16]

12. The famous Tanna Rabbi Akiba declared, "The world was never as worthy as on the day that the Song of Songs was given to Israel, for all the writings are holy but the Song of Songs is holy of holies" (*Yadaim* 3:5). Another Tanna said, "Everyone who reads a verse of the Song of Songs and makes of it a kind of song . . . brings evil into the world" (*Sanhedrin* 101).
13. Already in the time of Ḥasdai Ibn Shaprut farming was so widespread among the Spanish Jews that some scholars, e.g., Schipper, believe that agriculture was the major factor in the economic life of the Jewish community in Spain of that period.
14. *Tarshish*, 32.
15. *Ibid.*, 54.
16. *Selected Poems of Moses Ibn Ezra*, p. 74.

Beautiful is the loved one
As she sways in the dance
Like a bough of the myrtle,
Her unbound tresses
Billowing about her.
She slays me with the arrows of her glances—
They are drunk with my blood—
But she shows no mercy.[17]

Love and spring, the beauty of woman and the splendor of nature—these old and gray but eternally youthful themes of the poetry of the world are woven by Ibn Ezra into an ingenious tapestry that dazzles the eye with its vivid colors. Especially characteristic in this respect is the lovely epithalamion "Ha-Reah Mor Meahez Ha-Afasim"[18] which the poet sent to his friend Solomon ben Matir. The poem begins with a description of how spring awakens in the South, how all nature is drunk with fragrant odors and even "the silent mountains sing." Every leaf is full of joy, and even "the most melancholy faces" are bright and happy. On this background, drenched with light, the poet depicts in sculptured images passionate love, wrapped in a veil of bashful modesty, and the lovely bride with her "dove-like eyes intoxicated with the strong wine of love."

But the poet's years of happiness did not long continue. All too soon he had occasion to learn how filled with bitter drops is life's cup. Like most poets, Ibn Ezra was a very poor businessman. He suddenly lost his entire fortune, and thereupon immediately encountered ingratitude and deceit. Men whom he had considered his best friends turned away from him and became his enemies. This baseness so enraged the impoverished poet that even in old age, many years later, he could still not forget the "evil deeds" of the "insolent men" who "speak peace and at the same time bite with their teeth."[19]

After the first misfortune, a second quickly supervened. The poet fell in love with his elder brother's daughter. This was not a flirtation but a genuine love, "strong as death." It appears that Ibn Ezra's love found a response in the heart of his niece, but the family was not pleased with the proposed match. Ibn Ezra was not "substantial" enough, for he had lost his money and generally had little knowledge of practical life and business matters. His former friends worked against him, and his three elder brothers definitely

17. *Ibid.*, p. 75.
18. H. Brody in *Shaar Ha-Shir* (1905), pp. 68–70.
19. In his prayer "Nafshi Iviticha Balailah."

informed him that they would not consent to the marriage. The desolate poet then decided to leave his home and, before his departure, sent his beloved a song of love:

No one wishes to understand our love; all look on it with astonished eyes. . . . Deep is the wound that you, my beloved, have opened in my heart, but I have locked my heart, that men may not laugh, that they may not say: a foolish love-sickness. True, I am sick with love, and, separated from you, my pain will grow all the more. Without you the whole world is a prison, a sorrowful desert. There, where I shall not see your steps and your face will not hover before my eyes, men may be like gods—to me they are like wild asses. . . . Sweet as honey are your lips, but they bring no refreshment to me, who languish in sorrow; your perfumed breath makes others happy, while I yearn to breathe fresh air. . . . How lovely you are, how full of grace your youthful beauty! You are a trembling doe; proud lions bow before your glance, and innocently bloodied are all hearts that you take captive. Farewell, my beloved! The greater your fault, the more my love for you grows. My heart, my soul, my thought—all belong to you alone. In burning fire is my broken heart, and the flame is not extinguished through my tears. I forgive you for everything, my ardently loved one! Your very anger is like the grace of God in my sight. I am desperately ill, but I do not wish to be free of my sickness. I will remain faithful to you as long as the dew falls from the heavens and spring decks the earth with flowers. Be happy, my beloved, as long as the nightingale's song sounds among the branches.[20]

Ibn Ezra left his birthplace and went to Christian Castile. There, in a foreign land with an inferior culture, far from his beloved, the poet found the inhabitants like "wild asses." His sorrow and despair are powerfully reflected in many of his poems. "Like a shadow has my youth passed away," he laments.[21]

Swiftly as a dream have the happy days that sprinkled my black locks with dew vanished. Before the cold breath of suffering joy has fled from my visage, and the light of my eyes is extinguished. My heart yearns for my home; to the mountains of my homeland I call, full of longing, "Come closer to me." But my cry is in vain. They remain rooted to the earth. Fate has driven me to a dark people, to whom the ways of truth and knowledge are unknown. When I hear their barbarous talk, I sit full of shame, and my lips remain sealed.

20. The poem *Lechol Ish*, published by Dukes in his *Moses Ibn Ezra* and also by Kämpf in his *Nichtandalusische Poesie*, II, 209.
21. The poem *Hayu Yemei Heldi Ke-Tzel Over*, published by Harkavy in *Hadashim Gam Yeshanim*, III, Nos. 7, 31.

Ibn Ezra complains in similar fashion in one of the poems that he sent to his young friend, the great poet Jehudah Halevi:

I live among wolves to whom the name man is strange. Better to meet a bear in the forest, better to pass the time with a tiger, than to live among men by whom the darkness of Egypt is called light and knowledge. They are incapable of distinguishing spiritual beggars and petty misers from bearers of wisdom and prophets of God's word. . . .

At the end he cries out, "Oh, how narrow has the world become for me! It chokes my soul like a stiff neckband."[22] There, in a strange land, the homeless poet recalls the deceit of his false friends, and with anger and hatred hurls his reproof at them: "Your vile deeds will I inscribe on the forehead of time, so that future generations may know what you have done."[23]

But Ibn Ezra did not lose hope. He still believed that he would be reconciled with his brothers and no longer have to be separated from his beloved. In one of his poems to Jehudah Halevi he complains about his brothers, who have committed "a sin so terrible that the world has never heard of its like." But he immediately adds that he hopes that time will again unite those who are now apart and rejoice their hearts. "Our enemies will see God's acts and be ashamed."

The verses that he sent to a friend in Granada who had remained loyal are full of joyous expectation:

O, beloved doves, you faithful messengers! Like little clouds you soar toward the west, to the land of my birth. By my love I adjure you: Give my greetings from afar to my friends who have remained faithful. Far away from them, homeless am I, but their tent is firmly spread out in my heart. Tell them how beloved they are to me, how pained my heart is with longing and misery. Tell also the swallow, my beloved, who has built her nest in the depths of my soul, how, without her, life is odious to me and death becomes my hoped-for liberator. Tell her how, on her account, I am caught in the net of exile; for the sake of her, my dearly loved one, I have drunk to the dregs the cup of affliction, and my soul is a plaything for the sling of homelessness.[24]

But the poem ends on a happy note: "I hope to God that with my tears He will wash away my sufferings and cleanse my sins. I trust that He will grace my soul with rest and joy, and that I shall awaken to a new life."

22. *Otzar Neḥmad*, III, 50–51.
23. See Dukes' *Moses Ibn Ezra*, p. 106.
24. *Otzar Neḥmad*, III, 47–49.

Ibn Ezra's hope, however, was not realized. Soon afterward he received the news that his beloved, acceding to the wishes of her parents, had married another. His feeling of anger and offense overcame his pain, and proudly he directed to his enemies these contemptuous words: "Despite those who hate and envy me, I will proceed on my chosen way. They aimed at my heart, but the arrow did not strike; it flew by the mark. How dare hunchbacked thorns declare war against the cedars of Lebanon? How have little foxes the impudence to pursue the royal lion?"[25]

The poet now withdrew from the world. Life with its banal concerns, its pursuit of the deceitful phantoms of happiness and joy, became loathsome to him. This mood finds expression in his angry poem "Tevel Teni Libech."[26] Ibn Ezra portrays the world with its seductive pleasures as a debauched prostitute who decks herself out for her lovers in order afterward to deceive them.

The number of your lovers is equal to the number of those who have perished through you. To all of them you bear, with your false smile, the poisoned cup. You present the loveliest flowers, and under them scorpions lie hidden; if one enjoys your fragrant roses, he is struck by snake's poison. You decorate beds with the most beautiful covers, and pierce them through with thorns. You sing songs of joy, and forthwith the melody of mourning chokes them. You dazzle men with splendid palaces, and at the same time keep dark graves in readiness for them. You hold citharas and harps in your hand, and your loins are already encircled with the girdle of death. You are excluded from the commandment "Honor thy mother." No mother are you! The duty of your children is to reveal your disgrace, to rip off your mantle, so that you stand naked in your sin and shame.

Thereafter Moses Ibn Ezra devoted himself for a time entirely to scholarly pursuits. His only occupation was books and parchment scrolls. Philosophic ideas and systems temporarily displaced in him the desire for poetic creation. The experiences that occurred in the depths of his soul, where poetic images and tones were replaced by abstract ideas, found clear expression in the poem "Hekitzoti Mitenumat Raayonai."[27] The poet relates how "his thoughts awoke from their slumber, that they might put to sleep the restless desires of his soul." And he further recounts how he immersed himself in recondite philosophic secrets, how the nature of God and His power were revealed to him, and before his mind

25. See Dukes, *Moses Ibn Ezra*, p. 95.
26. *Ibid.*, pp. 100–101.
27. Published by H. Brody in *Shaar Ha-Shir*, pp. 70–71.

the light of heaven and the divine rays of eternal truth shone out of the darkness.

But Ibn Ezra was not an original thinker, and his religio-philosophical work bearing the long Arabic title *Al-Hadikah fi Ma'ani al-Mujaz wal-Hakikah*[28] is of no great interest. More important is his second work, *Kitab al-Muhadarah wal-Mudhakarah*,[29] on poetry in general and Hebrew poetry in particular, where he gives, incidentally, a historical and critical overview of the Hebrew poets who lived before him, especially Samuel Ha-Nagid and Solomon Ibn Gabirol.

At that time, it appears, Moses Ibn Ezra also composed his long poem of 164 verses, *Beshem El Asher Amar*. That he was the author of this poem remained unknown until recently. Leopold Dukes and David Kahana mistakenly considered it Abraham Ibn Ezra's work[30] and, indeed, saw in it the strongest evidence that the famous Bible commentator was also a great poet. In this poem the author celebrates, in forceful lines, the revelation of God's grandeur and power in His works, in the stars and planets on high and in the earth and man below. The influence of Gabirol's *Keter Malchut* is discernible

28. Ibn Ezra gave this work the Hebrew name *Arugat Ha-Bosem*. It was soon translated into Hebrew under this title.
29. The content of this work is given by Harkavy in *Hadashim Gam Yeshanim*, Nos. 7 and 29–31. Part of the Arabic original was published by the Leningrad professor P. Kokowzoff, in 1895. The Hebrew translation, *Sefer Shirat Yisrael*, was published by Ben Zion Halper in 1924.
30. The error derived from the fact that in *Shekel Ha-Kodesh* the beginning verse of Abraham Ibn Ezra's unknown poem *Beshem El Asher Yatzar* is quoted. When a long anonymous poem which begins with the first words of this verse were found in a Paris manuscript, David Kahana, as well as Dukes (in *Etzba Elohim* [1851], p. 31), concluded that this is the poem quoted in *Shekel Ha-Kodesh* under Abraham Ibn Ezra's name. The first verse of the poem in the manuscript, however, agrees only in its first half with the quotation from *Shekel Ha-Kodesh*; the second half is completely different. But even the first and similar half is also not Abraham Ibn Ezra's. This is the beginning of a poem of Samuel Ha-Nagid's, *Beshem El Asher Hehel Ve-Chilah Peulotav*. This poem was very popular, and many poets, it appears, wrote poems with these opening words. There is in Baron Günzburg's collection of manuscripts (number 19–821) an old copy of precisely this poem in complete form and with a more accurate text, as in the Paris manuscript, and it is expressly stated in it that the work was composed by Moses Ibn Ezra. Indeed, we have another proof that Moses Ibn Ezra is the author of this long poem. In the Leningrad Imperial Library there is an old manuscript (from the thirteenth century) of Moses Ibn Ezra's above-mentioned work, *Kitab Al-Hadikah*, and before the introduction the poem *Beshem El Asher Amar* appears. Regrettably, the first pages of the manuscript are missing, and therefore only the last forty-one verses of the poem have survived.

when Ibn Ezra, following the general medieval conception of the world, portrays the structure of the universe and when he concludes his poem with humble words of prayer and penitence. Gabirol's influence is also noticeable in the philosophic ideas reflected in this work. The poet asks,

How is it possible not to feel God's greatness in my heart when my thought and soul give testimony concerning Him? He is all, and all is in Him. Everything is permeated with Him, but His nature and ways remain hidden. . . . Everything bounded by time and place bears His stamp, yet He is beyond all place and time. Higher than every being. . . . He is the beginning, the cause of all matter and all form, and boundless are His creations, numberless the forms revealed by Him.

Moses Ibn Ezra composed several other learned works,[31] but he was not destined to find consolation in scholarly pursuits for long. Suddenly, in 1114, he received the news that his beloved had died in childbirth in Cordova. Before her death, she had asked that the poet be given her request that he cease roaming in exile and return to his birthplace. Ibn Ezra speaks of this in touching verses:

In pain and great labor was a child born, but it was left without a mother. She saw that death was already spreading its wings over her and tenderly besought her husband, "Forget not the covenant of youth, and with a loving hand knock on the doors of the grave. Be faithful and gentle to the little children who will call 'Mother' and whom she has left forever. Write also to my uncle,[32] who has suffered so much on my account. . . . Poor wanderer! With a deep wound in his heart has he suffered the hardships of exile in a strange land. Vainly has he sought the cup of consolation. Now he will find peace in the cup of sorrow."[33]

The death of his beloved profoundly shocked the poet, and filled with desolation is his cry of woe:

Wherever I go, wherever I turn, from all sides, only troubles and misery, misfortune and terrors, haunt me. My happiness is sunk into Sheol, my shining star lies hidden in the grave. Death has suffocated my hope, and my consolation has perished. Only the pain is alive, and it grows ever greater. . . . Would you see the most miserable among all the children of my people?—I am he.

31. For details concerning these works see Steinschneider, *Safrut Yisrael*, p. 119; Wilhelm Bacher, *MGWJ*, 1907, pp. 343–49.
32. The text says, "Write to my *dodi*." *Dodi* in Hebrew may mean "uncle" or "friend."
33. *Kerem Ḥemed*, VI, 92–93.

Ibn Ezra did not fulfill the request of his beloved and return to his homeland. He was a wanderer all his life and died in 1139[34] in a strange place, far from his own people. Brimming with quiet sorrow are the verses in which the poet recalls in old age the graves he was no longer destined to see: "The resting place of my parents and dear ones I saw in a dream. I greeted all of them, but received no answer. Have my father and mother forgotten their son? They only beckoned wordlessly and pointed out to me a place to lie down at their side."

The power of poetic creativity, however, did not abandon Ibn Ezra until the end of his life. But the death of his beloved had a tremendous influence on the mood and direction of all his later work. Spiritually broken, his heart filled with despair, Ibn Ezra ceased to believe in the power of scientific inquiry. Philosophic thought, which had previously seemed to him so great and exalted, became empty: "In vain does the seeker think that he will succeed in fathoming the hidden mysteries! How can a mortal understand Him who with His word created the heavens and by His will rules the world? Strive not, O man, to seek out what is higher than your reason! Ashamed and crushed will you return."

Ibn Ezra's youthful feeling of joy in life was choked by his sorrow before the burden of misfortune that rules the world. The melancholy poet became convinced that all his troubles were a just punishment for his former sins, for his frivolous youth. The joyous singer who, in his young manhood, had been filled with love of life now became the sorrowful, humble composer of religious hymns summoning men to repentance and piety. Ibn Ezra wrote over three hundred *piyyutim* (religious hymns)[35] and *seliḥot* (supplications for forgiveness or penitential poems) filled with lamentation over the vanity of earthly life. Not without reason did later generations give him the title "Ha-Salaḥ" or "Ha-Salḥan" (the author of penitential poems). The same motif is repeated in his hundreds of prayers and hymns: "pardon and forgiveness for the sin that I have sinned." His "great sin"—this is the tragic perception that will allow the poet who once wrote the *Tarshish* no rest. He, the crushed penitent, is convinced that he is a great sinner, that he had transgressed mightily in his youth when he was so enamored of this world. Ashamed and spiritually broken, he stands now before the God of judgment and mercy and begs forgiveness.

34. One of his last compositions is dated 1138 (published in *Ha-Goren*, VII, 69–75).
35. Landshuth in his *Ammudei Ha-Avodah* (pp. 239–55) lists 243 of Ibn Ezra's *piyyutim*. See also L. Zunz, *Literaturgeschichte*, pp. 202, 413, and 614.

"In grievous sin did my youthful years pass; I have misspent my youth, my life."[36] "I am filled with shame for my foolishly spent youthful years."[37] "From childhood on I have sinned and done evil, and pained is my heart and sick my soul."[38] This cry of woe resounds in most of his prayers. Ibn Ezra turns to God with a moving petition:

With heart purified,
Greatly shaken,
I approach God
At the time of my arising;
It counsels me and guides me
To confess my transgressions.
Behold, to expiate mine iniquities,
I offer my fat and my blood;
And I make confession and supplication,
For my sinfulness
And for the sinfulness of my people.
Who can fittingly praise my King?
Who can picture His power and majesty?
Lo, everyone that must speak with human mouth
Is of uncircumcised lips before Him.
Even the wisest cannot attain
By thought to the knowledge of His greatness;
And if the creature of dust essay
To tell of the least of the ways of his Lord,
He will be crushed by the endeavor.
For man is a dream,
And death the interpretation thereof;
But the eyes of God saw my unformed substance,
And from Him, my form cannot be hidden.
. . . .
O God, cause wrath to depart,
And lift up Thy steps to the ruins.
With the waters of love,
Oh, blot out guilt;
Tear in pieces the records of sin.
Oh, show grace to Thy servant,
That day, when before Thee,
He stands among Thy creatures to be judged—
The day that the pure are made known

36. In the prayer "Zeman Havli."
37. In the prayer "Nafshi Iviticha Balailah."
38. In his "Tochehah."

Before the Lord of Hosts,
That their souls may dwell among the holy ones
As a sign and a wonder—
The day that a voice passes among my people,
Crying: "Who are they that go?"[39]

"For my great guilt," the poet declares in another prayer, "I have torn my heart in two and the flame of sorrow has burned the pieces to ashes." Permeated with quiet, calm sorrow is his lovely prayer "Adon Ha-Yoshev Al Ḥug Ha-Aretz," which is read at the Neilah service of Yom Kippur:

Great in His holy omnipotence is the Creator of the world, and small and vain are the inhabitants of earth. I stand and pray that my song, which the congregation raises to God from early morning until the stars appear, find acceptance and favor among all the songs of the earth. The whole day through it waters the earth with tears and beseeches mercy from the Lord of the world, from early morning until the stars appear.

These quiet tones, however, sometimes pass into cries of indignation and reproof. Here the pious poet admonishes his brethren not to let themselves be led astray by the vanities of the world and earthly desires. The poet's fervor attains its peak in his famous "Tocheḥah," which is recited on Yom Kippur:

Ye deaf, hear from my lips of awes to be;
Take thought to pierce the world's deep mystery;
And ye, O blind ones, look—that ye may see!

Ye deaf, to all
Your multitudes I call,
Their Maker that deny,
On wealth their trust to build.
On power to rely;
Though wealth and power be
The very stumbling blocks of their iniquity.
Alas! how shall they hear,
That, wilful, stop the ear?
Or how shall ears with the world's tumult filled,
Heed wisdom's cry!

Take thought, O heritors of the joys of youth,
Who deem that earth's delights shall never pall—

39. *Selected Poems of Moses Ibn Ezra*, pp. 108–10. [More of this poem is given here than in Zinberg's text. —B.M.]

Unmindful of the days that must befall,
Sad days of whitening head and trembling hand—
  Will ye not learn the truth?
  Can ye not understand?
Your way accustomed unto sin is bent,
When right ye do, it is without intent!
Ye blind are they,
Bemused with worldly pride,
Who think to flourish upon earth alway;
While fate, relentlessly,
Sharpens the arrows that shall pierce your side.
And none there is, to see—
None to arouse you from your lethargy!
  Yet what shall sight avail,
  If understanding fail
To form the vision of the things to be?

Ye deaf are they that from instruction turn—
Watchmen who cannot see and will not learn;
Who deem ye bide in safety, whilst ye haste
Adown the pitward path. Ye have ears, indeed,
But hear not; neither will you heed.
  Go! leave the thronged heights
  Of sensuous delights,
And meditate within the lonely waste![40]

Ibn Ezra's poem in which he describes how the prophet Jonah
ben Amittai, who wished to flee from God, realized that one cannot
hide from Him, that there is nowhere to flee for God is everywhere, in the highest heavens and in the deepest abysses, is saturated
with the same feeling: "O, Lord of the world, I would flee from
Thee, but if I ascend to the heavens, there I find Thee, and if I
make my bed in the nether world, there art Thou."

The homeless poet who endured so much in life has only one
request, forgiveness for his sins and rest: "rest my soul desires, to
return to its source, its sacred home."[41] "Let man remember his
whole life long," he admonishes, "that death is his fate. Every day
the way becomes shorter, but man thinks he is not moving from
his place. He is like a man on board a ship; he stands immobile, yet
is carried on the wings of the wind."

But even Moses Ibn Ezra, the most typical poet of the personal
"ego," for whom the substance of his creativity was the innermost

---

40. *Ibid.,* pp. 157–58. [Again more of the "Toceḥah" is here given than
   in Zinberg's text. —B.M.]
41. The prayer "Nafshi Iviticha Balailah."

experiences of his soul, could not forget the community, the congregation of Israel. As in Ibn Gabirol's, so also in Ibn Ezra's religious lyrics national tones are frequently heard. The fate of the exiled people elicits from the wandering poet a bitter cry: "To bewail the magnitude of our misfortune is beyond our powers! If all the seas became ink, all the heavens parchment, and all the forests pens, even then it would not be possible to describe the least part of our suffering."

In all of medieval poetry there is not another poem so permeated with hopelessness as these lines in which Ibn Ezra laments the fate of his people:

Over their pitch-black night the morning star does not appear. The day of their exile knows of no tomorrow. The star of their redemption is hidden under the earth and does not appear; it has hidden itself in nethermost Sheol. False are all their hopes; their books have lied. All their lights—snuffed out; their days—passed away; their dreams—buried. There is none to console them, none to heal their wounds. Without a redeemer are the homeless, without a protector the oppressed.

It is almost incredible that such despairing verses could have been written by the pious Salḥan.

The young Moses Ibn Ezra was extremely proud of the role and significance of the poet. He celebrated the power and greatness of poets in general, and his own creativity in particular, in a special chapter of his *Tarshish*. The poet, he insisted, is endowed with a marvelous capacity "to raise unknown men to the summit of honor and greatness; with his power he crowns kings and breaks the might of rulers and princes."

Among the Arabic poets of that time it was the custom not to be parsimonious in self-praise, in glorifying one's own work to the heavens. In this respect Moses Ibn Ezra was also no miser.[42] He compares his poems to "God's script and tablets" that one should carry on one's heart; his verses are "queens that the goddess of song has borne," and in comparison with them all others are "plain maidservants."[43] "My golden songs," the poet declares, "will not be forgotten by men as long as night follows day. They are created out of words, refined by prophetic fire and irradiated with God's spirit. At their birth the ink was the darkness of night, the pen the golden ray of the sun, and the paper the ocean."[44]

In any objective estimate of Moses Ibn Ezra's work, more modest expressions and analogies would certainly have to be employed. It

42. See, e.g., *Otzar Neḥmad*, II, 183–84.
43. The introduction to *Tarshish*.
44. *Otzar Neḥmad*, II, 184.

must be said that in the poems of his early period there is too much artifice; they lack simplicity and clarity. As an aesthete, the young Ibn Ezra endeavored to use the most artificial and complicated forms. Consequently, his poems attained a high degree of metrical technique, but they lacked the warmth and fervor of genuine poetic inspiration.

In this connection it is worthwhile to dwell briefly on the structure of his *Tarshish*. The poem is written in the unique Arabic style called *Tajnis* (paranomasia), which consists in having the verses end with words that have different meanings but the same phonetic sound.[45] In addition, Ibn Ezra manifests great ingenuity in making all the similarly sounding words follow the strict order of the alphabet. The entire work bears the name *Tarshish* (a precious stone) because it consists of as many lines of verse as the letters of the Hebrew word *tarshish* form when they are understood as numbers, i.e., 1210. The poem consists of ten chapters, and each chapter ends with the name of a different precious stone (ruby, jasper, etc.) and itself consists of precisely as many lines as the Hebrew name of the stone in question equals when its letters are considered as numbers. When, with such overwhelming artifice, the poems in *Tarshish* still do not lose their charm and continue to enchant one with their beauty and the splendor of their imagery, we have clear proof how highly gifted Ibn Ezra was.[46]

In his later years, when the poet-aesthete was transformed into the pious Salḥan, Ibn Ezra discarded artificial forms, and his poems thereafter, particularly the religious poems, impress one with their earnest simplicity and genuine sentiment. Not without cause do the prayers and hymns of the Salḥan occupy such an honored place in the Sephardic Holy Day Prayer Book. But even in these the ingenious master of style and technique is clearly discernible. Rhyme is employed in all possible variety of forms. Aside from the customary rhyme at the end of the verses, the first half of the verse (*delet*) is often divided into two parts which have their special rhyme, e.g.:

> *Metei sechel / beli techel / renanot orchu negdo*
> *Asher yatzar / kol notzar / vetzar kol rum be-yado.*

45. For example, *al mah* and *almah*, *tzinah* (coolness) and *tzinah* (shield). Alḥarizi calls this form "words that sound alike but have a different content."

46. Not without cause did the poet and critic of the thirteenth century, Jehudah Alḥarizi, when he read the *Tarshish*, enthusiastically note on the manuscript that Moses Ibn Ezra is "like the lily among the thorns." See *Literaturblatt des Orients*, 1846, p. 810.

The Salḥan

Sometimes the first halves of the verses have a special rhyme, as is the case in the poem "Mi-peat Afelati." Some of Ibn Ezra's poems are so constructed that every line is divided into three parts and all three have the same rhyme, e.g.:

Im ḥasodecha shachaḥnu / vetoratecha zanaḥnu / zechor ki afar anaḥnu.
Echa tifkod beḥemah / alei tolaat verimah / afar min ha-adamah.

At times Ibn Ezra also employs special rhythmic effects that make a strong impression, e.g., in his well-known "Ofan Le-Parashat Shekalim," where he describes how hosts of angels and seraphim praise the Lord of the world. Because of the unique construction of the verses and the rhythmic sounding-together of similar words and names which quickly follow one another, the poet succeeds in masterfully rendering the swift, loud rush of hosts of seraphim with their mighty wings, all joining together in a joyful, triumphant cry of praise:

Kadosh, kadosh, kadosh!
Malachim mamlichim / maaritzim bechol peot
Makdishim marishim / margishim berov teshuot.
Noraim ve-en nirim / niflaim, ve-niflaot—
Omrim: Kadosh, kadosh, kadosh, Adonai Tzevaot!
Shemo lo-ad berov raad / be-emah hen yaaritzun
Sheon serafim berum afim / ke-verakim yerutzun. . . .

CHAPTER FOUR

Jehudah Halevi
The Poet

N O matter how highly Moses Ibn Ezra esteemed himself and his poetic talent, he gladly deferred to a younger colleague. This colleague was the glory of medieval Hebrew poetry, and the loveliest personality of medieval Judaism —Jehudah ben Samuel Halevi.[1] As in the case of many great Jewish figures, very little is known of Halevi's life. Even the years of his birth and death are not certain. It has merely been conjectured that he was born in 1080 and died in 1142. What has definitely been established is only that he was born in Toledo in Christian Castile and that his father sent him to Arabic Spain, the major cultural center of that time, that he might receive a broad education. Halevi studied Talmud and other Jewish subjects in the rabbinic academy of Lucena under the famous Rabbi Isaac Alfasi. He also studied medicine and thoroughly familiarized himself with Greek-Arabic philosophy. His favorite occupation, however, was poetry. Even as a thirteen- or fourteen-year-old, he had acquired a considerable reputation with his poems, and Moses Ibn Ezra, who was then already a renowned poet, enthusiastically declared that "out of Castile has risen a star that will light up the

---

1. In Arabic his name was Abu al-Ḥasan al-Lawi.
2. *Kerem Ḥemed,* IV, 86.

whole world."[2] It was then that the cordial friendship between the two poets, which lasted until Ibn Ezra's death, was sealed.[3]

When Halevi returned to his native city, he achieved fame there as a practicing physician. It is even probable that he was for a time body physician at the court of Castile. In one of his poems he declares, "I am a man friendly to all; hateful to me are only the court officials with their flattery."[4] But the relatively backward cultural atmosphere of Christian Castile, it appears, did not please the young poet; he was drawn to Arabic Spain and settled in Cordova.

While few details of Halevi's biography are known to us, the experiences of his soul and the treasures of his inner world were preserved for later generations in his spiritual and intellectual legacy. It is difficult to find another medieval poet in whom were forged so completely, in one harmonious cast, his poetic creativity and his life, the nature of his soul and his relationship to the world and his environment. To separate Halevi's poetic legacy from the purity of his spirit and the remarkable beauty of his life is impossible. His noble and gentle soul, with all its profundity and grace, was simultaneously reflected in his work and in his life. Halevi knew of no contradiction between what *is* and what is only *longed for*. What *should* be, *must* be. This marvelous integrity and beauty are blended into a glorious song, an immortal poem that bears the name Jehudah Halevi.

The famous poet Heinrich Heine recognized the incomparable grace of Halevi's soul, and in his well-known poem "Jehudah Halevi" celebrated the medieval singer's talent and soul, both together. His eulogy reads:

> Pure and just, without the least fault,
> Is his song, as is his soul.
> When God created
> This soul, satisfied with His work,
> He kissed the first-born;
> And the echo of that kiss
> Lives in every song of the poet
> Anointed with God's grace.

Halevi himself speaks feelingly of the integrity of his spirit:[5]

3. As a result of this friendship Hebrew poetry was enriched with a series of lovely songs that the two poets sent each other. A tender elegy by Jehudah Halevi in which he laments the death of the friend of his youth has also come down to us.
4. Brody, *Diwan*, I, 49.
5. *Ibid.*, II, 164–67.

How shall I be afraid of any man? There is no lion that can make my soul tremble. How shall I be concerned about want and need? In the depths of my soul are mountains of richest treasures. Strange to me is hunger—my soul obtains for me the best of foods; protected am I from thirst—her marvelous springs quench it; longing and misery alike are unknown to me—the sweet tones of her harps drive them away. I require no company; the cleverest talk of near ones and friends can only choke the melody of my soul.

A single ideal radiated before the poet's eye throughout his life—the ideal of beauty. This was the goal of all his hopes, desires, and dreams. The keener and more profound Halevi's gaze became, the more brightly did the star of his life shine, the more exaltedly did his song resound.

Halevi's youthful poems show clearly that his early years were filled with joy and love of life. "The days dance their merry cycle for me," the poet himself says. "I," he declares, "am the sea with its stormy waves"; "broad and full as the sea is my heart." Avidly the young Halevi imbibed from the overflowing cup and expressed his sentiments in his poems celebrating nature, feminine beauty, and love of women. He also sang guild and drinking songs and proposed to "drown the pain of sorrow in the red, sparkling beaker." He composed ingenious riddles and clever epigrams and honored his numerous friends with poems of praise and witty letters in verse. But even such occasional songs and friendly gifts are often literary gems as, for example, the poem that Halevi sent to Moses Ibn Ezra when the latter left his birthplace and went into exile. In the final stanza of his poem are these lovely lines:

You who are pure of speech, what do you among stammerers?
Or what has the blessed dew of Hermon to do with the cursed
  mountains of Gilboa?

While Halevi was writing a poem of praise to one of his friends, Solomon Farissol, he received the sad news that this friend had been killed. The shattered poet then concluded his song with elegiac verses of lamentation. A whole series of his poems of friendship (*shirei yedidut*) are adorned, in the style of the Arabic poets, with classically beautiful portrayals of nature. In the long poem that Halevi sent to his comrade Solomon Ibn Giat, when he describes his longing for the distant but dearly loved friend, he gives incidentally a magnificent portrait of a southern summer's night—how, at its dying, the beaming, laughing dawn is born in gold and purple.[6] The poem sent by Halevi to his friend Isaac Al-Yatom be-

6. The poem *Ayyin Nedivah* in Brody, *op. cit.*, I, 137–41.

gins with a paean to the loveliness of the southern spring that dazzles the eye with its splendid colors:

But yesterday the earth, like a child, avidly sucked the cold drops of an angry, gray-white cloud; like a bride wrapped in a winter veil, she yearned quietly with trembling heart and dreamed of passionate embraces, born of love and desire. But now spring is come, and the earth has been liberated from her sweetly painful longing. She dazzles with her golden, silken trickeries; she glistens with her decked-out flower beds, and shines joyfully in her colorful robe. Extravagantly she changes her garments without cease, adorns everything with silken cloth, and at every dawn the flowers look out with newly opened eyes. Now mother-of-pearl eyes sparkle, now ruby colors dazzle us, and forthwith these disappear under the samarkand cover. Now the world is adorned in white; anon it decks itself in bright purple like a beautiful young woman when the kiss of love trembles bashfully on her lips. . . . Ah, how lovely are the flowers of the earth! As if she had robbed the heavens of their most beautiful stars. . . . We wander quietly among the shadows of the fragrant avenues of the garden. With a happy smile the earth greets the pearly tears of the morning dew; she laughs and the tears glisten and sparkle, like precious stones on a woven breast cover. She joyously receives the song of every bird and listens to the turtledove singing to its beloved. She sings and rejoices through every leaf and the least little grass, like a young bride under the veil. And everything dances and rejoices in a happy circle. . . . My soul trembles joyfully and receives the lovely secret, brought by the dawn wind, freshly dipped in fragrant odors. Mischievously it runs further, and the myrtle's fragrant odor it takes along to refresh hearts. The myrtle branch that had just risen, greeting the welcome guest, bows again to the earth, and the palm branches tremble happily, enchanted with the song of birds.[7]

Halevi's sensitive ear registered the slightest movement of the quietest blade of grass, the humble breath of the most modest floweret. His heart was intoxicated with nature's gifts and, master that he was, he embodied in clear images the richness of the vivid colors, the joyous, triumphant cry of nature bubbling with life.

Against this colorful background the young poet, intoxicated with the spicy odors and warm breath of the earth drenched with southern sunlight, sings his song of earthly love. Raised in the milieu of an Oriental people, with its harem life, our poet celebrates in ardent verses the beautiful young inhabitants of the harems:

Greet, you singers, the lovely ones! Come, all you masters of the fiddle, the harp and other instruments! Sing a song of praise to the maidens

7. *Al Shoshanei He-Aviv* in Harkavy, *Diwan*, II, 58–59.

who look quietly through the windows of their palaces. They are graced with artless modesty like our mother Rebecca, and as lovely and pure are their bodies as their hearts and souls. If one of them accidentally throws a glance at a man's heart, he is at once mortally wounded. But they remain guiltless, these simple, lovely ones! Pure are their gentle hands; they have not touched the sharp poisoned arrows. . . . They desire no adornment, no luxurious clothing. Sadly, in sweet half slumber, they sit with lowered eyes. Were they to uncover their faces, even the sun would be blinded by their beauty. Their bright appearance tells the tidings: Day is coming; and among the ringlets of their locks the night with its dark shadows looks out. . . . For this host of beautiful stars my heart is the broad heaven, and each wanders freely on its way. How helplessly my dazzled eye travels among the garland of softly slim, blindingly bright, rosy red, radiantly white, lovely young women! How strictly they guard with their coral lips the two wondrous rows of polished pearls. Forgive, my heart, if their gaze often holds concealed falsehood and flattery—for they are so charmingly beautiful! Their odor is lovelier than the loveliest rose. They are slender and supple, like the noble palms kissed by the light morning breeze. Yes, they cruelly rob hearts and inflict deep wounds, but this is small payment for the joy when enchanted eyes absorb the brilliance and beauty of their faces. . . ."[8]

In similar colors Halevi portrays the young "mistress of magic," who is so dazzlingly lovely that if she were to throw off all her clothing, her body would still not be bare, for the magic of her artlessness and her peerless beauty would veil her naked form in their radiant, magical robe.[9]

Among all the beautiful women of the warm Southland Halevi found his only one, his chosen and passionately beloved. As the young poet drank from the cup of love, every drop of the liquid was transformed into charming love verses.

The beauty of the beloved, the joys of love, and the pain of longing—all receive in our poet plastic forms and vivid colors. And

8. Harkavy, *Diwan*, I, 47–48. These verses serve as an introduction to a long poem which the author sent to a close friend in Egypt on his way to Palestine. The verses are so different in mood from the rest of the poem that it has been conjectured that we have here two entirely different poems. However, it has also been pointed out that among the Arab poets it was generally the fashion, in a poem of friendship, to give first a description of nature or a paean to feminine beauty. We regard it as psychologically impossible that in the poet's mood on his way to Zion he should have undertaken to celebrate the lovely residents of the harems so enthusiastically. It is easier to believe that he placed, as an introduction to his friendship poem, one of the songs he had written in his youth.

9. *Ibid.*, p. 95.

over this "song of songs" of love hovers the grace of artless charm, at times mischievously mild, at times covered with a cloud of quiet sadness: "Wrapped in the night my beloved came. She showed me the flame of her cheeks and the gold of her locks that frame, like brilliant rubies, her polished crystal temples. Her enchanting form is like the rising sun when it adorns, with its radiant spears and golden purple, the joyful clouds of dawn." Of his own lovely one with "golden locks" Halevi sings in his graceful poem "Shalom Le-Tzeviah Naarah." "You golden-locked queen of splendor and beauty," the poet complains, "are a slender doe, but you devour like a lionness."

Dreaming and languid, the beloved sings: "On the light wings of the wind, at the end of a summer's day, I send greetings to my beloved. One thing only I ask of him: that he remember the day of parting, when we sealed the covenant of love under the shade of the apple tree."

But the love of the Southland is passionate, and through the gentle tones of love suddenly breaks the flame of burning desire. The fiery, sparkling speech of the Song of Songs, of the Biblical Shulamith, is heard: "Her cheeks like roses, these my eyes thirstily pluck; her breasts like pomegranates, these my hands avidly embrace; her lips, those glowing coals, my lips devour; and her locks, those black serpents, suffocate me with their sweet ringlets."[10]

The poet sings to his beloved: "My life would I gladly give for your night of love. . . . Ah, let me enjoy the taste of your lips, drink to the last drop the cup of love." And the beloved freely declares: "All the treasures of the world for that one night when, under the cover of its wings, I gave my love to my beloved! His breath intoxicated me like the strongest wine, and avidly I kissed his cheeks. He made me drunk with the burning caresses of his coral lips until wearily he besought me: "Enough, enough. I am wearied of kissing!"

But love is capricious, and her fragrant roses are not devoid of sharp thorns. The poet, in love, laments: "In my tears does she wash her clothing, and she drinks them under the rays of her shining face. She requires no springs—she has my eyes! She needs no sun with such dazzling beauty."[11] And the beloved declares with a cunning smile: "On my knees did my lover rest and saw his image in the mirror of my eyes. The naughty man covered my eyes with kisses. Not me, but my beloved did his lips kiss." "My dear one, my beloved," whispers the lover, "awaken quickly from your slumber!

10. Brody, *Diwan*, II, 44.
11. Harkavy, *Diwan*, I, 132.

Let me satiate myself with the brilliance of your starry eyes! Have you, perchance, dreamed of passionate embraces and caressing lips? —I am ready to be the interpreter of your dreams."

But now the sad day of parting has come, and the lover painfully cries:

You wish to part from me. Ah, but wait awhile. Let my gaze absorb the light of your radiant form. It is incredible that the cage of my breast should not be torn through by my heart, so that it may attend you on your way like a faithful servant. By our love I adjure you: Forget not our happy days, as I will always remember the nights of your embraces. . . . Your form will reign over all my hopes and dreams—so be you, too, loving and tender to me in your dreams. A seething sea of tears separates us, and I cannot come over to you; but when you, my beloved, lift your gaze to me, the depths of the sea will be split before my steps. . . . Even after my death, I will hear your soft steps with their sound of golden bells,[12] and at your greeting my cry of joy will come to you from the grave: "I love you!" Ah, my heart bleeds, and it is your hands that have shed its blood. Testimony of this are your red lips and the roses of your cheeks. . . . My heart has drunk both the honey-sweet liquid and the cup bitter as gall—these are your sweet kisses and the bitterness of parting. . . . Of all the treasures in the world, I desire only the smile of your lips and the band around your loins. My best spices, the refreshments of my soul, are your lips; my rest and joy—at your breasts! . . . Extinguished is your voice, it does not reach my ears—but its tones still sound over the strings of my heart. Only my shadow remains here now; my heart wanders after your steps. Ah, quickly unite the body with the soul! Return, my beloved, return home![13]

One of Halevi's most typical love poems ends on a completely unexpected note. The poet sings a love song to a beautiful inhabitant of the harem. In Oriental imagery he describes his love and his longing: "How lovely you are, how full of enchantment your gaze! Joined in your form are the grace of the smiling dawn and the dreamy loveliness of the summer evening, born in purple. When my eyes consider your radiant face and the night of your tresses, my lips reverently whisper: 'Blessed be the Creator of light and the Author of darkness.' " This poem further relates how the love-stricken poet begs for the hand of the "beautiful daughter of the sun and the moon" and wishes to seal the bond of love with her under the marriage canopy. Then suddenly Halevi concludes with

12. At that time it was the fashion to embroider women's shoes and dresses with little bells.
13. Fragments of the long poem *Mah-loch Tzeviah*.

these lines: "Oh, when will the poor daughter of Zion also find rest on the bridal bed, and when will God's voice resound, 'Arise, you who wander in strange lands; behold, the day comes and the sun has risen'?"[14]

This unexpected note is, however, not an accidental one. Closely connected with Halevi's love poems are his wedding poems, which he was accustomed to send as gifts to brides and grooms who were friends of his. A unique grace permeates these epithalamia celebrating the bashful love and ardent desire of young hearts, hidden under the veil of simplicity and innocence.[15] In one of these songs the poet again ends unexpectedly with a note of sorrow: "Ah, when will the day of joy and redemption come for my people also?"[16] This sad note is the first sign informing us that in the poet's soul, in his innermost ideas and feelings, a great change had occurred. The more powerful and mature Halevi's talent became, the more clearly was the sorrow of his people expressed in his poetry. The titanic struggle that took place in his day between the Christian and Moslem worlds in Spain as well as in Palestine, the sufferings which the Jews consequently had to endure from both sides, aroused in him profound grief over the fate of his defenseless people.

"There is no place," Halevi laments, "to flee. Neither in the east nor in the west do we find rest. . . . Whether Ishmael is stronger or Edom prevails, the fate of my people is equally bitter."

The world drama of the exiled people, its sorrow and sufferings, grieved the poet's sensitive soul and were transformed into chords of pain. But national pain and sorrow are in Halevi closely associated with the supreme ideal of his life, the vision of brilliance and beauty. As he became more mature and more profound, this vision of his youth gradually liberated itself from its earthly garment and took on ever more spiritual and nobler forms. In the soul of the mature poet a profound alteration took place, reminiscent of the transformation which the eternally youthful love poem, the Song of Songs, "the song above all songs," sustained in the consciousness of Israel. When the once youthful and powerful people, which ob-

14. Brody, *Diwan*, II, 49–50.
15. Several of Halevi's epithalamia are written in the Oriental style of clever riddles. As an example, we quote the poem which the author sent to a bride whose groom was named Jehudah (meaning in Hebrew a lion): "The marriage canopy is prepared; the lovely one's bridal tent shines in marvelous splendor. Mild as the Queen of Sheba, she distributes richest gifts and smilingly asks, 'Have you ever heard or seen that a gazelle should go live in the cave of a lion and not be fearful?' 'Ah,' they answer, 'you yourself are the gazelle coming to live in the lair of the young lion.'"
16. Brody, *Diwan*, II, 44; Harkavy, *Diwan*, I, 136.

tained a land for itself through the sword, became a "people of the spirit," the people of prophets and of "My son, My firstborn Israel," the verses of Shulamith and her beloved, flaming with the fire of love, were transformed into a mystical, sacred poem in which the union of the community of Israel and God is celebrated. The immortal song of earthly love and desire became holy; it lost its corporeal dress and became a "secret of secrets," a divine mystery. In Halevi also the song of earthly love and physical beauty was transformed into religious enthusiasm and mystical ecstasy.

The feeling of joy which the beauty of nature and the magic of love gave the poet in his youthful years gradually threw off its bodily garment and was changed into enthusiasm for the exalted greatness of the Creator, the eternal source of splendor and beauty. It was no longer earthly love and earthly beauty, but the God of love and beauty, that filled Halevi's soul and inspired his song.

The idea of God, for Halevi, was not an abstract concept, the conclusion of a syllogism. He experienced God within himself with the whole being of his poetic soul, with all the nerves and feelings of his great heart, with the sharp clarity of his power of imagination. "To forget God," the poet declares, "means to forget oneself"; "how can one live when he does not sense God as the source of life, light and joy?"; "only the servant of God is truly free"; "when He is angry, I am the lowliest slave; when He is gracious, I am king of kings."

No translation can render the power of Halevi's masterly verses:

> O Lord, where shall I find Thee?
> All-hidden and exalted is Thy place;
> And where shall I not find Thee?
> Full of Thy glory is the infinite space.
>
> Found near-abiding ever,
> He made the earth's ends, set their utmost bar;
> Unto the nigh a refuge,
> Yea, and a trust to those who wait afar.
> Thou sittest throned between the Cherubim,
> Thou dwellest high above the cloud-rack dim.
> Praised by Thine hosts and yet beyond their praises
> Forever far exalt;
> The endless whirl of worlds may not contain Thee,
> How, then, one temple's vault?
>
> And Thou, withal uplifted
> O'er man, upon a mighty throne apart,
> Are yet forever near him,

Breath of his spirit, life-blood of his heart!
His own mouth speaketh testimony true
That Thou his Maker art alone; and who
Shall fear Thee not, for lo! upon their shoulders
Thy yoke divinely dread!
Who shall forbear to cry to Thee, That givest
To all their daily bread?

Longing I sought Thy presence;
Lord, with my whole heart did I call and pray,
And going out toward Thee,
I found Thee coming to me on the way;
Yea, in Thy wonders' might as clear to see
As when within the shrine I looked for Thee.
Who saith he hath not seen Thee? Lo! the heavens
And all their host, aflame
With glory, show Thy fear with speech unuttered,
With silent voice proclaim.
And can the Lord God truly—

God, the Most High—dwell here within man's breast?
What shall he answer, pondering—
Man, whose foundations in the dust do rest?
For Thou art holy, dwelling 'mid the praise
Of them that waft Thee worship all their days.
Angels adoring, singing of Thy wonder,
Stand upon Heaven's height;
And Thou, enthroned o'erhead, all things upholdest
With everlasting might.[17]

This profound and powerful religious sentiment, which permeated the poet's soul, found expression in a large number of
prayer-poems which are among the most precious gems of Jewish
religious poetry. Halevi's intimate religious lyrics, however, bear
a clearly stamped national character. His religious sentiment does
not remain isolated within the narrow confines of his own ego; it
blends with the spirit of the community which lives in each individual and is the source from which the latter draws his life force.
Religious fervor, the experiences of a gentle and noble soul, are in
Halevi inextricably bound up with the strivings and hopes of the
people. God, the national community, and the trembling heart of

17. *Selected Poems of Jehudah Halevi*, translated into English by Nina
Salaman, chiefly from the critical text edited by Heinrich Brody (Philadelphia: The Jewish Publication Society of America, 1924), pp. 168–69.

the individual—all these are merged in the creative activity of the poet into a harmonious tri-unity, filled with splendor and beauty. Characteristic in this respect is Halevi's poem "Yam Suf Ve-Sinai Lamduni," one of his most beautiful and profound national-religious songs. Unfortunately, no translation can render the chords of half-dreaming, longing, and passionate love, filled with quiet sorrow, that resound so harmoniously in this incomparable hymn.

Even in religious poems so heartfelt, purely personal, and filled with lyrical effusion as "Ke-Niddah Haitah Tevel Lefani," "Adonai Negdecha Kol Taavati," "Yeshenah Be-Ḥek Yaldut," it is difficult to separate the individual from the community, the personal from the national. In the prayer "Bechol Libi"[18] the poet turns to God:

With my whole heart, with the flame of my soul, do I love Thee, my God and Creator! In dream and in reality Thy name accompanies me; how, then, can I wander lonely? Thou art my friend; how can I be solitary? Thou art my light; how can my star go down? How can I be tempted? — My God is ever my support! I am scorned and mocked by all, but they do not understand that everything I suffer for Thy name's sake is my pride and crown. O Source of my life, as long as I breathe, my lips will bless Thee! As long as my song resounds, it will remember and praise Thee!

In the sufferings of his people Halevi sees the surest sign of its eternity:

Lo! sun and moon, these minister for aye;
The laws of day and night cease nevermore:
Given for signs to Jacob's seed that they
Shall ever be a nation—till these be o'er.
If with His left hand He should thrust away,
Lo! with His right hand He shall draw them nigh.
Let them not cry despairing, nay, nor say:
Hope faileth and our strength is near to die.
Let them believe that they shall be alway,
Nor cease until there be no night nor day.[19]

In his famous philosophical-ethical work, the *Kuzari*, which we shall discuss later, Halevi declares that "we [the Jews] suffer more than all others because Israel among the nations is like the heart among the organs in the human body. The heart is more sensitive than all the other organs; therefore, it suffers more than all of

18. Harkavy, *Diwan*, I, 56.
19. *Selected Poems of Jehudah Halevi*, p. 167.

them."[20] Halevi becomes the inspired singer of the national sufferings, the poet who laments the fate of his people, the "quiet dove that has been driven from its nest and left suspended over the terrible abyss." With deep sadness he cries out to God in the name of Israel: "To Seir [the Roman empire] was I exiled, and driven to Kedar [Arabia]; tried in the crucible of Greece, and thrust under the yoke of Media. Thou, only Redeemer, as Thou art unique in Thy power, so is my hope unique and incomparable! Give me Thy help; I give Thee my love!"

Halevi, however, is not only the bearer of the people's suffering but also the singer of its hopes and dreams:

The poor prince must suffer under the hands of the robber and oppressor. He must wander lonely and miserable over the face of the earth, while the daughter of Edom lives in joy. The son of the king weeps while the son of the maidservant greets him with laughter. But sufferings are a proving stone; purified and refined will you soon awaken to a new, joyous life!

"How long," Halevi cries out in another poem, "will the light of Jesse's scion[21] be extinguished? — Let the harps of the sons of Levi break their long silence!" And this miracle actually occurred: the harp of the ancient Levitical singers awakened with wondrous power under the magical hand of the inspired Castilian poet.

It was this golden dream, the simple folk belief in the redeemer who would liberate the exiled people from its suffering and awaken the ancient land of the patriarchs to new life, that became the foundation of Halevi's later poetic creativity. The Muse of his poems encircled the historic ideal of the Jewish people with an imaginative garland of brilliant stars and fragrant flowers. The "harp of the Levites" did, indeed, break its silence, and on its strings the fondest hopes of the nation were brought to life in mighty chords that resounded in the hearts of Jews for centuries.

"Zion," in Halevi's eyes, was not only the historic land of the fathers. For his poetic spirit, which incorporated the ideal and abstract in plastic and concrete forms, the mountains of Judea became the symbol of the most beautiful and exalted, for which his own soul as well as the nation's longed.

As the doves hasten to their cotes, so lift up your hearts to the light that streams over Jerusalem, the source of your life, the loveliest crown

20. In the *Kuzari* the poet incidentally emphasizes that sufferings purify and refine the people, freeing it from all impurity and dross.
21. I.e., the Messiah, the son of David.

of your dreams and desires. Great is God's love for the gates of Zion; He has united them eternally with the gates of Heaven.

The longing for the supreme ideal of beauty and righteousness found its expression among the foremost poets of medieval Christendom in the mystical legend of the Grail, the cup which received the innocent blood of him who sacrificed himself for the sins of the world. The same ideal incorporated itself for the greatest Jewish poet of the Middle Ages in "the heart of the world," Mount Zion. The choicest spirits of medieval Christendom, the knights of the legendary round table of King Arthur, wandered over the world seeking the Holy Grail. The Jewish "knight" Jehudah Halevi also set out to seek *his* national "holy vessel," the cup of *Weltschmerz*, Mount Zion.

The harmoniously integral poet, who knew of no inner contradiction, dedicated himself with all the flame of his poetic spirit to this ideal. The stronger his longing for the distant land of his fathers became, the clearer his song resounded. The poems that Halevi wrote on his way to Jerusalem are among the loveliest gems of medieval Hebrew poetry. All are permeated with one basic sentiment, irradiated with one idea, which forges them into a unitary poem, a great ode to Zion.

The songs in which the poet's longing for the land of his fathers, "where every stone is burnt through with the fire of my heart and the dust is watered with my tears," is portrayed may be considered as introductions to this poem.

My heart is in the east, and I in the uttermost west—
How can I find savour in food? How shall it be sweet to me?
How shall I render my vows and my bonds, while yet
Zion lieth beneath the fetter of Edom, and I in Arab chains?
A light thing would it seem to me to leave all the good things
    of Spain—
Seeing how precious in mine eyes it is to behold the dust of
    the desolate sanctuary.[22]

Halevi's heart looks toward the distant East where, before his inspired gaze, David's city, "the heart of the world," Jerusalem, shines.

Beautiful of elevation! Joy of the world!
City of the Great King!
For thee my soul is longing from limits of the west.

22. *Selected Poems of Jehudah Halevi*, p. 2.

The tumult of my tenderness is stirred when I remember
Thy glory of old that is departed—thine habitation which is
  desolate.
O that I might fly on eagles' wings,
That I might water thy dust with my tears until they mingle
  together.

I have sought thee, even though thy King be not in thee and though,
  in place
Of thy Gilead's balm, are now the fiery serpent and the scorpion.

Shall I not be tender to thy stones and kiss them,
And the taste of thy soil be sweeter than honey unto me?[23]

The poet relates how his relatives and friends were all opposed to his journey, but he answered them proudly: "Is it good that the memory of our dead be treasured while the ark and the tablets remain broken? Shall we piously visit the place of corruption and worms and abandon the fountain of eternal life?"

With brilliant simplicity the poet further describes[24] how he leaves his home, parts with his only daughter and her son and his faithful pupils, and sets out on his long and difficult way. Later, we see him on board ship. He offers a prayer of love to God and addresses a petition to the west wind, which is to bring him to the longed-for land:

This is thy wind, O perfumed west,
With spikenard and apple in his wings!

Thou comest forth of the treasuries of the traders in spice—
Thou art not of the treasuries of the wind.
Thou waftest me on swallow's wings, and proclaimest liberty for
  me;
Like pure myrrh from the bundle of spices thou art chosen.
How must men long for thee, which for thy sake
Ride over the crest of the sea on the back of a plank!
Stay not thine hand from the ship
Either when day abideth or in the cool breath of the night;
But beat out the deep, and tear the heart of the seas and touch
The holy mountains, and there shalt thou rest.

Rebuke thou the east wind which tosseth the sea into tempest
Until he maketh its heart like a seething pot.

23. *Ibid.*, p. 19.
24. In the poem *Hetzikatni Teshukati Le-El Ḥai.*

What shall the captive do, in the hand of God,
One moment held back, and one moment sent forth free?

Truly the secret of my quest is in the hand of the Highest,
Who formeth the mountain heights and createth the wind.[25]

Now the poet is already far from home. He sees around himself
"only water, heaven, and the ship." The sea is angry, but Halevi's
soul is filled with quiet joy; the ship is "bringing it closer to the
sanctuary of its almighty God." Halevi, however, is not only a
pious pilgrim going up to God's holy city; he is also a great poet.
He stands on the ship enthralled by the sea with its splendor and
powerful beauty. His soul leaps up for joy, and he composes on
the ship a series of marvelous sea poems that have no peer in all of
medieval literature.

Now the sea is still. It lies calmly in the arms of the graceful
southern night. The incomparable beauty of the dreamy night on
the quiet sea fills the poet's soul with reverence, and he sings a
paean to the almighty Creator. But the sea does not know of any
long rest or stasis. Now it shines with a thousand reeling suns and
dazzles with millions of dancing rays. Now it storms, and fearful is
its anger and cruel its judgment. A terrible windstorm had arisen
and deathly terror had seized all on the ship. But our poet remained
calm. His faith is firm. He *must* reach his ideal, he *will* see "the
heart of the world," the goal of his hopes, the Holy Land!

I cry to God with a melting heart and knees that smite together,
While anguish is in all loins,
On a day when the oarsmen are astounded at the deep,
When even the pilots find not their hands.
How shall I be otherwise, since I, on a ship's deck,
Suspended between waters and heavens,
Am dancing and tossed about? — But this is but a light thing,
If I may but hold the festal dance in the midst of thee, O Jerusa-
lem![26]

I say in the heart of the seas to the quaking heart,
Fearing exceedingly because they lift up their waves:
If thou believest in God who made
The sea, and whose Name doth stand unto all eternity,
The sea shall not affright thee when the waves thereof arise,
For with thee is One who hath set a bound to the sea.[27]

25. *Selected Poems of Jehudah Halevi*, pp. 24–25.
26. *Ibid.*, p. 29.
27. *Ibid.*, p. 28.

These verses are fragments of the great symphony in which Jehudah Halevi portrays with tremendous poetic power the storm wind on the sea, the fierce roar of the waves that boil and seethe, the demonic laughter of the bottom of the sea that has sundered the chains of the abysses. On the ship, which is hurled by the waves like a chip of wood over mountains and valleys, helpless men with icy despair in their hearts lie in terror. But now the storm dies down, the sea is calmed, the ship is saved, the men are freed from their terror and gratefully lift their eyes to their Protector and Redeemer. And Halevi concludes his poem with a tender chord: "Ah, when will the tidings of redemption also come for the people that languishes in exile and is pursued by all, like the ship by the waves and the storm? When will the proclamation be heard: 'Go forth, my faithful one, from your dark prison! God's grace will light up your bitter fate!'?"

For a while the west wind died down, and the ship had to remain at anchor for a long time on the shores of North Africa near the egress of the Nile. The splendor of Egypt awakens the poet in Halevi, and he sings of it in lovely verses:

Praise, above all cities, be unto Egypt
Whither came first the word of God.
There a chosen vine was planted,
Whose clusters became a peculiar treasure;
There the envoys of God were born,
Envoys of God, as from bridegroom to bride;
And there God's glory came down and walked
In a pillar of fire and cloud, swathed in thick darkness;
And there the offering of the Lord was made,
And the blood of the covenant given, and redemption found.
There stood Moses to supplicate—
And verily no assembly is like unto this for prayer,—
And Israel is to be, unto Egypt and Assyria,
A third, and a highway between them.
Yea, an altar of the Lord hath been in the midst of Egypt
To exalt His name above all praise,
And such signs and wonders and fame,
That the world is filled with the glory of His memory.
Even her river is of the rivers of Eden,
And the goodness of her soil may be weighed against the garden of
    Eden.[28]

28. *Ibid.*, pp. 33–34.

The Jewish communities in Egypt welcomed the famous poet with great honor and pleaded with him to stay with them. Halevi's answer was brief: "How can Egypt hold me when all my thoughts and desires are woven around Mount Zion?"

The closer the poet came to the shores of the land of Israel, the greater his impatience, and he begged the waves to bring him quickly to his goal. "Soon I shall see the dwelling of my beloved who has left her nest. The doves are driven out of their nest, and crows have settled there." The land of the patriarchs and the desolate sanctuary dominated Halevi's imagination so strongly that he saw in a dream before his enchanted eyes the sanctuary as it once was, in all its splendor and glory, when the priests performed the sacrificial service and the Levites sang their songs and prayers.[29]

Now the powerful longing for the Holy Land, for the incarnate symbol of the loveliest and most exalted in the world, reached its peak and surged in the immortal ode to Zion *Tziyyon Ha-Lo Tishali*, which to this day is read throughout the Jewish world on the Ninth of Av, when Jews mourn the destruction of their sanctuary:

> Zion, wilt thou not ask if peace's wing
> Shadows the captives that ensue thy peace,
> Left lonely from thine ancient shepherding?
>
> Lo! west and east and north and south—world-wide—
> All those from far and near, without surcease,
> Salute thee: Peace and Peace from every side.
> . . . .
> I with the jackal's wail have mourned thee long,
> But dreaming of thine own restored anew
> I am a harp to sound for thee thy song.
> . . . .
> There the Shekhinah dwelt; to thee was given
> Thy Maker's Presence when He opened there
> The gates of thee toward the gates of Heaven.
>
> And only glory from the Lord was thine
> For light; and moon and stars and sunshine waned,
> Nor gave more light unto thy light divine.
>
> O, I would choose but for my soul to pour
> Itself where then the Spirit of God remained
> Outpoured upon thy chosen ones of yore.

29. See Halevi's poem *Elohai, Mishkenotecha Yedidot.*

Jehudah Halevi

Thou art the royal house; thou art the throne
Of God; and how come slaves to sit at last
Upon the thrones which were thy lords' alone?

Would I were wandering in those places dear
Where God revealed Himself in ages past,
Showing His light to messenger and seer!

And who will make me wings that I may fly,
That I may take my broken heart away
And lay its ruins where thy ruins lie?

Prostrate upon thine earth, I fain would thrust
Myself, delighting in thy stones, and lay
Exceeding tender hold upon thy dust.
. . . .
The life of souls thine air is; yea, and thou
Hast purest myrrh for grains of dust; and deep
With honey from the comb thy rivers flow.

Sweet to my soul 'twould be to wander bare
And go unshod in places waxen waste—
Desolate since thine oracles were there;

Where thine Ark rested, hidden in thine heart,
And where, within, thy Cherubim were placed
Which in thine inmost chambers dwelt apart.

I will cut off and cast away my crown
Of locks, and curse the season which profaned
In unclean land the crowns which were thine own.

How shall it any more be sweet to me
To eat or drink, while dogs all unrestrained
Thy tender whelps devouring I must see?

Or how shall light of day at all be sweet
Unto mine eyes, while still I see them killed—
Thine eagles—caught in ravens' mouths for meat?

O cup of sorrow! gently! let thy stress
Desist a little! for my reins are filled
Already, and my soul with bitterness.
. . . .

Zion! O perfect in thy beauty! found
With love bound up, with grace encompassing,
With thy soul thy companions' souls are bound:

That they rejoice at thy tranquility,
And mourn the wasteness of thine overthrow
And weep at thy destruction bitterly.
. . . .
And thine anointed—who among their throng
Compareth? Likened unto whom shall be
Levites and seers and singers of thy song?

Lo! It shall pass, shall change, the heritage,
Of vain-crowned kingdoms; not all time subdues
Thy strength; thy crown endures from age to age.

Thy God desired thee for a dwelling-place;
And happy is the man whom He shall choose,
And draw him nigh to rest within thy space.

Happy is he that waiteth: — he shall go
To thee, and thine arising radiance see
When over him shall break thy morning glow;

And see rest for thy chosen; and sublime
Rejoicing find amid the joy of thee
Returned unto thine olden youthful time.[30]

On this note Halevi's ode to Zion is interrupted and, with it, his
entire poetic activity. One easily comes to the conclusion that so
it *had* to be, considering the nature of the poet. Halevi was one of
those noble, romantic spirits of whom a Russian poet says that they
dedicate themselves with all the ardor of their soul to the "golden,
unreachable dream." They yearn their whole life long for what
cannot be attained, what is "beyond our powers," because what is
attainable is thereby no longer the ideal; it is the common, the everyday. Hence, it is quite understandable that the poet's song had to be
broken off precisely when the golden dream of his life revealed
itself in all its sadness and degradation. He saw before him a terribly impoverished and wasted land, where the fanatical Crusaders
ruled arrogantly and displayed their wickedness.

30. *Selected Poems of Jehudah Halevi*, pp. 151–56.

What afterwards happened to Halevi is unknown,[31] but Jewish popular imagination has woven around the last moments of its favorite poet a garland of suffering. Legend relates that when Halevi arrived at Jerusalem he set out for the Western Wall, singing his ode to Zion. On the way a Moslem horseman ran him down and struck him through with his spear. The poet fell dead on the spot with his ode on his lips.

The enthusiasm, admiration, and wonderment that the poet of Castile called forth in his lifetime were also transmitted to later generations. Not only his friends, such as Moses Ibn Ezra and Joseph Ibn Zaddik,[32] wove laurel wreaths for him and declared that "all the sons of Jacob became Jehudahists,"[33] i.e., followers and admirers of Jehudah, but writers of later generations also celebrated the poet of Zion with intense fervor. "The song that Halevi sang," declares the thirteenth-century poet Alḥarizi,

shines like a crown over the congregation of Israel, adorns its neck like the most precious strand of pearls. He is the light and greatest pride in the palaces of song, the chief pillar in the sanctuary of wisdom and knowledge. He is strong and mighty, and before the lightning of his talent the giants of poetry bow. Nothing can compare with the beauty of his song. The rays of his glory have obscured the names of Asaph and Jeduthun, and the songs of the sons of Korah have lost their charm. He penetrated into the most hidden vaults of the poetic art, took all its riches away, and locked the door. All are his followers and attempt to sing in his manner, but they do not reach even the dust

31. The author of this work conjectures that the poet returned home, where he died shortly thereafter. We base this on certain accounts of Halevi's pupil, the scholar Solomon Parḥon. In his book *Maḥberet He-Aruch*, which he completed in 1160, Parḥon quotes an opinion of Halevi's which the latter expressed after he was in Egypt. From this it follows that Parḥon, who then lived in Spain, had some intercourse with his teacher even after his journey to Jerusalem. Parḥon also relates in the same book that not long before his death Halevi vowed to write no more poems. We know, however, that just at the time of his journey to Jerusalem Halevi's creativity attained its highest level. Apparently Parḥon is here speaking of the *later* period of the poet's life, i.e., after his journey to Palestine. It makes sense to assume that Parḥon could know such details of Halevi's last days only if the poet returned to Spain and Parḥon had precise knowledge of when his teacher died. That Parḥon did, indeed, know exactly when Halevi died we see from a further remark of his in which he tells of a learned discussion that he had with his teacher. "After his death," Parḥon adds, "I became persuaded that he was right, not I."

32. In his poem, *Avi Ha-Shir*. Of Ibn Zaddik we shall speak at some length later.

33. This was said of Halevi by Jehudah ben Abut. See *ZHB*, III, 177–79.

of his chariot, and humbly they kiss his feet. . . . His prayers capti-
vate all hearts. His songs refresh like the morning dew and burn like
glowing coals. His songs of lamentation rend the clouds of tears and
flood the earth.[34]

A later poet, Abraham Bedersi, calls Jehudah Halevi the Urim
and Tummim of Jewish song, and the poet of the nineteenth century, Heinrich Heine, writes:

> He was a great poet,
> The light and star of his generation,
> The lovely candelabrum of Jacob's house,
> A wondrous pillar of fire,
> Of song and poetry,
> Who went before
> The homeless people, Israel,
> In the darkness of exile.

34. *Taḥkemoni*, Gate Three.

CHAPTER FIVE

Religious Philosophy From Saadiah Gaon to Maimonides

EHUDAH HALEVI occupies an extremely important place in the history of Jewish literature in Spain. With him medieval Hebrew poetry reaches its zenith; after him comes the period of decline, the time of twilight when the sun of poetic artistry begins to set. Halevi, however, was not only a great poet but also a thinker who played a very significant role at that historical moment when Jewish thought found itself at a crossroads and the controversy between the neo-Platonist school and the followers of Aristotelianism erupted.

We referred earlier to the considerable influence of Arabic literature on the development of Hebrew poetry. But this influence was exercised to no lesser extent in other realms as well, especially the natural sciences and philosophy. The first generations of Islam, when the Koran and Mohammed's flag conquered half the world, constitute one of the most fascinating periods in the history of civilization. Nomadic Arab tribes had lived in anterior Asia for centuries under primitive cultural conditions. Gradually, hidden and unobserved by any outside eye, immense moral and spiritual powers developed among these children of the desert. Then suddenly, like the eruption of a volcano, these powers disclosed themselves to an astonished world. The Koran rallied around itself the previously separated and often hostile tribes, and united them into a powerful people which quickly conquered a major part of the civilized world of the time and created a strong caliphate that extended its sovereignty over numerous peoples and lands in Asia, Africa, and the Iberian peninsula in Europe. The power of the early caliphate, however, did not rest on the sword alone. The capital city of the caliphs, Baghdad, quickly became a center in which the arts and sciences flourished; it fully deserved the title given to it, "the Athens of the Middle Ages."

Among the adherents of Islam, interest in philosophic questions soon awakened. Through the mediation and under the influence of Syrian Christians (many of whom were employed by the Arabs as physicians), the Arabs became familiar with the rich legacy of the Greeks in the fields of philosophy and science. As early as the beginning of the ninth century, at the command of the caliph Al-Mamun, numerous philosophic works which familiarized the Arabs with the details of Aristotle's system were translated. Among the philosophers of the later Roman period Aristotelianism had been mingled, to a significant degree, with Platonic ideas; hence, it was also transmitted to the Arabs in neo-Platonic dress. Plato and Aristotle soon began to play an important role in Arabic culture. Arab scientists and scholars studied the ideas and systems of the great Greek philosophers assiduously and sought to expound and interpret them.

The Arabs, however, did not wish to confine themselves to the role of disciples and mere interpreters of the ancient Greek thinkers. They also sought to enlarge the treasures which the latter had bequeathed and undertook independent investigations in many areas of knowledge. They enriched mathematics with a new science which, to this day, bears the Arabic name algebra. A new period also began in physics. Such brilliant investigators as Al-Ghazali, the author of the famous work *The Scales of Wisdom,* and others created new paths for natural science, discovered new instruments, and pointed to new possibilities for conducting experimental investigations by weighing and measuring everything in the most precise manner. It was from their school that the father of experimental chemistry, Geber or Jabir, stemmed.[1] When one casts even only a cursory glance at the number of discoveries for which the European world is indebted to Arabic civilization, one must agree with the famous German scientist Alexander von Humboldt, who characterized the Arabs as "the true creators of the modern physical sciences."[2]

Given such a high degree of civilization and scientific knowledge,

1. For details about him, see A. Miller, *Der Islam im Morgen-und-Abend-land* (1886), I, 509–14; P. Valden, *Nauka I Zhizn*, III, 45 (Russian).
2. See his *Kosmos* (Russian translation) (1851), II, 208.

it is understandable that in educated circles a certain incompatibility between scientific concepts and principles, on the one hand, and the religious notions and ideas that had been received through tradition from the fathers, on the other, gradually began to be felt. The Koran, with its poetic language and Oriental imagery, refers very frequently to God in anthropomorphic terms. God's hands and feet are spoken of, God laughs, He is angry, He is offended, etc. But everything in the Koran, in the eyes of the faithful Moslem, is sacred; every word was written by the prophet Mohammed at the direction of the holy spirit. The prophet is truth, and his teaching is truth. To escape these contradictions, the philosophically educated and devout Moslem had to seek a solution and effect a reconciliation between faith and free speculative thought, between the principles of religion and the conclusions at which philosophy and the natural sciences had arrived. It was this that gave rise among the Arabs, in the ninth century, to a religious-philosophical school called the Kalam,[3] which set itself the task of defending and justifying the principles of faith in the face of the results of philosophical inquiry. Among the representatives of this school, who bore the name Mutakallimun[4] (i.e., "students of God's word"), a schism eventually occurred, and a group of thinkers separated from it, calling themselves the Mu'tazila,[5] who denied the idea of fatalism that occupied such an important place in the Moslem world of thought. The fatalists held that man cannot alter his destiny, which is predetermined by Providence, a power above and beyond his will. In opposition, the schismatics proclaimed the principle of free choice and endeavored to prove that man has free will, for only so can he be held morally responsible for his deeds, whether good or bad. They also sought in a rationalist manner, i.e., through common sense and logical argument, to resolve the contradictions between faith and philosophy.[6]

It is readily understandable that the Jews who lived in the lands over which the Arabs extended their sovereignty could not remain unaffected by the great intellectual development that Moslem civil-

3. *Kalam* has the same significance as the Talmudic term *Memra*, i.e., God's word. In time, however, the word *Kalam* obtained the meaning of religious-philosophical speculation in general.
4. In medieval Jewish literature the Mutakallimun bear the name *medabberim* or *baalei ha-dibbur* (men of the word).
5. For a more extensive discussion of this sect, see S. Munk, *Mélanges de philosophie juive et arabe* (Paris, 1859), pp. 310–12.
6. Among the philosophically learned Moslem theologians who sought to effect a compromise between faith and philosophy, the scholars of the school of advanced studies in the city of Basra became particularly renowned.

ization spurred. We have indicated that after the close of the Talmud the Jewish community existed for a time in a state of intellectual sterility, its cultural creativity temporarily at a standstill. The famous Talmudic academies in Sura and Pumbeditha, which represented the pinnacle of Jewish spiritual life, then became, as it were, congealed. No fresh breath of life was felt in them; no interest was taken in any studies other than Talmudic, and even in this realm no independent, creative spirits who sought to chart new paths appeared. Everything proceeded according to the old order. Men held fast to the ideas of former generations and did not deviate by a hair's breadth from the principles of study that had been inherited from the ancients.

Now, suddenly, a novel world of ideas, to which Moslem civilization had given rise, irrupted into their environment. Entirely new problems were created. Unexpectedly, profound inconsistencies, which it was impossible to resolve with the old ideas and subtleties that held sway in Sura and Pumbeditha, revealed themselves. Many of the more thoughtful among the Jews experienced an intense inner conflict, a genuine "rent in the heart." Their ancestral heritage was deeply precious to them, but they had become familiar with an alien world of ideas that evaluated in an entirely different way the spiritual treasures of man and sought to arrive at truth in altogether new ways. With sorrowing hearts they sought guides who might help them out of their spiritual and intellectual confusion, but they did not find them. Hence, in many Jews a feeling of indignation and bitterness arose against the "shepherds of Israel," the spiritual leaders of the people, who had not matured to the demands of the troubled times and were in no position to serve as guides at such a critical juncture.

There were other factors as well. The Exilarchs, who were the leaders and rulers and, together with the heads of the Talmudic academies, the judges of the Jewish community in Babylonia, exercised their office harshly and arrogantly, and not always justly. This elicited intense dissatisfaction among certain strata of the population. The historical writer Abraham Zacuto describes how the Exilarchs would purchase their offices from the Babylonian authorities with money and bribery, and then exercise their power for purposes of financial gain. "They used to oppress the people mightily, and were false judges and unrighteous leaders."[7]

7. *Yuḥasin* (Filipowski's edition), Chapter 3, pp. 206–7: "For these Exilarchs were not men of truth, and they purchased their offices from the kings like tax gatherers. . . . From the days of Ishmael, the Exilarchs did not conduct their offices properly, but purchased them with much money from the kings, like tax gatherers, and were worthless shepherds."

These social factors, along with some adventitious personal motives, produced a schism in the Jewish community in the second half of the eighth century. An entire branch of Jews, led by the learned Anan ben David, broke away from the stock of Judaism and formed a separate sect, known as the Karaites. The Karaites carried their antagonism toward the contemporary representatives of rabbinic Judaism over to rabbinism in general, and indeed, to the entire Oral Torah and its major element, the Talmud. They set forth the view that, in interpreting the laws and statutes of the Torah, one was not to rely on the authority of the ancients but on his own common sense and on the literal meaning of the Biblical text. In this way they came to reject many of the laws which had been introduced by the sages of the Talmud. It must be borne in mind that at that time the historical development of civilization had still not been scientifically explored. The theoreticians and spiritual leaders of the new sect had not the slightest understanding that the numerous laws and customs that had arisen among the Jewish people during the post-Biblical era were not at all "accidental" inventions of this or that Tanna or Amora, but rather a product of the people's life in its organic development under the influence of the environment. The Karaites, who maintained that one should recognize common sense alone and investigate the ideas of every scholar individually, actually lost the ground under their feet and eventually blundered into such spiritual and intellectual confusion that there could no longer be any question of normal development among them.[8] In their polemic against the Rabbanites, the theoreticians of the new sect made use of the philosophical arguments and theories of the Arabic Mu'tazila, and, under their influence, endeavored to ground the principles of the Jewish faith through philosophical assumptions and logical arguments.

The Karaites, however, were not the only ones at this time who declared war on rabbinic Judaism. Within the Jewish community itself there arose, in that era of confusion, adversaries who went much further than they. The Karaites were men of strong belief; the Torah of Moses was no less precious to them than to the most orthodox and pious rabbi of the period. But under the influence of philosophical speculation there appeared among the Jews thoroughgoing freethinkers, heretics, and atheists, who scoffed at faith in general and the Jewish faith in particular. These were men of brilliant capacities and sharply honed minds, but without any inner core or firm roots. Of tragic and heroic stature in their fervor are

8. For details, see Munk, *op. cit.*, p. 472; A. Geiger, *Gesammelte Schriften,* II, 135–41.

those battling heretics who rise, as did Abraham in his time, with ax in hand to cut down the dead gods of their ancestors in the name of the new truth which they have experienced in their own hearts. But the heretics of the period in question were of a completely different stripe. They were basically indifferent not only to faith but also to the values of inquiry and knowledge. It was not the enthusiasm of seeking and attaining truth that was precious to them, but the play of clever thought, invention, mere ideas; they scoffed at everything enveloped in the mantle of sacredness and toward which others had an attitude of reverence. The role and significance of such heretics is twofold. Like acids that consume rust and destroy mildew, so these awaken critical thought and rouse in the hearts of men those doubts which are the origin of genuine searching and striving for knowledge. But along with this they also do great harm, in that they apply their criticism not only against what is mildewed or dead but against everything, not only against idols but against gods, not only against the dried-up and withered but also against the roots and sources of life.

One of the most significant freethinkers who lived among the Jews of that period was the Bible exegete Ḥiwi Al-Balchi (his enemies in hatred called him Ḥiwi Ha-Kalbi, meaning "Ḥiwi, the dog-like"). Ḥiwi sought to show that the Torah is not divinely revealed and that the miracles recounted in it are not miracles at all, since they occurred normally, according to the laws of nature. For example, the Jews crossed the waters of the Red Sea not because it was divided by God but because, just at that time, as a result of the attractive power of the moon, the waters over a certain area receded. When the Pentateuch relates of Moses that "the skin of his face shone," Ḥiwi again explains this naturalistically: because of long fasting, Moses' skin became translucent.[9]

Some time ago a fragment by another anonymous heretic of that era, who composed a tract against the Bible in the form of a poem in which he attempts to prove that the Bible was not written through the agency of the holy spirit because it is full of contradictions and exaggerations, was discovered.[10] Such critics achieved a certain success. There were even some teachers who expounded the Torah to the pupils in their schools according to Ḥiwi's system.

These antagonists finally roused rabbinic Judaism from its temporary slumber. It realized that the danger confronting it was

9. For details about Ḥiwi Ha-Balchi, see the work of S. Poznanski in *Ha-Goren*, VII, 112–37.
10. This fragment was discovered and published by S. Schechter in *JQR*, XIII. We do not agree with Poznanski's conjecture that this writer lived not in Ḥiwi's time but two hundred years later.

extremely serious, that it must fight for its very existence, and that it could triumph in this struggle only if it employed the same weapons as its opponents, i.e., philosophy and science. Rabbinic Judaism promptly demonstrated that it still possessed the spiritual and intellectual powers required to protect itself against these internal and external adversaries. A considerable number of Jewish scholars and thinkers arose who ventured on the path that the thinkers of the Kalam had marked out and who sought to effect a compromise or reconciliation between faith and philosophy, to establish the principles of religion on philosophical foundations, and to defend the ancestral legacy with the aid of speculative thought.

Thus, Arabic civilization brought it about that the Jewish community, for the second time on its long historical road, encountered the Greek world of ideas. We have indicated, in the introduction to this work, how in Alexandria, in the days of the Second Temple, two different worlds, the Hebraic and the Hellenistic, met. The Jews educated in Greek culture tried to reconcile these worlds; they endeavored to remove the inconsistencies between Greek philosophy and Judaism and to synthesize them, in order to set their own minds at rest and free themselves from inner conflict. For, no matter how dear the faith of their fathers was to them, in all their thought and inquiry the Greek world of ideas was already predominant. The most significant of these harmonizing thinkers was Philo of Alexandria. Jewish faith was certainly very precious to him, but he drew nourishment from Greek culture and was an ardent adherent of Plato's philosophic system. To harmonize this system and the Torah of Moses, he undertook the first attempt to create a new structure, to establish on Jewish ground the foundations of religious philosophy. Philo sought (and, indeed, it seemed to him that he really found) in the Bible the entire Greek world of ideas; he attempted to show that the profound philosophic conceptions to which the Greek spirit had given birth had already been revealed centuries earlier in the Torah of Moses. This feat Philo performed in a very singular way. While one of the rabbis of the Talmud once remarked about the Book of Job that "Job never existed but was a parable," for Philo it is not Job alone who is merely a parable. He is quite certain that "Moses is truth and his Torah is truth"; but there is another truth, philosophic truth, which was revealed by the great Plato (the "holy man," as Philo calls him). This truth must also be present in the Torah. And for the extraordinarily gifted dialectician Philo it was not at all difficult to show that this is in fact so. Under the simple and literal meaning of the Biblical text, he declares, lies a deeper, hidden allusion; every story recounted in the Bible is not simply a story but a parable with a philosophic content and significance. The altar and the sanctuary, for instance, are an allusion to the upper worlds; the Garden of Eden is divine wisdom; the four rivers surrounding the Garden of Eden are the four virtues which this wisdom bestows; the rain mist that fructifies the earth is the intellect which, like a spring, waters our feelings and conceptions. In this way Philo sought to combine two completely different and alien worlds, to make them seamless. Moses, for him, was not only the lawgiver commissioned by God but also the great philosopher and thinker, the mirror image of Plato.

Now, centuries later, the Jewish world again encountered Greek philosophy—this time, however, in Arabic dress. As in the Alexandrian period, so also now, when Jewish scholars, under the influence of Arabic civilization, endeavored to reconcile faith and philosophy, they did so not in the Hebrew language but in the cultural language of the era, Arabic.

A highly significant point must, however, be underscored here. The Jewish community of Alexandria in the days of the Second Temple was only a small branch of the Jewish stock. The Greek forms of creativity in this community did not have any noticeable effect on the Palestinian center, which then constituted the majority of the Jewish people and in which the national culture developed in its own original way. Very different was the situation in the Middle Ages, when Arabic civilization spread its dominion over the lands where the most important and largest part of the Jewish population lived. The influence of this civilization on the majority of the Jewish people and its intelligentsia produced, as we have already indicated in our introduction, an entirely new epoch in the development of the national literature. The individual overcame the community; Jewish literature ceased to be anonymous, to bear the exclusive stamp of the community. What once occurred in the Alexandrian center, in an isolated branch of the Jewish people, was now repeated in the major center—the "metropolis," as it is called in the Talmudic expression, of the national settlement. No longer the community but individuals—poets, thinkers, and scientists, who stand in their spiritual and intellectual development far above the collective—create works on their own account according to their personal taste and conception of the world, assemble under their own names national treasures on which they set their own impress and their individual creative spirit. The specific quality whereby the old Hebrew-Aramaic literature was so sharply distinguished from its sisters was lost. From the Arabic period on, a definite distinction between national literature and popular literature, i.e., collective and anonymous folk creativity, is clearly discernible among Jews also. These two golden threads, which weave the texture of Jewish culture, are no longer joined together but are spun each by itself.

This was one of the major reasons why the new vernacular of the largest Jewish community, Arabic, did not manage to achieve the honored place in Jewish civilization that the Aramaic dialect had had in its time, despite the fact that Arabic has no lesser affinity to the language of the Bible than Aramaic. The Targum, the Aramaic translation of the Torah, became sacred among Jews, and to this day the Pentateuch is read weekly by the devout Jew "twice in Hebrew and once in the Targum." The Arabic translation of the Bible, however, remained as profane a thing as the Greek Septuagint. Aramaic was interwoven with Hebrew, the ancient national language of the Jewish people; they became twin sisters. Arabic, however, became not the sister of Hebrew but its rival, a mirror of the relationship of Hagar to Sarah. For centuries, Arabic was, for the major segment of the Jewish people, the most significant factor in general culture but not in national creativity. To this the factor to which we referred in the first chapter also contributed heavily. The flowering of Arabic, considered sacred by the Arabs since it was the language of the Koran, elicited a certain feeling of envy among the Jews. It awakened in them the desire to strengthen and develop the language of *their* sacred possession, the Bible. We have already noted how clearly this mood was expressed in the first great Hebrew poet of the Arabic period, Solomon Ibn Gabirol.

It was because of this that the fate of the literary legacy of the Jewish thinkers and scholars who wrote in Arabic differed from the fate of the books written in Alexandria by Philo and his colleagues. Philo's works remained for the Jewish people "like a stone that none turn over." Written in the little-understood Greek language, they had a very slight influence on Jewish thought, and even this influence was exercised in circuitous ways, at third and fourth remove. The religious-philosophic works that the medieval Jewish thinkers wrote in Arabic, however, were quickly translated into Hebrew and became an organic part of the national literature. For centuries these works dominated the Jewish spirit and Jewish thought, and their influence is still discernible.

The first Jewish thinker who attempted to present systematically in Arabic the foundations of Jewish religious philosophy was the famous Gaon of Sura, Rav Saadiah ben Joseph Ha-Fayyumi (born in Fayyum 892, died c. 952).[11] Despite the restless and disturbed

11. Until modern times it was thought that Saadiah died at the age of fifty. A letter of that era (published in *JQR*, n.s., XI, 424–25) shows, however, that this is an error and that he died at the age of at least sixty.

life that this scholar led, he left a large legacy in various fields of knowledge. Saadiah translated and commented on the Bible in Arabic and wrote works on Jewish philology (best known is his Bible lexicon, *Agron*). He also wrote a commentary on the famous mystical work *Sefer Yetzirah*, which we shall later discuss at some length. But, above all, he obtained renown as an incomparable polemicist and champion of the Jewish faith.

Saadiah had occasion to fight on three fronts. First, he struggled against the Karaites. In this area he had no peer. The Karaites never again encountered an opponent such as he, and for many generations their theoreticians and scholars endeavored to refute his arguments and ideas, fruitlessly exerting themselves to restore the foundations that Anan and his followers had laid down and that the Gaon of Sura mercilessly destroyed.[12] Saadiah also carried on a stubborn battle against the heretics and atheists, and wrote a polemic against the greatest of them, Ḥiwi Al-Balchi. He realized, however, that even more threatening to the survival of Judaism were the serious doubts that had been aroused under the influence of Arabic culture among many Jews who wished to remain loyal to the faith of the fathers but could not resolve the contradictions revealed by critical speculative thought and the light of the burgeoning sciences. The allaying of these doubts was Saadiah's major task. To reconcile Jewish faith with the world of philosophic ideas, to demonstrate that Judaism has nothing to fear from speculative thought, was the goal he set himself in his work *Kitab al-Amanat wal-I'tikadat*, which gained fame among the Jewish people under its Hebrew title *Sefer Ha-Emunot Veha-Deot*. Written by Saadiah in 933, it was translated into Hebrew by Jehudah Ibn Tibbon in 1186.

The author explicitly states in his introduction the motives that impelled him to write this religious-philosophical work:

I saw men sunk, as it were, in a sea of doubt and overwhelmed by the waters of confusion, and there was no diver to bring them up from the depths and no swimmer to save them. But since my Lord has given me some knowledge that I can employ for their support and endowed me with some ability that I might use for their benefit, I felt that to aid

12. That is why the enmity of the Karaite writers of that time toward Saadiah is so intense. They expressed their hostility in many bitter tracts. The best known of these is the *Milḥamot Adonai* of Salmon ben Jeruḥam. A complete manuscript of this tract, which is extremely interesting from a cultural-historical point of view, is contained in the Harkavy Collection in the library in Leningrad of the Society for the Dissemination of Enlightenment Among Jews.

them was my duty and guiding them correctly my obligation. As the prophet says, "The Lord God hath given me the tongue of them that are taught, that I should know how to sustain with words him that is weary" (Isaiah 50:4). Though I confess to the shortcomings of my knowledge, which is far from perfect, and admit the deficiency of my understanding, which is far from complete, realizing as I do that I am not superior in knowledge to my contemporaries, but can offer my contribution only to the best of my ability and according to my lights: as the prophet says, "But as for me, this secret is not revealed to me for any wisdom that I have more than any living" (Daniel 2:30). Nevertheless, I cherish the hope that He who knows my intentions and the desire of my heart will grant me success and sustain me according to my purpose, not according to my gifts and abilities, as has been said by another prophet, "I know, my God, that Thou searchest the heart and hast pleasure in uprightness" (I Chronicles 29:17).

From the spirit of Saadiah's work, from the character of his premises and conclusions, it is easy to discern the influence of the Arabic thinkers of the Mu'tazilite school. Saadiah's goal is to show that human reason is fully entitled to express its views on religious questions and matters of faith. He dwells on the three stages that lead man to the attainment of truth: first, *sensations*, which give man representations of everything in the world; secondly, *conceptions*, which the mind receives through these representations; and, finally, *logical conclusions*, which the mind draws on the basis of the conceptions. To these three sources of knowledge the author of *Ha-Emunot Veha-Deot* adds a fourth, which in his opinion is the most important, namely, the holy spirit, the revelation of God present in the Torah and in the books of the prophets. Belief in the divinely revealed character of the Torah, however, Saadiah emphasizes, does not bar for man the way of achieving truth through his own powers and intellect. On the contrary, one's personal thought and investigation can confirm the truth revealed through the holy spirit by the prophets, and it can also provide the logical proofs required to refute the arguments of the heretics who deny the truth given on Mount Sinai. This foundation of Jewish faith, the divine revelation at Sinai and the revelatory character of the Torah, is firmly proven, in Saadiah's opinion, through historical tradition. This tradition, which has been transmitted from generation to generation and relates the great historic theophany that occurred in the sight of all Israel, has no lesser significance than any other experience based on the evidence of the senses. Judaism, Saadiah insists, has nothing to fear from philosophical thought. The truth of divine revelation can even be strengthened through rigorous scientific inquiry, and philosophical reflection can contribute importantly to confirming the bonds of peace and amity between faith and reason.

The further development of Jewish religious philosophy occurred not in Saadiah's native land and not under the leadership of the Geonim and Exilarchs of Babylonia but in Arabic Spain. The first philosophic work produced there by a Jewish thinker was Solomon Ibn Gabirol's *Fons Vitae* or *Mekor Hayyim*, discussed above. But Ibn Gabirol did not undertake to serve as a defender or advocate of the Jewish faith or to make peace between religion and philosophy. As we have observed, in his neo-Platonic, pantheistic system there is no room for any dogmatic religion with strictly defined principles and premises.

A completely different character is manifested by the work of one of Ibn Gabirol's contemporaries, the *Hovot Ha-Levavot*[13] of Bahya ben Joseph Ibn Pakuda. Bahya was one of the most popular personalities among the Jews of the Middle Ages, yet virtually nothing is known of his life. Not even precisely when he lived has been established. It is only a matter of conjecture that he lived in Ibn Gabirol's time and completed his famous work in Saragossa in the second half of the eleventh century.[14]

Bahya was a man of broad philosophical learning. He was especially influenced by the Arabic order of ascetics called the Pure Brethren and their well-known encyclopedic work.[15] But it was not philosophical questions as such nor a reconciliation of philosophy and faith that mainly interested the pious *dayyan* or rabbinic judge of Saragossa. To be sure, in the first chapter of his work, "Shaar Ha-Yihud," in which God and His attributes are treated, he employs the philosophical arguments and premises of his time. His major task, however, is not speculation. Bahya knows that the truth of the Jewish faith rests on three foundations: on revelation (*Torah*

13. The Arabic original bears the name *Kitab al Hidayah ila Faraidi al-Kulub*. It was translated into Hebrew by Jehudah Ibn Tibbon. Another Hebrew translation by Joseph Ibn Kimhi was almost entirely lost. The Arabic original was first published by A. S. Yahuda in 1912.

14. David Kaufmann attempts to show (*Gesammelte Schriften*, II, 1–2) that *Hovot Ha-Levavot* was completed in 1040. But Professor Kokowzoff (see his work, *The Date of Life of Bachja Ibn Paqoda* [1927]) has demonstrated that Bahya's work was written after 1055, most likely in the years 1080–90.

15. Bahya calls the representatives of this order simply "the philosophers." The order was active in the tenth century in the major centers of Arabic culture in anterior Asia, Basra and Baghdad. Bahya also often quotes, under the name *perushim* (ascetics), the well-known mystical order of the Sufis. The ten sections or "gates" of *Hovot Ha-Levavot* are divided according to the ten levels which the Sufi must traverse in order to reach true love of God.

min ha-shamayim), on the tradition of the fathers, and on the arguments of human reason; but that is not his point. His chief concern is to show that Judaism must be, above all else, a Torah of the heart and feeling, a religion that will be a comfort, support, and guide for the soul in its innermost world, with all its longings and strivings. The "duties of the heart" (*ḥovot ha-levavot*) are far more important than observance of laws and statutes, the "duties of the limbs." Purity and reverence of heart transcend the mechanical fulfillment of commandments. That the ritual law must be subordinate to the moral imperative is the leading motif of Baḥya's work. In *Hovot Ha-Levavot*, moreover, an attitude that became dominant in Jewish ethical-religious literature only in later times is distinctly present. This is the ascetic mood, the constant admonition that one must renounce the pleasures of the world. The pious, melancholy author never wearies of repeating how vain and sinful life on the terrestrial globe is, that this world is no more than a sorrowful and dark passageway (*prozdor*) that man is compelled to traverse in order that he may merit entry into the wondrously beautiful, light-filled palace (*teraklin*) of eternal life. "As it is not possible to hold fire and water together in one vessel," explains the author, "so desire for the pleasures of this sinful world cannot live together peaceably in the heart with longing for the heavenly world of pure spirituality." This thought, which permeates the whole book, is further expounded by Baḥya in the following parable:

In one of the Indian islands there was a state whose citizens decided to appoint over them each year a stranger as ruler. When the year had elapsed they would banish him, and he would then have to return to the status he had occupied before having been appointed. Among those elected one was a fool who knew nothing of their secret plans for him. He accumulated much money, built palaces which he fortified, and sent nothing out of their country. On the contrary, whatever he had outside the state, his money, his wife and his children, he brought into it. And when the year ended, the citizens dismissed him, stripped of all his possessions and deprived of all that he had built or acquired before he entered office up to the time he relinquished it. And so when he left, he had nothing of what had belonged to him, either in the city or outside it. He grieved and regretted the trouble he had taken and the efforts he had expended on the buildings he had erected and the treasures he had accumulated and that would now go to another person. Subsequently, the people of the state decided to appoint as their ruler a stranger who was wise and understanding. After he had been appointed, he selected a person to whom he showed kindness and inquired of him concerning the customs of the people and the laws which they observed with regard to the one who had preceded him in office. The favorite revealed to the new ruler their secret plan and what they intended to do to him. When he learned this, he did not act as did his predecessor, but strove and worked to take everything valuable in the country to the land where he had placed all his other treasures. He did not trust his subjects' exaltation of him or the honor they showed him. During the whole time he remained in their country his mood vacillated between grief and joy. He was grieved that he would soon have to leave the people and that the treasures he could bring out were, in his estimation, so few. Could he have remained longer, he would have been able to bring out more. But he was glad that he would soon leave and be able to settle in the place where he had put his treasures and would be in a position to use and enjoy them in various ways, with quiet mind, confident spirit, and without interruption. After his year was finished, he was not troubled at leaving, but prepared for the event speedily, calmly and joyfully, with approval of his work and with diligence. He was going to great good fortune, honor and abiding joy.[16]

In order to inscribe in the memory of the reader the basic motifs of his *Hovot Ha-Levavot* Bahya repeated them at the end of his work in a humble prayer:

My son, devote thy unique [soul] wholly to thy Rock, when thou declarest the Unity of the One who formed thee.

Search, investigate and ponder His wonders; let understanding and the law of righteousness be thy girdle.

Fear God. His testimonies and statutes keep forever, so that thy feet shall not slip.

Let thy heart be confident and assured, trusting in God, the Rock, that He will be thy help.

With pure heart fulfill His statutes for His sake; exalt no human being in thy generation.

Observe that the end of [the earthly] creature is to return to earth. Be lowly, for sand and a clod of earth will be the place where thou wilt sojourn.

Let thine understanding contend against thy folly; repent of thy heart's presumptuousness and thine [evil] inclination.

The ways of God, in just judgment and rectitude, wisely search with thy mind and inward being.

Put out of thy heart the follies of childhood and early youth, nor yearn for the desires of thine adolescence.

16. *Hovot Ha-Levavot*, Gate 3, Chapter 9. This same story is also found in *Ben Ha-Melech Veha-Nazir, Makama* 12, and much later also in *Simhat Ha-Nefesh*, but in another version.

Then in thy yearning thou wilt see the everlasting God and thy unique [soul] will be united with thy Rock.[17]

Because of the sincere, tender tone and the profound spiritual and religious sentiment with which Bahya's work is permeated, his *Hovot Ha-Levavot* became for centuries one of the best-loved ethical books among the Jewish people. Knowledge of the work became especially widespread when it was translated into Yiddish at the beginning of the eighteenth century, and the rabbinic judge of Saragossa achieved the status of one of the most popular heroes in Jewish life.[18]

An entirely new path for Jewish philosophy was attempted by the celebrated poet of Zion, Jehudah Halevi. Halevi considered it pointless to seek, as Saadiah Gaon had done in his day, a reconciliation or compromise between speculative thought and faith, to show that the philosophic and other secular sciences do not contradict the foundations of Judaism. It was clear to him that the essence and the chief value of the Jewish religion consist not in the fact that it may also be philosophically substantiated with the aid of logical theories and arguments, but rather in its moral content and in its educative power. The meaning and importance of the Torah consist, in Halevi's view, not in the fact that speculative thought and its conclusions are not inconsistent with it, but that it gives something that philosophy does not have and cannot give.

Halevi developed his religious-philosophical conceptions in his famous Arabic work *Kitab al-Hujjah wal-Dalil fi Nusr al-Din al-Dhalil,*[19] known among Jews under the title of its Hebrew translation, *Sefer Ha-Kuzari.*[20] The book is written in the form of a dialogue between the king of the Chazars and a Jewish scholar

17. Bahya wrote other religious poems besides. Especially well known is his poem "Barechi Nafshi" (reprinted in many editions of *Hovot Ha-Levavot*), in which the fundamental principles of his ethical work are presented in poetic form.
18. To be sure, to this a very special circumstance, or more correctly a special error and misunderstanding, contributed. In the fourteenth century one of the pupils of Rabbi Solomon ben Adret, the mystical Rabbi Bahya ben Asher, wrote a commentary on the Pentateuch. This commentary became extremely well known among Jews, and the author of the famous "women's Torah," the *Tze'enah U-Re'enah,* frequently quotes it. In almost every section the author quotes "what Rabbenu Bahya says." The simple reader mistakenly thought that this Rabbenu Bahya and the author of *Hovot Ha-Levavot* were the same person.
19. The Arabic original was first published by Hirschfeld in 1887.
20. In 1911 A. Zifronovitz published a new critical edition of Jehudah Ibn Tibbon's translation, edited according to the Arabic original. From another Hebrew translation that Jehudah Ibn Kadrinal made only fragments have come down to us.

(*ḥaver*). Halevi took as the basis of his legendary dialogue the historical fact that in the eighth century, in the kingdom of the Chazars on the banks of the Volga, the royal family, as well as the upper classes of the populace, had been converted to Judaism. The king of the Chazars, according to Halevi, heard in a dream a voice calling to him, "Your intention is acceptable to God but not your deeds." To interpret his dream, the monarch applied to a philosopher, a Christian theologian, and a Moslem scholar. None of these, however, satisfied him. He then summoned a Jewish scholar. The latter charmed the king with his wise words; to all questions he gave clear and appropriate answers. This produced such a great impression on the king of the Chazars that he decided to make the Jewish faith his own.

In the *ḥaver* it is Halevi himself who speaks. In the Jewish scholar's speeches the poet develops his own world outlook and his view of the nature of Judaism, as well as his criticism of many assumptions and doctrines of Greek-Arabic philosophy. Halevi had a thorough knowledge of the philosophy of his time, and his overview, in the fifth section of the *Kuzari*, of the Arabic Kalam has a definite scientific-historical value. He speaks with great respect of the Greek philosophers (especially Socrates), yet sharply attacks Greek philosophy, which dominated the minds of the intellectuals of his day. Philosophy, in his view, gives a great deal to the intellect, the sharply honed reason, but nothing to the heart and its feelings. Nevertheless, it proudly claims that only in itself, only in reason, inquiry, and speculative thought, lies the source of human perfection.

In Halevi's day the controversy between two philosophic tendencies, neo-Platonism and Aristotelianism, was intensified in Arabic culture. The works of the renowned Arab thinker and profound expositor of Aristotle, Avicenna (Ibn Sina), first became known in Moslem Spain in that generation and were widely accepted in the circles of the Jewish intelligentsia. The Aristotelians had not yet, in Halevi's time, overcome their opponents and their conceptions had still not achieved absolute dominion; but for anyone with an attentive eye it was not difficult to foresee their speedy triumph. Halevi perceived a serious threat in the extreme rationalism of the Aristotelian system, which seeks to subject all realms of the human spirit to the exclusive sovereignty of reason. The poet, for whom the ethical world, questions of morality and justice, were so closely associated with profound religious sentiment, could in no way assent to this absolute and boundless dominion of reason. With all the ardor of his poetic soul he felt that reason alone is not the whole essence of man, not the only nor, in his opinion, even the major source of knowledge. Proceeding from this view, Halevi, already in the first chapters of his work, criticizes the philosophers of Aristotle's school,[21] who argue that man can achieve the summit of perfection only through accumulating philosophical knowledge and that only through exploring and becoming familiar with the various sciences is man united with the *sechel ha-poel* or "active intellect,"[22] the reflection of God's light on earth.[23]

For the philosopher, says Halevi, the chief thing is inquiry itself, theoretical inquiry and reflection about God, just as the astronomer seeks to trace the course of the stars and planets in the heavens. His purpose is not moral progress or improvement, not the victory of right and justice, but the acquisition of a constantly larger sum of knowledge. Quite different is the attitude of the man permeated with the fervor of profound religious feeling. Such a person does not strive merely to understand the nature of the Creator; he longs for God to be his guide, the measure and criterion of all his deeds and of his conceptions of right and justice. The religious person cannot be content with acquiring ever greater knowledge; his desire is to embody in life, in concrete deeds, the truth that he has attained. The philosopher, on the other hand, considers only how to sharpen and refine his thinking, how to bring his reason to the peak of perfection. In this he sees the supreme joy of man. Because he perceives in inquiry and knowledge the sole way to the summit of perfection, the philosopher isolates himself from other men, removes himself from ordinary life and everyday concerns. The religious man, however, is imbued with the awareness that only in life itself, in deeds and relationships to other persons, lies the way that leads man to perfection and brings him close to the Creator. Halevi sharply emphasizes the vast difference between the abstract conception of God attained through cold reason and its logically clear ideas, and the ardent, heartfelt sentiment which permeates the soul of the believer with his longing, prayerful enthusiasm. "How," he has the king of the Chazars ask, "can one compare the God of Abraham with the God of Aristotle?"[24]

21. Characteristic of Halevi's attitude to Greek philosophy is the following verse in one of his poems to Moses Ibn Ezra:
    And let not yourself be led astray by Greek wisdom,
    For it bears no fruit but only flowers.
22. For more about the concept of the active intellect, see the following chapter.
23. *Kuzari*, I, 1. Some scholars, such as David Kaufmann (*Geschichte der Attributenlehre*, pp. 123–40) and others, insist that in this struggle against philosophy's ambition to be the sole ruler in the realm of the human spirit, Jehudah Halevi took as his model the famous Arabic theologian Al-Ghazali (died in 1111) with his work *Tahafut al-Falasifah*.
24. *Kuzari*, IV, 18.

Halevi underscores the distinction between the divine power which the Torah calls Elohim and the God of the Tetragrammaton, Yahweh. Elohim is the God of speculative thought, the God who is the Cause of causes, i.e., the origin and First Cause of all that exists. This is the God of Aristotle, who is conceived as pure wisdom and understanding and who affects the world, not through His deeds and thoughts, but through what He *is*.[25] But the God of Abraham, the God of the Tetragrammaton, Halevi declares, is the Creator who embraces the whole world and is concerned with it, the guide of the universe, the ruler and judge, who receives all prayers and regards all tears. This is not the distant, detached, and indifferent God of Aristotle, whose providence reaches only the highest stars and spheres in the heavens, but the God who lives in men's hearts, who is experienced in every corner of the soul.

Elohim, the God of Aristotle, may be understood through thought and scientific inquiry. Not so Yahweh, the God of revelation, the God who disclosed himself at Mount Sinai. Only through profound intuition, through religious fervor and enthusiasm, can one catch a glimpse of His light.[26]

He who seeks God through speculative thought, says Halevi, cannot understand the ardent love for the Creator with which the believer is permeated. Philosophy strives to grasp the nature of divinity through speculation and inquiry, by way of logical ideas and intellectual arguments; the Torah, however, teaches one how to know God so as to love Him, so that the soul shall be filled with the sweet sentiment of cleaving to Him, of surrendering oneself with one's whole body and soul to Him and being prepared to sacrifice oneself for His name's sake. Just as a ray of light, says Halevi, is reflected more clearly through a good mirror or finely polished crystal than through gray and opaque bodies, by so much the more is the passionate God-feeling of the religious believer clearer and sharper than the abstract and cold God-concept attained through detached speculation.

To illuminate the great role and significance of Judaism, the author of the *Kuzari* especially insists that in the ethical culture of

25. Aristotle's philosophy denies that the divine will or providence affects the world and nature. No God with creative and active willpower influences the order of the world. God, says Aristotle, is not the guide or ruler of the universe. The fact that the world runs according to established and purposeful laws does not derive from the Cause that stands above and beyond the world, not from the Creator, but rather from the fact that the universe bears in itself the laws of regular motion and purposeful order.
26. Halevi expresses the same idea in many of his poems.

humanity, in the development and refinement of its moral consciousness, historical-psychological factors are extremely important. When the principles of morality and justice live in the awareness of a community for centuries and are sanctified through the tradition of the fathers, they obtain all the more weight and influence, and their historical-cultural significance grows ever greater. The supremely important place that the "categorical imperative" held in the thought of the greatest philosopher of modern times, Immanuel Kant, was occupied in the mind of the medieval Jewish poet Halevi by sacred tradition, the religious legacy of the fathers. Kant was convinced that the foundation of morality lies in the depths of our feeling and consciousness, and that it is impossible to demonstrate the truth of this foundation on an experimental level. Within ourselves, in the depths of our soul, we carry the law, the criterion that evaluates all values and commands us to do thus and not otherwise. For Halevi the religious foundations that live in the garment of tradition through a long chain of generations are hallowed and transformed into the "categorical imperative" of the heart, of the innermost consciousness, which liberates man from doubts and gives him the assurance that so must be done and not otherwise. It was Halevi's conviction that religious tradition is the major factor in the moral improvement and development of man, because only the tradition of revealed faith has persuasive power that is free of doubts and has no need for proofs or arguments. Philosophy lacks these sure foundations and this unconditional authority. One philosophical system contradicts another; what was earlier accepted as absolute truth is today declared false; and in the realm of philosophy there is not a single theory or assumption, a single idea, that is recognized by all philosophers as indisputably true.

The Greek philosophers, says Halevi, necessarily erred in many questions because they could not rationally understand, and therefore rejected, such events as were confirmed by Jewish tradition and by the Hebrew prophets. The philosophers "denied all matters" that cannot be explained through reason. The prophets, however, "confirmed these matters," because they could not deny what was revealed to them and what they perceived with their inspired eyes.[27]

Halevi insists that the prophet, unlike the philosopher, does not strive to comprehend God through ingenious speculation and inquiry, for he feels God in every corner of his heart and every spark of his soul. His whole being is imbued with the consciousness that God is in the world—not the distant God of philosophical thought,

27. *Kuzari*, IV, 3.

but the compassionate Near One, who is constantly and continuously experienced, every minute and every second. And the prophet's holy spirit, what he perceives with his inner eye, is, in Halevi's view, a much purer and more reliable source of truth than the hair-splitting dialectics of the philosopher. When the Torah declares that the prophets and the entire Jewish people were witnesses of God's revelation on Mount Sinai, this must be and can be explained not by way of philosophical speculation or scientific inquiry but in a psychological manner.

For Halevi Judaism is, above all, the disclosure of the self-consciousness and self-determination of the Jewish people. His whole work is permeated with the idea that the Jews are not only a religious community but also a psychologically unique ethnic individuality, with an extremely rich national-historical, spiritual-cultural heritage. But Halevi does not emphasize merely the national character of the Jewish faith; he also attempts to show that Judaism can exercise its full moral influence and disclose all its educative power precisely among the Jewish people because only among them did the ethical foundations of the Torah of Moses pass from generation to generation and operate uninterruptedly on a long chain of generations, training their moral sentiment in an ethical environment. Thanks to their religious-ethical environment, the sacred tradition transmitted as a legacy from generation to generation for thousands of years, the Jews became the "chosen people." They became the chosen people, says Halevi, not because of Moses but vice versa. Moses' greatness drew nourishment from the high moral level at which the masses of the children of Abraham, Isaac, and Jacob lived.[28]

Halevi, therefore, asserts that even when one belonging to the gentiles "joins himself to us," he does not "become equal to us."[29] Despite the fact that the ethical foundations of the Torah of Moses have a universal and all-human significance, Halevi believes that the Torah remains the exclusive possession of the Jewish people, to which it is bound by thousands of psychological-cultural threads. Because of this, he points out, in the Torah even the promises and rewards for obedience to the commandments and the performance of good deeds bear a decisively *national* character. "It does not say in the Torah that if you will observe this or that commandment I will bring you after death into beautiful orchards, where you will have much pleasure, but rather, 'you will be My people and I will be your God.' "[30]

28. *Ibid.*, II, 56.
29. *Ibid.*, I, 27; see also 115.
30. *Ibid.*, I, 109.

It must, however, be underscored here that in Halevi's view the individual is not lost in the community. He is not drowned in the collectivity, like a drop in the sea, without his own independent value. Halevi sees in the nation or people the essential environment in which the personality of the individual obtains the potentiality of developing normally and fully, of revealing all its beauty and the riches it has received as a bequest from earlier generations. The national religion with its sacred tradition, it is Halevi's firm conviction, does not destroy the personality of the individual; on the contrary, it is this that creates its moral worth, enriches it, and endows it with immortality. Halevi therefore strongly assails the followers of Aristotle's philosophy who take the view that ordinary mortals, whose reason does not concern itself with philosophical speculation and scientific investigation of nature, are like animals and that their souls perish with their bodies. He cannot, under any circumstances, agree that only philosophers merit immortality of the soul. "We," Halevi declares, "do not deny to anyone his reward for his good deeds, no matter to what nation he may belong."[31] Every moral person is worthy, according to him, of "the world to come." For the Jew, however, the way to immortality is made considerably easier by psychological-historical factors, by national-ethical foundations hallowed by tradition.

These factors, the long past which stretches from Abraham through Mount Sinai to the end of all generations, give the Jewish people, according to Halevi, tremendous strength and integrity, despite the fact that Jews are scattered over the world and likened "to a dead object." When the king of the Chazars says to the *ḥaver*, "You [Jews] are like a body without a head and without a heart," the latter answers, "No, we are not a body but scattered bones. . . . Yet, in these dried bones the spark of life is still not extinguished. . . . We are not like a dead man but like a terribly sick person, in whom only the faith that the great miracle will occur and that the dried bones will live again is strong."[32] "We suffer more," says the *ḥaver* further, "than all others because the people of Israel among the nations is like the heart among the other organs. It is more sensitive than all the rest, and therefore also suffers more." Sufferings, however, the *ḥaver* insists, are like a crucible; they purify of all dross.

Halevi frequently repeats this idea: "Only souls that suffer and are greatly tried are illuminated by God's light."[33] But he is very far from Baḥya's ascetic view. He insists that the Law of Moses

31. *Ibid.*, I, 111.
32. *Ibid.*, II, 30, 32.
33. *Ibid.*, IV, 22.

opposes abstinence and teaches that man must develop all his powers, both the physical and the spiritual equally, because he cannot make any distinction between these powers that are so closely connected with each other.[34] Here Halevi incidentally expresses an idea that played a very prominent role in later Hasidism, namely, that God may be served not only through prayer and fasting, but also through joy, dance, and song.[35]

The conclusion of the *Kuzari* is characteristic of the poet of Zion. After the *ḥaver* has answered and clarified all the questions the king of the Chazars puts to him, he tells the king of his determination to migrate to the land of Israel, "the heart of all lands." At first the king tries to persuade his teacher to remain with him, but when the latter refuses to change his resolve, the king says to him,

Your words have convinced me that to dissuade you from this journey would be a sin and that to help you in your undertaking would be a good deed. May God help you. May He be your guardian and protector, as you have deserved. May He spread His grace over you and over all who share your view. Amen.

So ends the *Sefer Ha-Kuzari*. The *ḥaver* who carries on the discussion with the king of the Chazars is, as we have noted, Jehudah Halevi himself. And shortly after he finished his work, Halevi took up the wanderer's staff and set out "for the heart of the world," Zion.

The *Sefer Ha-Kuzari* was a sharp protest against arrogant rationalism, against the tendency to give reason boundless dominion over the realm of spirit and culture. Jehudah Halevi was a courageous warrior, but he did not win this struggle. His work, though written with great emotion and skill, was nevertheless unable to check the progress of Aristotle's ideas which, thanks to Avicenna's work, quickly spread in that era among the Jews of Spain. Indeed, shortly after the *Sefer Ha-Kuzari* appeared, one of Jehudah Halevi's friends and an admirer of his poetry, Joseph ben Jacob Ibn Zaddik, stepped forth as an ardent protagonist of rationalism.

Of the life of this interesting personality we know little. His contemporary, the author of the *Sefer Ha-Kabbalah*, Rabbi Abraham Ibn Daud (Ravad I), relates that Ibn Zaddik was a rabbinic judge in Cordova from 1138 to his death in 1149. From a poem that Jehudah Halevi sent to Ibn Zaddik we know that the latter had three sons. These are the only particulars we have of his biography. Jehudah Alḥarizi praises Ibn Zaddik's poetic talent highly. But

34. *Ibid.*, II, 50.
35. *Ibid.*

very little of his poetic legacy has come down to us. His lovely poem beginning with the mischievous lines

> Where is the old wine that renews joy,
> Where are the songs of desire and love?
> All kinds of blood are forbidden to us,
> Save the blood of grapes

for many years erroneously carried Abraham Ibn Ezra's name.[36] In any case, he became renowned not as a poet but as the author of an Arabic philosophic work in four chapters, *Al'Alam al-Saghir* (The Microcosm), better known under the title of the Hebrew translation, *Olam Katan*.[37]

In this work, which was produced in a time of transition[38] when philosophic thought found itself at a crossroads, it is easy to distinguish the influence of the most diverse streams of thought—of Plato's philosophy, of the Arabic Pure Brethren (in *Olam Katan* they are called "the pure philosophers"), of the mystical work *Sefer Yetzirah*, and of Gabirol's *Mekor Ḥayyim* or *Fons Vitae*. Most sharply and clearly discernible, however, is the influence of Aristotle's system—above all, his strongly enunciated rationalism.

Of the two commandments of the Torah, "Thou shalt know the Lord" and "Thou shalt love the Lord thy God," Ibn Zaddik preferred the former. "Knowledge of God" is, in his view, the chief commandment, the supreme duty of man. One who wishes to attain the highest truth, says Ibn Zaddik, must first explore and know himself.[39] For the essence of man, his inner world, is a mirror of the great outer world. He who knows himself is also in a position to understand the world outside himself; but he to whom his inner world is not clearly and accurately known can also not understand the external world. This idea which we have already encountered

36. See *JQR*, n.s., IV (1913), 89.
37. It has not been definitely established who the translator was. A. Jellinek believes that *Olam Katan* was translated by Moses Ibn Tibbon, M. Steinschneider believes it was done by Naḥum Ha-Maaravi, and S. Pinsker thinks Moses of Narbonne was the translator. Against Jellinek's theory, see J. Reifmann in *Otzar Tov*, 1884, p. 32. Jellinek first published the translation in 1854. A new critical edition was published by S. Horovitz in 1903. We have made use of Jellinek's edition and of David Kaufmann's textual corrections (*Geschichte der Attributenlehre*, pp. 225–337).
38. *Olam Katan* appeared in 1145, three or four years after the *Kuzari*.
39. The same idea is expressed by Solomon Ibn Gabirol at the beginning of his *Mekor Ḥayyim:* "And what one should especially seek from knowledge is to know one's self, for through this he will also know what is outside himself."

in Ibn Gabirol's *Mekor Ḥayyim*, the analogy of the *olam katan* (the microcosm) to the external world (the macrocosm), is the central theme of Ibn Zaddik's work, and he repeats it frequently with various explanations. The investigation of his own nature can be undertaken by man only with the aid of philosophy, that "wisdom of wisdoms" which is, according to Ibn Zaddik, the only sure way leading to knowledge of the Creator. Only with the aid of the sciences and philosophy can man free himself from his blindness and rise above the multitude "which gropes in darkness."[40] He who does not strive to attain the heights of scientific inquiry and philosophy is not worthy of bearing the name man,[41] because man was created for this: to seek out wisdom and attain eternal truth.[42]

In total antithesis to Jehudah Helevi, the author of *Olam Katan* recognizes no distinction between the philosopher or detached thinker and the prophet. From Ibn Zaddik's point of view the prophet is also, first of all, a philosopher, a man of speculation and inquiry. And only these, the philosopher and the prophet, he declares, can truly serve the Cause of causes. Only they have a proper conception of divinity and of the divine attributes. Only they understand that the God-concept cannot be associated with any analogies or attributes, not only with corporeal or material ones, such as "great," "strong," etc., but also not even with purely spiritual attributes, such as "wise," "intelligent," "gracious," "eternal." For "to whom shall I liken Thee?" God cannot be likened, His being cannot be grasped.[43] Only one who recognizes this truth can serve God perfectly, for only such a man can fulfill with complete consciousness all the commandments and laws, which aim at bringing one closer to God's deeds and works. Only through *muskalot*, i.e., abstract concepts attained by way of speculation and inquiry, can man obtain a clear comprehension of the nature of the "perfect good." Only with the aid of philosophy, Ibn Zaddik insists, can we understand that the whole world as God's creation is "the result of goodness, grace and wisdom." And we strive to imitate His deeds and work: "The origin of all our good deeds is wisdom, for this alone gives us the possibility of comprehending the Creator, and this comprehension arouses in us the will to serve Him."

40. *Olam Katan*, p. 21.
41. *Ibid.*, p. 42.
42. *Ibid.*, p. 64.
43. See the third chapter of *Olam Katan*, p. 56 ff. This chapter, in which the author gives a very profound exposition of the problem of God's attributes, is the most important part of the entire work, and it is because of it that Ibn Zaddik occupies an honored place in the history of medieval Jewish philosophy.

As a faithful protagonist of the "sovereignty of reason" and an intellectual aristocrat recognizing only the rule of speculative thought, Joseph Ibn Zaddik speaks with great contempt of the "multitude," which cannot understand that the corporeal expressions and images which the prophets employ in relation to God are only parables and allusions, and must not be construed literally. He explicitly declares that only the philosophic, thinking soul is immortal; this means, he explains, that "it returns to its source and is illuminated with the reflection of the infinite light which the Creator of the universe bestows." And this, he insists, "is the true reward of good deeds, not as the fools and deniers of reason think."

"I know," says Ibn Zaddik, "that people will surely argue: 'What do you mean? Why, this is an actual denial of the resurrection of the dead.' 'No,' I will answer, 'we do not deny it; on the contrary, we confirm it more than you, for we have in this matter a much more accurate conception than you.' " Ibn Zaddik concludes, as it were, with a mocking smile: "We cannot deal with this question in more detail, when the people of our generation are so blind and foolish."[44]

Ibn Zaddik, the rabbinic judge of Cordova, was the first harbinger of the new tendency that was destined to play a tremendously important role in medieval Jewish intellectual life. Shortly after him the first systematic Aristotelian among the Jews, Rabbi Abraham Ibn Daud, better known under the name Ravad I, appeared.

Born in Toledo in 1110, Abraham Ibn Daud, like Jehudah Halevi, was educated in Moslem Spain. In Cordova, the major center of Arabic civilization, he studied mathematics, astronomy,[45] and Aristotle's philosophy in Avicenna's interpretation and exposition. He was also interested in that science which, among the Spanish Jews, was a neglected stepchild—history. To be sure, even Ibn Daud concerned himself with history not for its own sake but out of external, polemical motives. The Karaites at that time were attempting to carry their quarrel with rabbinic Judaism from anterior Asia into the new center of Jewish civilization, Spain. They sought to show that since the institution of the Gaonate had succumbed in the East, Talmudic Judaism had lost its lawful representatives and spiritual leaders and, along with this, the long "chain

---

44. *Ibid.,* p. 74.
45. An astronomical work which Abraham Ibn Daud wrote not long before his tragic death in Toledo in the year 1180 has survived in manuscript. He died as a martyr in an uprising. The details and causes of this uprising have remained unknown (see the *Sefer Ha-Kabbalah* of Solomon of Turtial and A. Neubauer's *Seder Ha-Hachamim Ve-Korot Ha-Yamim*, I, 102.

of tradition," the heritage of the fathers, in which the Rabbanites so gloried, had also been broken.

To refute this argument Abraham Ibn Daud composed his *Sefer Ha-Kabbalah*, in which he presents an account in chronological order, generation by generation, like links in a chain, of all the Jewish teachers of religion, the lawgivers and exponents of the Torah of Moses, beginning with the Tannaim and Amoraim up to his own time, the middle of the twelfth century. He insists that spiritual hegemony and religious authority passed by inheritance and tradition from the East to the West, and that the rabbis of Spain are the legitimate heirs and successors of the earlier Geonim in Babylonia. Here Ibn Daud introduces the legend, so well known because of him and quoted ever since by all historians, about the "four captives," the four Jewish scholars of Sura who were captured near Bari while traveling on an Italian ship. These founded new Talmudic academies in distant Jewish communities and created new centers for study of the Talmud. One of the four was Rabbi Moses ben Enoch, who, in the time of Ḥasdai Ibn Shaprut, was head of the new *yeshivah* or Talmudic academy in Cordova.[46]

The information that Ibn Daud provides about the cultural situation of the Spanish Jews is of great historical value. Thus his book, which aimed at polemic and apologetic goals, became one of the most important and reliable sources for the history of the Jews of Spain in the first period of their cultural flowering.

Ibn Daud also set himself an apologetic goal in his philosophic work written in the year 1160, *Al-'akidah al-Rafiyah*, better known under the title of Solomon ben Labi's Hebrew translation, *Emunah Ramah*.[47]

In the introduction the author asserts that he intends to provide a solution to the difficult question that agitates so many souls and arouses grievous doubts in so many hearts: how can a reconciliation be effected between the idea, on the one hand, that God is omniscient—that for Him all secrets, all events hidden in the womb of the future, in the infinite chain of coming generations, are revealed, and that everything that happens is the result of His will—and, on the other hand, the belief in man's power of choice and free will? It is clear that this problem is intimately connected with the very foundation of morality and ethics—man's responsibility for his deeds. For if man is not endowed with free will, if everything is

---

46. See *Sefer Ha-Kabbalah* (Neubauer's edition), pp. 67–69.
47. Published with a German translation by S. Weil in 1852. In manuscript there is also another translation by Samuel Motot under the name *Sefer Emunah Nissaah* (see J. Guttmann, *Die Religionsphilosophie des Abraham Ibn Daud*, p. 8; also *Iggerot Shadal*, p. 836).

foreseen and predetermined, then reward and punishment have no justification whatever, for there is no reason to reward the righteous or punish the wicked.

Ibn Daud's answer is very characteristic of the man, who is capable of touching upon important problems but does not possess sufficient profundity to examine them thoroughly and provide satisfactory solutions. He explains man's power of choice in the following way: The Creator presents men with various and opposing "possibilities," from among which he has the alternative of choosing freely whichever he wishes; God does not know beforehand for certain which of these opposing possibilities the human will will select. To be sure, Ibn Daud himself realizes that there may be a "stubborn maker of difficulties" who will raise the question how it is possible that God should not know beforehand man's deeds and fate. This difficulty he attempts to dispose of by putting, on his part, a question to the "stubborn one":

How, then? If one says that everything happens according to a predetermined decree, that opposite choices cannot be at one and the same time "possibilities" belonging to the free human will, then one denies man's power to choose. But without free choice, the world can have no existence, for man's freedom of choice is the foundation of reward and punishment and of "the world to come."[48]

Thus Ibn Daud obviously begs the very question which it was his task to answer. In fact, however, he had no intention of giving a definite solution to this question, and it is not this that is central in his *Emunah Ramah*. Ibn Daud only cites it as an example, to show how many religious problems and contradictions had been disclosed and remained unresolved in his generation simply because men abandoned philosophical investigation out of fear that it would remove them from the right way. Men, he complains, are afraid to hold simultaneously in their hands "both lights," Torah and philosophy, and therefore when they take up one of them they extinguish the other. He is therefore "happy" to show that between these "two lords" that rule the world, there is no enmity or jealousy, for between the Torah and divine revelation, on the one hand, and true philosophy, on the other, there is no inconsistency whatever. It is, therefore, not to be feared that philosophy may lead man away from faith; on the contrary, true philosophy can only strengthen and confirm faith.

"True philosophy"—this, for Ibn Daud, is the philosophy of Aristotle. He is strongly opposed to the neo-Platonists in general

48. *Emunah Ramah*, p. 99.

and the Jewish neo-Platonist Ibn Gabirol in particular, accusing the latter of having spoken "rebellious words against his people." Both Aristotle's philosophy and the Torah of Moses, Ibn Daud insists, lead to the same goal, the attainment of moral truth. The Jewish faith has, however, the advantage that the great truths which philosophic thought disclosed to the peoples of the world only after many generations of blind seeking and groping on false paths were obtained by the Jewish people at the very beginning, thanks to divine revelation and the prophets.[49]

Like Saadiah Gaon in his day, so Ibn Daud insists that this foundation of the Jewish faith, the revelation at Mount Sinai, can in no way be denied, for it is proven and confirmed through ancient tradition. This tradition, which passes from generation to generation and recounts the great historical event that occurred in the sight of all Israel, under the control and testimony of a large assembly, has such great value and significance and possesses such convincing power that it is impossible to refute it through the keenest logical theories.[50]

49. *Ibid.*, p. 63. See also p. 4.
50. *Ibid.*, p. 81. Concerning Jehudah Halevi's influence on Abraham Ibn Daud, see D. Kaufmann, *Geschichte der Attributenlehre*, pp. 241–52.

CHAPTER SIX

Maimonides

BRAHAM IBN DAUD was not an original, independent thinker. He was merely the emissary and harbinger of the new tendency which was then penetrating into the Jewish world of ideas. Shortly after him, however, appeared the great prophet of this tendency,[1] the true sovereign of the domain of thought, the keen thinker who imposed his powerful spirit on the whole subsequent period of Jewish culture and whose influence was also felt in the medieval Christian thought world. This was Rabbi Moses ben Maimon,[2] better known as Maimonides or Rambam, the

1. On the influence of the author of the *Emunah Ramah* on Maimonides, see J. Guttmann, *Die religiöse Philosophie des Abraham Ibn Daud*, pp. 9–11, and also his article in the *Cohen-Festschrift*, pp. 135–44.
2. His Arabic name was Abu 'Imran Musa ben Maimun Ibn 'Abd Allah. Joseph ben Eliezer, a writer who lived at the end of the thirteenth century, gives Maimonides' lineage in his commentary to Ibn Ezra's *Tzofnat Paaneah:* "Rabbi Moses, the chief of the princes, the teacher of righteousness, was the son of Rabbi Maimon the *dayyan*, the son of Rabbi Joseph the *hacham*, the son of Rabbi Isaac the *dayyan*, the son of Rabbi Joseph the *dayyan*, the son of Rabbi Obadiah." (We quote the manuscript of *Tzofnat Paaneah* that is found in the Leningrad Imperial Library in the Firkovich Collection, I, No. 67.)

author of the *Mishneh Torah* and *Moreh Nevuchim* (A Guide for the Perplexed).

Maimonides is the only one among the great Jewish personalities of the Middle Ages whose biography is known to us in all its particulars. Even the day and month in which he came into the world were noted down for posterity.[3] He was born in Cordova on the day before Passover at 12:40 P.M., March 30, 1135. His father, Rabbi Maimon, a capable Talmudist, was a *dayyan* or rabbinic judge in that city. When Moses was thirteen years old the fanatical Almohades conquered Cordova, and its Jews were confronted with the alternative of converting to Islam or going into exile. Rabbi Maimon and his family left the city, wandered over Spain for twelve years, and then settled in Morocco in the city of Fez. There also they had to suffer much from the Almohades, who ruled the land, and five years later, in 1165, the Maimon family set out for Palestine. Maimonides stopped for a brief sojourn in Jerusalem, and then settled in the city of Fostat (Old Cairo), where he spent all the remaining years of his life and composed his famous works. In time he became the chief rabbi (Nagid) of all Egypt, but he earned his living through the practice of medicine. He was court physician to the vizier Al-Kadi al-Fadil, and afterwards to the sultan Al-Fazael, the famous Saladin's son,[4] for whom he wrote a special work on hygiene.[5]

Maimonides provides an interesting portrait of his activity as a practicing physician and his life at the sultan's court in his letter to Samuel Ibn Tibbon. When Ibn Tibbon was engaged in translating the *Guide for the Perplexed*, he wanted to travel to Fostat to see Maimonides and consult with him about numerous details of his work. Maimonides, however, dissuaded him from the journey. "I must tell you beforehand," he wrote,

that you will not be able to spend a single hour with me in private, neither by day nor by night. . . . This is the order of my day: I live

3. See Saadiah Ibn Danan in *Ḥemdah Geunzah*, 30; also Azariah dei Rossi, *Meor Enayim*, the end of Chapter 25, where the report of Maimonides' grandson Rabbi David is quoted.

4. Maimonides' contemporary, the Arabic scholar Al-Kufti, relates that the English king, Richard the Lion-Hearted, is supposed to have invited Maimonides to become his court physician, but that the latter declined. See *Literaturblatt des Orients*, 1846, p. 341.

5. As the author of numerous medical works, Maimonides occupies an honored place in the history of medieval medicine. For details concerning Maimonides as a physician, see M. Steinschneider, *Hebräischen Übersetzungen*, pp. 762–74; Vogel, *Maimuni als medizinischer Schriftsteller* (in the collection *Moses ben Maimon*, I, 231–47); and J. Eiger in the anthology *Yevreyskaya Misl*, II.

in Fostat and the sultan in Cairo, which is a distance of about two Sabbath-limit walks. According to court protocol, I am obliged to visit the sultan every morning. In case he or any of his wives or children are sick I spend most of the day in Cairo at court. At times I must also attend the sultan's officers and servitors. In general, I have to spend every morning in Cairo, even when everything is in order, and I return home to Fostat after midday very hungry. There a great crowd both of Moslem and Jews is already waiting for me, among them prominent persons and distinguished officials, and also persons of the common multitude, some strangers and some known to me. I alight from my donkey, wash my hands, go out to them, excuse myself and ask them to wait a little until I eat something. Afterward, I go out to the sick, ask each one about his ailment, and prescribe remedies for them. These people go away, others come, and so it goes until late at night. Sometimes I engage in a discussion till 2:00 in the morning and even later. I lie down because of great weariness and in a lying position give the necessary explanations. . . . In short, throughout the whole week I do not have any opportunity to speak with an Israelite privately, face to face, except on the Sabbath. Then the members of the community come to my house after morning prayers, and I transmit to them all the necessary orders for the coming week.[6]

Maimonides' years of wandering were also years of learning. With great diligence this brilliantly gifted figure accumulated vast knowledge. One of the greatest authorities in the realm of Jewish scholarship, he was also in full command of the general science and research of his day. In the major medieval branches of science he was not only an expert but also an acute investigator, an ingenious architect and builder who knew how to put together individual bricks and stones into a solid edifice dominated by a single idea. He was blessed with that marvelous aptitude that one finds so rarely among Jews—the art of building, of orderly and harmonious architecture.

But what Maimonides was able to accomplish was beyond the capacities of his generation. The contemporary Jewish intelligentsia could not control and harmonize the broad general culture of that day with the powerful but confused structure of Jewish learning, of Talmudic-rabbinic knowledge. Minds became perplexed and could not, with the best will in the world, fulfill the ancient principle "It is good that thou shouldest take hold of the one; yea, also from the other withdraw not thy hand" (Ecclesiastes 7:18). They could not help but perceive inconsistencies between the two worlds, the Talmudic-rabbinic and the general-scientific. Mai-

6. Maimonides wrote this letter in his old age in the year 1199. It has also been published in Yiddish in *Kevod Ḥachamim*.

monides, with his keen eye, realized this and considered it his duty to come to the aid of his contemporaries, to liberate them from spiritual and intellectual confusion and not only point to, but with his own hands lay out, a broad, smooth path that might lead the men of his time to the truth.

While still a youth wandering with his father over Spain, Maimonides began a gigantic undertaking: to investigate Jewish religious literature systematically, according to a definite plan, to introduce order into the immense legacy produced by the ceaseless productivity of centuries, to collect in one work all the laws and statutes connected with the religious-moral life of the Jewish community that are scattered, without any organization, in the chaotic pages of the Talmud. Maimonides devoted about twenty years of hard labor to this task. First he wrote (in Arabic) a comprehensive commentary to the Mishnah. Only then did he approach his famous work the *Mishneh Torah*, also known under the title *Yad Ha-Ḥazakah*, with its fourteen books.[7]

For ten years Maimonides labored day and night on this work.[8] "I, Moses ben Maimon, the Spaniard," he declares at the end of his introduction,

have girded up my loins and, relying on the help of God . . . I have composed this work in which are collected all the laws and statutes, with the enactments, customs and decrees that were introduced from the days of Moses our teacher to the redaction of the Talmud and that are expounded in the work of our Geonim who lived in later generations. I have given my work the title *Mishneh Torah* because any one who will first study the Written Torah and thereafter this work will, through it, become thoroughly familiar with the entire Oral Torah and not need to consult any other book for this purpose.

This work, which was planned as a compendium of the entire Oral Torah, was written by Maimonides in Hebrew, and its language serves to this day as a model of Hebrew scientific style. Every word is in its proper place, every sentence polished and measured, everything clear and lucid. Like the style, so is the content and organization of the enormous mass of material. As architect

---

7. A small Arabic work, known by the Hebrew title *Sefer Ha-Mitzvot*, serves as an introduction to the *Yad Ha-Ḥazakah*. This work has come down to us in two different versions, and of each version there is a Hebrew translation, one by Solomon ben Joseph Ibn Ayub and the other, better known, by Moses Ibn Tibbon.
8. So he reports in his letter to Jonathan ben David Ha-Kohen. The work was completed in 1177.

and builder Maimonides has no peer in the whole of religious-scientific Hebrew literature. His *Mishneh Torah* is truly a masterpiece of classical structure, so ingeniously are its parts adapted to each other. The enormous number of laws and commandments found in the Torah and Talmud are divided by Maimonides into fourteen groups. Each group is dealt with in a separate book, and each book is divided into chapters and paragraphs.

In the *Mishneh Torah* or *Yad Ha-Ḥazakah*, as well as in Maimonides' commentary to the Mishnah, a characteristic trait is immediately obvious. The author does not confine himself to the role of the commentator and codifier who sets forth and expounds the laws. He also avails himself of every opportunity to enlighten the reader, to open his eyes, and to demonstrate to him the harmfulness of superstition, with its bizarre notions and formulas that lead men astray and corrupt their intelligence. Maimonides makes no secret of the fact that his enlightening discussions have in most cases a very slight relationship to the law in question. "I realize quite well," he admits in one place, "that what I explain here does not belong to the subject; but I have done it deliberately because I consider it the most essential of duties to give the reader a clear concept of how rightly to appreciate the value of the laws and statutes." Therefore, it happens quite frequently that where, in the Gemara, the explanations of a given law are connected with obsolete superstitions and ancient prejudices, Maimonides scorns these explanations and gives, instead, a new, more rationalistic, "more correct" explanation.

Maimonides' *Mishneh Torah* created a tremendous sensation. Wherever the work appeared, it elicited the greatest enthusiasm among Jews. "Rabbi Moses ben Maimon," writes his contemporary Aaron ben Meshullam of Lunel, "has led his people out of the sea of foolishness. He has implanted God's sacred Torah in all hearts. There has been no one like Moses ben Maimon since Rabina and Rav Ashi" (*Taam Zekenim*, 67). "Maimonides' work," writes another contemporary, Rabbi Sheshet Beneveniste, "has, with its clear language and marvelous order, opened the eyes of all. Everyone hastens to make a copy of the work for himself. Old and young come together to study it. Thanks to the *Mishneh Torah*, many have become competent in all the laws and are able by themselves to decide questions and express their views concerning every precept and statute."

To be sure, Maimonides' work also called forth, in certain circles, strong opposition. Some of its antagonists were motivated by external and petty motives—jealousy, envy, and pride. Certain scholars saw in the *Mishneh Torah* a kind of insult to themselves, and endeavored to show that experts such as they had no use whatever for such "helping" books.[9] Maimonides himself speaks with philosophic calm, in a letter to his beloved pupil Joseph Ibn Aknin, of these pedantries and petty attacks. "Know," he adds,

that not out of a desire for glory nor in order to acquire fame for myself among Jews, have I written this work . . . I realized that the people do not have a single law book in which all the laws are clearly and logically explained without errors and without controversy. . . . And what I have done was done only for the honor of God . . . I know of a certainty that in time, when jealousy and the pursuit of glory will be stilled, my work will be accepted by the Jewish people, and they will make use of it alone and no other book.[10]

Precisely this expectation of Maimonides that eventually people would content themselves with the *Mishneh Torah* alone had to call forth intense dissatisfaction on the part of many pious rabbis and scholars. These were afraid that it might displace the Gemara, and that men would no longer consider it necessary to be versed in the Talmud. They also complained that in his work Maimonides had not indicated the original sources on which he had relied in explaining any given law. This made it extremely difficult to look up and compare his view with the texts in question, if one wished to convince himself that the law had really been explained properly and that the author had not erred. Maimonides himself had to admit that this complaint was, indeed, justified,[11] but he sharply rejected the other charge against him, namely, that his intent was that Jews should pay less attention to the Talmud and its commentators. "I have never, God forbid, said: Do not occupy yourself with the Gemara and with the *Halachot* of Rabbi Isaac [Alfasi] and others."[12]

It must, however, be noted that this statement is not altogether candid or correct. It is true that in public, to the masses, Maimonides never taught that less time should be devoted to study of the Talmud. However, individuals, his chosen disciples, whom he considered capable of receiving a philosophic education, he advised "not to waste time on the discussions of the Gemara and the commentators on the Talmud, for it is better to devote oneself to useful sciences and to sharpen the mind through philosophical inquiry."[13]

9. Among these opponents was the head of the Talmudic academy in Baghdad, Rabbi Samuel ben Ali.
10. *Iggerot Ha-Rambam*, 21–22.
11. In his letter to the *dayyan* of Alexandria in Egypt, Rabbi Pinhas ben Meshullam.
12. *Iggerot Ha-Rambam*, 22.
13. In a letter to his favorite pupil Joseph Ibn Aknin.

A loyal adherent of Aristotle's system and a strict rationalist, Maimonides, in his commentary to the Mishnah and especially in the *Mishneh Torah*, endeavored to persuade the reader that the only correct and sure support in questions of faith and morality is reason or logical understanding. In his famous "creed" he sought to express the essence of Judaism in thirteen basic principles, and along with this insisted that one should not only believe in these principles but must also (except in the case of two of them, the resurrection of the dead and the coming of the Messiah) justify them philosophically and comprehend them with the mind, for only clear, logical understanding provides the possibility of penetrating into the true substance of each principle.[14] Belief, for Maimonides, is strictly bound up with thought and investigation, and he therefore considered it essential to give in the first part of his *Mishneh Torah*, in the *Sefer Ha-Madda*, a complete religious-philosophic system in which he tries to justify "through reason," with the aid of logical premises and conclusions, the fundamental religious conceptions of Judaism.

Maimonides, however, could not be content with the *Sefer Ha-Madda*. In it only the "major headings" of the problem of critically illuminating the Jewish faith through philosophic thought are touched upon. The *Sefer Ha-Madda* may be considered merely an introduction or prelude to Maimonides' later work, his famous *Moreh Nevuchim* (A Guide for the Perplexed).[15]

In no other work does Maimonides' personality express itself so clearly as in this great philosophic treatise, which was written in Arabic in the form of a gift to his favorite pupil, Joseph ben Jehudah Aknin. Characteristic is the introduction to the *Guide for the Perplexed*, in which the author insists that the book is written neither for the general public nor for the scholars who pore all their days only over the Gemara: "my work is written solely for those who have immersed themselves in philosophic study and are greatly confused because it appears to them that there is a contradiction between philosophic truth and certain particulars of the Torah."

Maimonides also explains that he has deliberately not expressed his thoughts in easily comprehensible and systematic form, so that the "truths" that are investigated in this book may remain hidden for the "multitude." "God is my witness," he says further,

14. On these "thirteen principles" an anonymous medieval poet constructed the famous hymn *Yigdal Elohim Ḥai*.
15. Completed in the year 1190. The Arabic text, *Dalalat al-Ha'irin*, was published with a French translation in three volumes by Solomon Munk, 1856–66.

that I have long wrestled with the question whether I should publish this work in which, for the first time among our people, are discussed such important and recondite matters. . . . It is written, however, "It is time to work for the Lord; they have nullified Thy Torah." It is a duty to act for the sake of God's name when the Torah is in danger. . . . In a word, I am a man who cannot do otherwise. No matter that I have come to the conviction that the truth established through reason can be taught only in such form and manner that it will satisfy and inspire merely the chosen individual and, at the same time, provoke tens of thousands of fools; I shall nevertheless speak the truth openly to enlighten and aid this single individual, and I shall not let myself be frightened by the attacks of the multitude.

It is erroneous to believe that Maimonides set himself the task of making peace between Greek-Arabic philosophy and Judaism. The *Guide for the Perplexed* is not at all an apologetic book. In complete opposition to Jehudah Halevi, Maimonides was convinced that the religious beliefs of the Jewish people fully corroborate Aristotle's philosophic ideas, and that the truths disclosed through divine revelation cannot in any way contradict the conclusions to which man's rational inquiry has come. He had no doubt that philosophy is no less sure a source for grounding truth than divine revelation. "Where truth is clear and sharp," he declares, "it makes no difference whether it has been revealed by prophets through the holy spirit or whether it has been expressed by non-Jews" (*Yad Ha-Hazakah, Hilchot Kiddush Ha-Hodesh*).[16]

Maimonides could in no way agree with Halevi's contention that the "God of Abraham" is sharply distinguished from the "God of Aristotle." On the contrary, he was convinced that, with regard to the idea of divinity, there are no differences of opinion between Aristotle and the Torah of Moses, and that all the truths that philosophy teaches are also expressed and confirmed in the Bible and Talmud. Those who believe that there are, indeed, contradictions between philosophy and faith are simply in error, and the error arises, in Maimonides' view, from the fact that people misconstrue the meaning of the Bible. He therefore speaks deprecatingly of the "poor commentators" who consider it the most important task to explain the text word for word.[17] He himself regards as essential and primary not the translation of the words, not the simple or literal meaning, but the "parable" and the "allusion." For harmony between the Mosaic Torah and Greek philosophy was attained by Maimonides in the same way as it was by Philo in his

16. End of Chapter 17.
17. *Moreh Nevuchim*, II, Chapter 29.

day, i.e., through expounding the Biblical text allegorically.[18] In all the stories of the Bible Maimonides, the strict rationalist, perceived only allegories which disclose, by way of parable and allusion, the very ideas and thoughts on which Aristotle constructed his philosophical system.[19]

"The teaching that is suited to the multitude," Maimonides already insists in his first work, his commentary on the Mishnah, "must be by way of riddle and parable."[20] For every commandment and statute of the Torah he endeavors to find a rational motive or practical effect, because all that is written in the Torah is pure truth, and that which is true must also be useful and can and *must* be explained through reason and logical argument.[21]

In this connection it must be noted that in those days men still had no conception whatever of the *historical development* of religious and other cultural phenomena. Maimonides in particular lacked all historical sense. To occupy oneself with history and with music, he said, is "a foolish and useless pastime."[22] It is, therefore, not surprising that when he seeks to estimate the value and significance of religious laws and practices, he considers them exclusively from their practical and utilitarian side. In this way Judaism, the faith of divine revelation and great miracles, is transformed into a practical-religious and rationalist-utilitarian legislation. All the "thou shalts" and "thou shalt nots" of the Torah are nothing but simple demands of the natural human understanding, useful principles of practical hygiene. Maimonides did not realize that the two world outlooks that are so clearly expressed in the Bible on the one side, and in Aristotle's philosophy on the other, are two independent and entirely *different* manifestations of the human spirit. Firmly convinced that there is only *one* truth—philosophical, logical truth—Maimonides also saw in Judaism merely a set of philosophical ideas and concepts. Because the Torah of Moses is pure truth, it must in all particulars confirm the assumptions of philosophic truth, of the one true philosophy—the Aristotelian. Unconsciously, Maimonides found in Judaism and in the Bible merely a rationalistic commentary to Aristotle's philosophy. To discern something more, something different, in the Bible, his

18. Whether Maimonides was familiar with Philo's philosophy has not been determined. In any case the Arabs certainly knew of Philo. See A. Harkavy, *Izvestia Kirkisana*, 1894, pp. 255, 267, and 276.
19. *Moreh Nevuchim*, III, Chapter 50.
20. Introduction to the Commentary on the Mishnah, *Seder Zeraim*.
21. *Moreh Nevuchim*, III, Chapters 35–49.
22. Commentary on the Mishnah, Tractate *Sanhedrin*, Chapter 10, *Mishnah* 1.

brilliant but one-sided mind was incapable of doing. Without any poetic sentiment, alienated from and contemptuous toward the inner world of human dreams and spiritual enthusiasm, he recognized only the *rational* or *intellectual,* only that which can be *logically proven.* That the Bible and Aristotelian philosophy derive from two different worlds could not even cross his mind.

Rightly to appreciate this great philosopher, however, it must be noted that he did not follow his teacher and guide, Aristotle, with blind self-disparagement or altogether uncritically. Maimonides was, indeed, thoroughly persuaded that everything Aristotle had taught concerning the terrestrial world, i.e., our sublunar world, is pure truth, and that whoever attempts to deny it does so simply out of "lack of understanding"; his intellect is not able to grasp the profound thoughts of Aristotle's system.[23] "Aristotle's opinions," said Maimonides, "are, in general, the acme of human knowledge."[24] Nevertheless, he was not willing always and in all cases to rely on the great authority, for he had discovered that the major stumbling block on the path of free inquiry is blind and pusillanimous belief in authorities.

The noted eighteenth-century Jewish thinker Solomon Maimon, in his autobiography, relates with great enthusiasm that for all the knowledge and enlightenment he had attained, he was indebted exclusively to Maimonides. But he adds: "This great influence was exercised on me not so much by Maimonides' system as by the daring flight of his thought, which refused to acknowledge any limits besides those of the mind itself, and by his love for the truth which, for him, was higher than anything else in the world."

To convince oneself how accurate this characterization is, it suffices to read through the pages in the *Guide for the Perplexed* in which Maimonides battles against the routine and cowardice of human thought, against self-disparagement and blind, unquestioning trust in authorities and ideas taken over from one's ancestors. In the love of the multitude for the common, the old-time, the familiar, and in its suspicion of and hatred for the new and extraordinary, he perceives the worst enemy of true knowledge, the most dangerous obstacle on the path of seeking and attaining truth.[25]

23. *Moreh Nevuchim,* II, Chapter 22.
24. See his letter to Samuel Ibn Tibbon. The same idea is expressed by Maimonides' contemporary, the famous Arabic thinker, Averroes.
25. *Moreh Nevuchim,* I, Chapters 31, 73, and many other places. In this particular Maimonides is a predecessor of the famous medieval scientist and philosopher Roger Bacon. Authority, says Bacon, explains nothing; it merely demands belief. It commands the mind but does not enlighten it.

Maimonides' critical eye sought to penetrate into the essence of any given subject, and ruthlessly rejected every unproven assumption, refusing to take account of any authority whatsoever. For this reason he strongly denied Aristotle's view concerning the eternity of the world and the eternity of matter; the proofs that the Greek thinker adduced in this connection seemed to him insufficient. In this connection he insisted that he declines in this matter to accept the view of Aristotle, not at all because the latter contradicts certain verses of the Torah in which it is affirmed that God created the world out of "the waste and void," i.e., out of absolute non-being;[26] he does so only because the idea of *creatio ex nihilo*, set forth in Genesis, commends itself more to reason than Aristotle's idea of the eternity of the world.[27]

Maimonides' religious-philosophic system is undoubtedly a harmoniously integral structure; every part is congruent and ingeniously fitted to the next. The air in this structure is bright and clear, but it is cold and uncongenial to the yearning, fervently believing soul. Maimonides recognized only that which can be proven by reason and to which speculative thought gives its assent. In his view, the major goal of man lies in philosophical inquiry, in seeking out the laws of nature and, above all, in recognizing and understanding the Creator of the universe.

But how can man know and understand the Creator? We have already observed how the Jewish thinkers Saadiah, Ibn Zaddik, and others protested in the sharpest possible manner against corporeality and anthropomorphisms in relation to God, i.e., against clothing Him with human forms and attributes. No one, however, until Maimonides[28] showed so profoundly and brilliantly that the conceptions which man can have of divinity must be limited exclusively to negative attributes. Human speech is pallid and poor; it cannot give a true and accurate idea of the nature of the objects and phenomena that surround man and fill the space of the world. Man employs words, which are pictures and symbols, and with their aid arouses in another person certain representations and concepts. But how is it possible to give, through pictures and signs, a conception of that which has no form or image? How can one speak of divine attributes when all praises and words of laudation in human speech are suited to purely human conceptions and reflect human feelings and desires? The nature of God, however, is wholly other; it is absolutely different from the human. Man, with

26. *Moreh Nevuchim*, II, Chapter 25.
27. *Ibid.*, Chapters 22–25.
28. *Ibid.*, I, Chapters 50–60. These chapters are among the finest in Jewish religious philosophy.

his picture speech, is, therefore, in no way able to portray the nature of God and, willingly or unwillingly, cannot but clothe Him in a garment of materiality. When we associate the God-idea with such qualities as "unique," "pure," "perfect," "exalted," and the like, we unconsciously express concepts based on our feelings and on our corporeal representations. We say, for example, that God is one; God's oneness, however, is of a totally different kind than the concept of oneness which man has. The latter is the concept of one among many, a part of a larger, more complete entity. Such a notion is in no way appropriate to divinity. We say further that God "lives," but the concept of "living" is, among men, strictly associated with the representation of feelings and movements, as well as the end of life, death. But the antithesis of life and death applies only in the material world and can have no relationship whatsoever to the idea of God. Again, we say God is eternal. The concept "eternal" is, however, connected with the concept of time, and God is *above* and *outside* time.

It is clear, Maimonides concludes, that man's speech cannot express God's perfection. We shall, therefore, come closer to the truth when, with regard to God's nature and attributes, we make use not of affirmation but of negation. It is much more correct to say God is *not* one among others, He is *not* limited in power, He is *not* corporeal, etc.[29]

Maimonides, therefore, strongly assails the "singers and poets" who, in their compositions, crown God with praises and images. These poets he calls "fools," and their prayers and poems in which God is spoken of in pictorial language he regards as nothing but "blasphemy."[30] In his legal *responsa* Maimonides expresses his strong opposition to the recital of *piyyutim* in the synagogue, since these were composed not by "scholars" but by simple poets, and the latter are incapable of raising themselves to God.[31]

From Maimonides' standpoint the poetic effusion of the soul of an Ibn Gabirol or a Jehudah Halevi is thus nothing more than blasphemy committed by "fools." To his acute but more systematic than creative mind, the emotion of the poetic spirit, the trembling of the longing soul, the soaring of the human imagination, were completely alien. The rich world of human feelings and desires, the best consolation of men—poetry, with its dazzling colors and golden dreams and hopes, everything that illuminates

29. *Ibid.*, Chapters 57–58.
30. *Ibid.*, Chapter 59. S. Sachs (*Ha-Tehiyyah* [1850], pp. 3–5) has shown that Maimonides here aimed mainly at the author of *Keter Malchut*, Solomon Ibn Gabirol.
31. A. Geiger, *Melo Chofnajim*, p. 70.

and adorns man's life was disparaged by Maimonides' steel-sharp but ice-cold thought. He did not understand that precisely in the passionate striving for the exalted and the ideal, which man himself has created in spirit, do the noblest aspects of his soul disclose themselves. He did not realize that Ibn Gabirol's and Halevi's hymns flow out of the depths of the inspired religious soul and strive toward the divine, about which man dreams in the highest moments of his life.

According to Maimonides, one can serve and know God not through prayer, and not even through good deeds and a morally pure life, but chiefly through philosophical searching and reflection. And to this level only those who are proficient in all branches of positive science, such as mathematics, physics, logic, etc., can attain. Even in the commandment of the Torah, "And thou shalt love the Lord thy God with all thy heart and soul and might," Maimonides saw only the commandment that man should *comprehend* God with the acuteness of thought; for to love, he asserts, means to seek out. And it is the understanding of God, he further declares, that provides the greatest pleasure imaginable (*Sefer Ha-Mitzvot*).

Especially characteristic of Maimonides' philosophical outlook is his attitude toward the belief in the immortality of the soul and the resurrection of the dead. We have observed that, on the question of the eternity or creation of the world, Maimonides agrees with Jewish tradition and opposes Aristotle's doctrine. In his understanding of immortality, however, he inclines more to Aristotle's views and expresses ideas that are clearly incompatible with traditional Jewish teaching.

In Aristotle's philosophy God is not the guide of the world. He does not direct the order of the universe and He has not created the material world. Aristotle sees in God not the Creator but the highest ideal, the Perfect Being who affects the world only by the fact that He *is*. As Perfect Being, the most exalted level of wisdom, He is the supreme goal and purpose of all that exists; everything strives and moves toward Him. It is clear that in Aristotle's system divine providence does not rule over the individual, for man is associated with corporeality, with the material world, which was not created by God; hence, his fate cannot be under God's providence.

Such a view is obviously in total contradiction to Jewish tradition. "All Israelites have a share in the world to come"—this Talmudic dictum is highly typical of the entire Jewish world outlook. Maimonides, however, in fact denies it. In his opinion, not every human soul is endowed with immortality. Man, he declares, is distinguished from other living creatures by the fact that he possesses the potentiality or capacity to perfect himself in knowledge and the sciences;[32] but only if man employs this capacity properly, only if he studies the sciences and immerses himself in philosophical investigations, does the potentiality become actuality. Only under these conditions does man's soul unite with the "active intellect," the "earth spirit" which governs the terrestrial world and which alone is truly immortal.[33]

The concept of the "active intellect" occupies such a central position not only in the Maimonidean system but in medieval Jewish religious philosophy in general that a brief explanation of it seems necessary. According to Aristotle, the universe consists of a number of heavenly "spheres" in constant motion. This motion, in his view, can be called forth only by immaterial substances, i.e., by eternal and immortal spiritual powers. The number of these independent spirits (intelligences, separate intellects) is equal to the number of the "spheres." Aristotle also considers the stars as spiritual substances endowed with divine intelligence. The Arabic Aristotelians, who took over the Aristotelian system in neo-Platonic dress, believed that between divinity (the First Cause) and the terrestrial world there are ten such spheres (in medieval Hebrew literature they are called *galgalim*). The first "intelligence," which brings the highest "sphere" into motion, is a direct reflection of the First Cause, of God Himself. The second intelligence is a reflection of the first, and so on to the last, the tenth intelligence, which is connected with the lowest sphere, that of the moon. This is called the active intellect (in Hebrew, *sechel ha-poel*).

Maimonides, who firmly believed in this Aristotelian conception of the universe, came with strict consistency to ideas that are utterly inconsistent with the understanding that Judaism has of the role of man in the world order. According to Biblical tradition, not only all earthly creatures but even the stars and planets were created for man's sake. Maimonides strongly opposes this idea. Let man not delude himself, he explains, and think that everything was created for his sake, that even the intelligences, the spheres, and the angels exist only for his benefit. Compare man's petty reason with the great intelligences of the "spheres," and you will

32. *Moreh Nevuchim,* I, Chapter 70. The profoundest expositor of the *Moreh,* Moses of Narbonne, writes: "Rabbi Moses, peace be upon him, followed Alexander of Aphrodisias in this matter and believed that the soul is only a power and potentiality."
33. From this it is clear that Maimonides actually denies individual immortality, i.e., the survival of the particular person's soul as an independent spirit.

immediately understand how foolish it is to believe that everything exists only for the sake of vain, little man.[34]

Maimonides, however, realizes quite well that only now does the problem become truly difficult: For the sake of what *was* the terrestrial world created? The conventional theological explanation of the rabbis, that the world was created for the sake of man and man created to serve God, did not satisfy him.[35] This, he maintains, explains nothing, for one may again ask: Why does God need man to serve Him? Does He thereby become more perfect?[36] Maimonides arrives at the conclusion that the question is really insoluble and that one must be content with the answers "So God willed" or "So His wisdom decreed."

Man ought to accustom himself to the quality of humility, Maimonides teaches, and realize that he is not the major element and most important link in the world order. Only by toilsome searching, by perfecting his understanding through the sciences and philosophical inquiry, is the chosen, extraordinary person worthy of having his soul united with the "active intellect." And in the fact that the soul becomes a small part, a spark, of this eternal spirit does its deathlessness consist. But the soul of the common man, whose mind has not sought after philosophic truth, is not immortal and goes down to destruction.

Aristotle denied that divine providence governs individuals. Maimonides did not go this far,[37] but he also believed that not every person is under God's providence. Providence, he maintains, is strictly connected with the intellect, and the more perfect a man's intellect the greater the influence of Providence on his fate.[38] Hence, only those persons whose minds are perfected to the highest degree are fully under divine providence. But the "rebellious fools," whose minds have not been illuminated and who are therefore not under the influence of divine providence, Maimonides concludes, are like all other living creatures and like cattle, as is said in Psalms 49:13: "He is like the beasts that perish." Under certain circumstances it is even permissible to kill them for the sake of the general good.[39]

These cruel words seem almost incredible coming from the

34. *Moreh Nevuchim*, III, Chapter 13.
35. Only in his younger years, when Maimonides wrote his Commentary on the Mishnah, did he still take his stand on the rabbinic theological view. In the introduction to *Seder Zeraim* he insists, "For the purpose of the world and all that is in it is the wise and good man."
36. *Moreh Nevuchim*, III, Chapter 13.
37. *Ibid.*, end of Chapter 18.
38. *Ibid.*, end of Chapter 17; cf. Chapter 51.
39. *Ibid.*, Chapter 18.

mouth of the great philosopher, yet they are, in a sense, a logical result of Maimonides' world outlook. Zealous for his only possible rationalist truth, Maimonides, the champion of free thought, necessarily becomes the fanatical oppressor of those who think otherwise. He divides human beings into six degrees,[40] and in the second of these includes persons with "false opinions." These persons, he adds, should, under certain circumstances, be destroyed and their opinions rooted out, so that they may not mislead others.

This arrogant scorn and contempt for the "foolish, ignorant multitude" is very clearly discernible in Maimonides' work generally and in his *Guide for the Perplexed* particularly. Even the ancient Hebrew prophets, those ardent champions of the oppressed and fighters for justice and righteousness, are transformed by him into philosophers and scientific investigators who hold themselves aloof from the "multitude" and are constantly absorbed in the upper worlds of the "active intellect." In his view, the prophet is a man who keeps as far away as possible from the masses and seeks neither glory nor praise from them. With cold detachment he considers and investigates the deeds and desires of ordinary men, who are, in certain respects, similar to the beasts. The man of complete perfection maintains his distance from the multitude and considers only how to avoid the injury that the latter can cause him when he comes in contact with it, or in what way he can make use of it when this is necessary to him.[41] The function of the "multitude," of common flesh-and-blood mortals, which justifies their existence, is, first, to serve the "actualized man," the person perfected in all kinds of wisdom, to take care of his needs so that he may quietly and uninterruptedly occupy himself with speculation and philosophical truths, and, second, to entertain him so that he may not feel lonely and forsaken.[42]

Not moral perfection, but knowledge and inquiry, fathoming the nature and essence of all that exists, is, according to Maimonides, the supreme goal of man. Only the soul of the thinker who penetrates into the depths of the world of thought is immortal. Man approaches God not through good deeds, but on the wings of speculative thought. Genuine service of God consists in the acquisition by the mind of true ideas and opinions.

"The sovereignty of reason!" Reason alone is the measure of all values. It governs human fate. Only with its aid does man create a bond between himself and divine wisdom. He, however, who does not delve into philosophic problems, even if he is a perfectly

40. *Ibid.*, Chapter 51.
41. *Ibid.*, II, Chapter 36.
42. See the introduction to the Commentary on the Mishnah, *Seder Zeraim.*

righteous man and his whole life one of self-sacrifice and love of fellowman, does not deserve to have the rays of divine providence illuminate his fate. This attitude of Maimonides is reflected in the last chapter of the *Guide for the Perplexed*, in which he speaks of four degrees of perfection. The first and lowest degree is material wealth; the second, bodily perfection; the third, moral perfection. But, he declares, even the third level must be considered only a means, not an end in itself. Morality and righteousness, Maimonides maintains, are effective only in social relationships, only between man and his neighbor. But when one considers man as an individual, outside the community, they lose all value and significance. The highest level of perfection is the fourth, the perfection of the mind, through which man penetrates into the profundities of the world of ideas and obtains a true conception of divinity. "This," says Maimonides, "and only this is genuine perfection. Only with this does man purchase immortality and deserve to bear the name man."

We have observed that Jehudah Halevi considers the sacred tradition, the religious-ethical legacy of the fathers, as the "categorical imperative" of the heart and inner consciousness which liberates man from doubt and provides him with the assurance that so it *must* be, so and not otherwise *must* be done. The poet's conception of the world is founded on historical, collective development. Its focus is not the isolated individual but the entire community, the people in its historical evolution. Maimonides, however, is convinced that the surest road leading to perfection is the solitary way of the individual, of the proud, single human personality. The supreme perfection is the perfection of speculative thought, whose bearer is not the community but the individual person. Not the tradition of the fathers, but the unfettered philosophic thought of the individual who stands above the community, separated from the multitude, elevates human personality to the highest level and endows it with immortality.

As far as the moral duties of man and the goals of human personality are concerned, Maimonides is a faithful disciple of Aristotle. Like the Greek philosopher, he sees man's supreme happiness and pleasure in speculation, in the activity of the mind. Morality is only the product of the practical understanding and its functioning. It holds our will in check and prevents it from departing from the "middle way." It must not allow itself any injurious extremes but hold fast to the "golden mean."[43]

In Maimonides' work, medieval Jewish philosophy attained its zenith. His *Guide for the Perplexed*, the cornerstone of Jewish

43. See Maimonides' *Shemoneh Perakim*.

theology on philosophical-rational foundations, guaranteed the hegemony of Aristotelianism over Jewish thought for centuries. More than any other Jewish thinker, Maimonides is responsible for the fact that the Jews became the mediators between Greek-Arabic philosophy and the medieval Christian world. The *Guide for the Perplexed*, which, at the command of the Emperor Frederick II,[44] was translated into Latin as early as the first decades of the thirteenth century, had a considerable effect on the Christian thinkers of the Middle Ages, the Scholastics.[45] Albertus Magnus quotes in his work entire chapters from "Moses the Egyptian's"[46] *Dux Neutrorum* (Guide of the Perplexed).[47] An even greater influence was exercised by the *Guide* on another great genius of medieval Scholasticism, Thomas Aquinas,[48] who employed Maimonides' arguments and logical ideas in his discussion of major philosophical and theological problems. Even in modern times the *Guide for the Perplexed* made a significant impression on the famous Leibniz, who declared enthusiastically that in the book "of the distinguished philosopher, mathematician, physician, and Bible commentator Rabbi Moses Maimon" he found more philosophical profundity than he could have imagined.[49]

The influence of the *Guide for the Perplexed* was also extensive in the Islamic world. Even in Maimonides' own lifetime the book had Moslem commentators,[50] and in the fourteenth century in Fez, as well as in other cultural centers and Moslem schools of advanced studies, his philosophic work was diligently studied.[51]

In Judaism itself Maimonides inaugurated an entirely new era. To

44. See M. Steinschneider, *Ha-Mazkir*, VI, 31, and *Hebräischen Übersetzungen*, p. 433. The Latin translation was made not from the Arabic text but from Alḥarizi's Hebrew translation.
45. See J. Guttmann, *Die Scholastik*, pp. 85–120; *Der Einfluss der maimunischen Philosophie auf das christliche Abendland* (in the collection *Moses ben Maimon*, I, 135–230); D. Kaufmann, *Der Führer Maimunis in der Weltliteratur* (*Gesammelte Schriften*, II, 152–89).
46. Among the Scholastics, Maimonides was called Moses the Egyptian.
47. See J. Guttmann, in the collection *Moses ben Maimon*, I, 153–75; M. Joel, *Das Verhältnis Albert dem Grossen zu Moses Maimonides* (1876), and his *Etwas über den Einfluss der jüdischen Philosophie auf die christliche Scholastik*.
48. Concerning the influence of Maimonides on Thomas Aquinas, the French scholar Emil Saisset says, "*Maimonide est le précurseur de saint Thomas d'Aquin et le More-Neboukhin annonce et prepare la Summa Theologale*" (*Revue des Deux Mondes*, I [1886]); see also J. Guttmann, *Das Verhältnis Thomas von Aquina zum Judentum* (1891), p. 31.
49. In the collection *Moses ben Maimon*, I, 325–26.
50. See Steinschneider, *Hebräischen Übersetzungen*, pp. 361–62 and 415.
51. Joseph Ibn Kaspi, *Taam Zekenim*, p. 53.

the extraordinary impression that the great philosopher made on his own generation the inscription that an anonymous hand placed on his tombstone bears vivid testimony. It is almost unbelievable that a Jew should have written such words of deification: "A man and yet not a man; and if you were a man, your mother conceived you from angels on high; or God Himself, without man and woman, created you an angel in the terrestrial world."

The famous poet Jehudah Alḥarizi declared in the poem of praise that he sent to Maimonides in Egypt: "An angel of God are you, and you were formed in the image of God. And if you have our image, it was on your account that God said, 'Let us make man in our image and in our form.' " Another poet of that time likened Moses ben Maimon to the Biblical Moses, and asserted that Maimonides with his pen performed no lesser miracles than the son of Amram with his staff. "To whom can he be compared," cried a later poet, Jacob ben Ezra Gabbai, "for on earth there is none like him. Only in the heavens, among the divine seraphim, can one find a brother to him who might equal his worth."

In the lands of the East in many communities Maimonides' name was woven into the Kaddish prayer,[52] and special religious poems composed in his honor were recited.[53]

Maimonides' rationalist banner, with its proud device "the sovereignty of reason," later called forth a bitter struggle in certain strata of the Jewish people. But his works became for centuries the focal point at which the major streams in Jewish culture converged. His *Guide* was for centuries a sure and faithful "pointer of the way" for all who searched and struggled for freedom of thought. This profound work, with its soaring philosophic thought and its ceaseless quest for truth, was the awakener that summoned to new life and aroused from intellectual slumber not only such geniuses as Baruch Spinoza, Solomon Maimon, and Moses Mendelssohn, but also thousands of ordinary young men who, in Talmudic academies and houses of study, yearned for light and knowledge.

52. Naḥmanides refers to this in his well-known letter to the rabbis of France.
53. See S. D. Luzzatto in *Kerem Ḥemed*, IV, 32, and *Iggerot Shadal*, p. 421.

CHAPTER SEVEN

Abraham Ibn Ezra

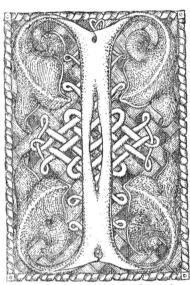

IN Jehudah Halevi medieval Hebrew poetry attained its zenith. The poet of Zion also had a vast influence on the development and enrichment of poetic forms. He himself indicates that verses and rhymes were born in him more swiftly than the flash of thought. In his poems we find a remarkable wealth of metrical forms and harmonic rhythms and sounds. Halevi, for example, very often employs the Arabic form *muwassaḥ* (in Hebrew it is called *ezor:* "band" or "girdle"), in which the structure and rhyme of the first verses are repeated in the poem after certain intervals. But the length of these intervals and their rhythmic structure are each time different and have new and unexpected effects. In the poem "Shelomotai Sei," aside from the general rhyme that unites all its verses, every double verse is also interwoven with two other rhymes of its own:

> *Shelomotai sei yonat reḥokim—leofer midberei edyo—revivim*
> *Legonev lev bemilov ha-ḥalakim—beshemen mor velo vedyo—*
> *ketuvim.*

A number of Halevi's poems consist of ten-line verses. The four closing lines have, in each of the verses, the same two rhymes; the first six lines, however, have their own separate rhymes.[1]

Halevi himself, in his *Kuzari,*[2] strongly deplores the fact that

---

1. For an extended discussion of Halevi's meter see H. Brody, *Studien zu den Dichtungen Jehudah Halevis,* 1895.
2. II, 70–78.

Arabic meter, which, in his opinion, is alien and disturbing to the
spirit and structure of the language of the Bible, has penetrated into
Hebrew poetry. But despite the fact that these Arabic forms are,
indeed, artificial and difficult, Halevi's poems have a remarkable
musical sound, and the heavy chains of the foreign meter cannot
(at least, not always) destroy the unique internal rhythm and harmonic delicacy of his verses. How graceful and musical, for example, is this little poem by Halevi:

> *Yom nod zehovi tzevi, orah u-vorah u-vi*
> *Moas ve-omar: ani sor me-al roshecha.*
> *Ve-omrah: mah beri, mah yesh beyodi meri*
> *Ki te'enaf bi? Ve-anah: meryecha reshecha.*[3]

Our poet also obtains splendid effects when he uses phonetically
like-sounding words that have different meanings, as, for example,
in the following love poem, where he playfully describes how
silken black curls frame the marble forehead and rosy cheeks of
the lovely one who is so frivolous that if she once takes pity on
you, she will, in exchange, betray you six times:

> *Lehi keritzpat esh beritzpat shesh*
> *Nirkam sevivov mor kerikmat shesh;*
> *Yosef belibi esh bekorvo li*
> *Ki yahamol paam veyivgod shesh.*[4]

In his famous Zion poem "Ha-Yuchlu Pegarim" Halevi expresses
his longing to see the blessed land of his fathers as soon as possible.
How beautifully the construction of this poem, with its two-
footed light lines, appearing as if fitted with wings, harmonizes
with the impetuousness of the poet's desire. The poet begs the
wind to spread its wings and swiftly bring the ship to the East.
And this petition trembles in, and hovers over, the unique meter
of the lines, in the harmonious sound of the tones and syllables:

> *Ali sefinah—vedirshi medinah*
> *Asher lashechinah—betochah hadarim.*
> *Vehushi veufech—veyad El tenifech*

3. Harkavy, *Diwan*, II, 74.
4. Brody, *Diwan*, II, 31. The same word *shesh* has in the first line the
meaning "marble," in the second line "silk," and in the fourth "six."

Vekishri chenafech—bechanfei shehorim.
Lenadim venaim—beruah kelaim
Velibot keruim—le-elef gezarim.

We have seen what angry contempt Solomon Ibn Gabirol had
for those talentless versifiers for whom poetry and art were a matter
of fashion and who saw in these, not the loveliest treasures that
exalt the soul, but colorful playthings and pastimes. In Jehudah
Halevi's era the number of such dabblers increased significantly,
for the "three great stars," as Heine called the three major Hebrew
poets of the Middle Ages, developed poetic forms and the technique
of poetry writing to such an extent that to compose verses was not
at all difficult even for dilettantes who lacked the smallest spark of
poetic talent. Halevi was also very scornful of these "rhyme-
makers." When his friends asked him in astonishment why he had
been silent for such a long time, he replied bitterly: "The fount
of poetry is corrupted and defiled; it awakens in me only disgust
and indignation. The lion can no longer walk in his path when little
foxes scrabble around in it."

But it was not only "little foxes" who walked in the "lion's path"
of poetry. Men of high culture and considerable literary talent also
often made use of poetic forms, despite the fact that they were not
true poets. To be sure, the flame of poetic feeling, the soaring of
poetic inspiration, is not discernible in their songs; nevertheless,
they make a strong impression with their wealth of ideas and with
the brilliance of sharply honed intellect which they reflect. It is
these virtues that many of the poems of Jehudah Halevi's younger
contemporary and close friend, Abraham ben Meir Ibn Ezra,[5]
possess.

Abraham Ibn Ezra (born in Toledo in 1092, died in Rome in
1167) is one of the most original and interesting personalities of
medieval Jewry. He was a man of encyclopedic knowledge who
was renowned as an outstanding mathematician, astronomer, Bible
commentator, philologist, and poet. His restless spirit did not allow
him to remain long in one place. He was a constant wanderer,
travelling through Asia and Africa and visiting numerous cities in
Italy, France, and England. And everywhere on his path he scattered the seeds of the rich Arabic culture. "I have been everywhere," Ibn Ezra says in his poem "Nedod Hesir Oni," "I have

5. In medieval Christian literature Abraham Ibn Ezra is known by the name
Abraham Judaeus or Abenare. The legend that Ibn Ezra was Jehudah
Halevi's son-in-law has no foundation. This legend is transmitted at
length, and in a naive, popular form in Yiddish also, in the *Maaseh-Buch*
and in *Kevod Hachamim.*

written books and revealed hidden secrets." Moving about constantly and living in poverty and want did not hinder Ibn Ezra in his ceaseless investigations. He wrote scores of books, the influence of which was long felt in various fields of knowledge.[6]

Nature endowed him with numerous gifts but omitted one. Ibn Ezra was a great scholar and an extraordinary stylist, but not a harmoniously integral person of solidly rooted character. He was full of contradictions and without measure and equilibrium—a clever skeptic who analyzed everything with his critical mind and, at the same time, lacked a firm standpoint; a fierce opponent of "heretics and deniers," and yet not seldom inclined to superstition; a brilliant, independent investigator, but also a devotee of astrologers, tricksters, and fortune tellers.[7]

It was Ibn Ezra who laid the foundations of critical Bible scholarship. His ideas in this realm later had a strong influence on Spinoza, who praises him as a "distinguished scholar and free thinker."[8] Ibn Ezra expressed epoch-making theories on the origin of the Pentateuchal text, as well as on the period when certain Psalms and the second part of the Book of Isaiah were written. But he was a very poor man, always dependent on patrons who supported him and kept him from perishing of hunger. Hence, he was afraid freely to utter his thoughts, which would have seemed highly heretical at that time, and became accustomed to expressing them in covert fashion, through allusions and hints.[9] "There is a secret here"; "and the wise will understand"; "and the wise will be silent" —these are his customary formulas. But Ibn Ezra phrased his conjectures so obscurely and in such disguised fashion that even the

6. One of the medieval writers testifies that Ibn Ezra composed over a hundred works (see *Kerem Ḥemed*, IV, 132). The list of Ibn Ezra's most important works and the dates when they were written is given by D. Rosin, *Die Religionsphilosophie Abraham Ibn Ezras*, in *MGWJ*, 1898, pp. 25–26.

7. For a list of Ibn Ezra's astrological works see D. Rosin, *MGWJ*, 1898, p. 250. On pp. 305–15 and 345–62 Ibn Ezra's astrological views are also given.

8. Spinoza, *Tractatus Theologico-Politicus*, Chapter 8.

9. For example, when Ibn Ezra explains the first verses of the Book of Deuteronomy he quotes several passages from the Pentateuch and indicates in an extremely veiled way that these passages show that the Pentateuch was edited considerably later than Moses: "And if you understand the secret of the twelve [the last twelve verses of the Book of Deuteronomy in which Moses' death is related]—'and Moses wrote' (Deut. 31:9); 'and the Canaanite was then in the land' (Gen. 12:6); 'in the mountain of the Lord it shall be seen' (Gen. 22:14); and 'behold, his bedstead was a bedstead of iron' (Deut. 3:11)—you will recognize the truth."

"wise" are frequently hard pressed to uncover the "secret."[10] An excellent popularizer who knows how to express the profoundest idea clearly and understandably, he often becomes deliberately obscure and baffling. Himself a free investigator, he often plays the pious zealot ready to give up his life for the least punctilio of the tradition, for every letter of the Torah.

Despite these inner contradictions, Ibn Ezra was a genuine promoter of enlightenment and culture, and his influence on the intellectual development of Jewry, especially of the Jews living in Christian Europe, was very considerable. He was one of the first Jewish scholars in Moslem Spain who utilized for scientific purposes not Arabic but Hebrew only. Of course, the fact that Ibn Ezra wrote his works in Christian lands (Italy, Provence, England), where Arabic was unknown, contributed much to this. Ibn Ezra set himself the task of familiarizing the culturally deprived Jewish communities of Italy and Provence, which did not read Arabic, with the scientific achievements of Spanish Jewry. His younger contemporary, the famous translator from Arabic, Jehudah Ibn Tibbon, emphasizes Ibn Ezra's important enlightenment role in relation to the Jewish community of southern France.[11] Much later, in the fourteenth century, the poet Jedaiah Ha-Penini, the author of *Behinat Olam*, speaks enthusiastically of Ibn Ezra's cultural work in Provence, where "he opened the eyes of all."[12]

To arouse among the Jews of Christian Europe an interest in and taste for scientific philology, Ibn Ezra translated Ḥayyuj's philological work into Hebrew and himself composed several books on Hebrew grammar: *Sefer Tzaḥot, Sefer Moznayim*,[13] and others. In his famous commentary on the Pentateuch,[14] on which he

10. In one place, his commentary to Daniel 1:4, Ibn Ezra himself indicates that there are scholars who do not openly express what is in their minds but do so only through allusions and in indirect ways.
11. In the introduction to his translation of Ibn Jannah's *Rikmah*, Ibn Tibbon writes that "the sage Rabbi Abraham ben Ezra came into their lands and aided them in this matter through short compositions containing pleasant and precious things."
12. In his *Ketav Ha-Hitnatzlut* Jedaiah Ha-Penini writes: "And our fathers have told us of the joy of the scholars of this land and its pious men and rabbis when he [Ibn Ezra] came to them and began to open their eyes in our regions."
13. In the introduction to this work the author gives a very valuable list of all of the Jewish grammarians who lived up to his time.
14. The text of Ibn Ezra's famous commentary is unfortunately very corrupt and erroneous in all editions. A critical scientific edition will be possible only when the text is compared with the old manuscripts. On textual emendations in Ibn Ezra's commentary, see S. J. Fuenn in *Gan Peraḥim*, I; W. Bacher in *Otzar Tov*, 1891, pp. 1–51.

worked until the last day of his life,[15] and in his commentaries on other Biblical books, investigation of the Biblical language takes first place. "Above all," he declares in the introduction to his commentary on the Pentateuch,

I shall be concerned with analyzing each word grammatically and only then proceed to the interpretation of the meaning. . . . I shall not dwell on the reasons and explanations by way of *derush* [homiletical interpretation] which the men of the tradition gave in their day, for these do not belong at all to the subject . . . and are useful only for young children in elementary schools. I shall also not make use of the emendations of the later scribes but take into consideration only the Targum [Aramaic translation], for its rendering is correct and made all the obscure passages clear and comprehensible.

Ibn Ezra also deemed it necessary to attack the older religious poets, mainly Eleazar Kallir, because they employed the Hebrew language barbarically, took no account of its structure and principles, and created strange and confusing terms whose meaning is difficult to obtain.[16]

A versatile scholar, Ibn Ezra wrote one book after another in various fields of knowledge—mathematics,[17] astronomy,[18] astrology, and religious philosophy—with extraordinary rapidity. To the last field mentioned belongs his work *Yesod Mora*, written in London in the year 1158 at the wish of his pupil Joseph ben Jacob. Ibn Ezra himself relates that he composed this book in a month's time, and the work, written in such haste, does in fact suffer much from this. Everything in it is in a state of confusion, and it is virtually impossible to obtain from the *Yesod Mora* any clear conception of

15. In Firkovich's manuscript collection there is an old parchment manuscript of Ibn Ezra's commentary on the Torah written in the city of Kaffa (modern Feodosia) in the year 1281 by a certain Solomon ben Jacob. On the last page of the manuscript there is a poem of Ibn Ezra's which indicates that he completed the commentary on the second day of Adar in the year 4927 (1167 c.e.). After the poem there is a note by the copyist that on the same day, the second of Adar 4927, Ibn Ezra died.

16. See his commentary to Ecclesiastes, Chapter 5.

17. *Yesod Ha-Mispar, Sefer Ha-Eḥad* (published by Pinsker and Goldhardt in 1867), and others.

18. *Sefer Ha-Ibbur, Sefer Ha-Luḥot, Keli Ha-Neḥoshet.* On discoveries made by Ibn Ezra in the field of astronomy, see M. Steinschneider, *Safrut Yisrael,* p. 280.

Ibn Ezra's philosophical and religious views. Much more interesting in this respect are his two short works written in rhymed prose, *Ḥai ben Mekitz*[19] and *Arugat Ha-Ḥochmah U-Pardes Ha-Mezimmah.*[20]

Ibn Ezra did not produce a philosophical system of his own but lavishly scattered in his works numerous profound and original ideas which were absorbed into Jewish religious philosophy[21] and found their further development only in later generations. In the conflict between the Aristotelians and the neo-Platonists, he did not take a firm stand. However, he was more inclined toward the neo-Platonist system, colored somewhat with Pythagorean notions. The latter were undoubtedly obtained under the influence of the *Sefer Yetzirah*, on which he wrote a commentary. The influence of Solomon Ibn Gabirol and his *Keter Malchut*[22] is also markedly discernible.

"As an exile languishing in captivity in a strange country longs for his homeland," says Ibn Ezra, "so man's spirit strives to the heavenly vaults."[23] He further declares: "It is because man is a reflection of the Creator of the world and feels Him constantly in himself that his drive toward the heights, toward the source of wisdom, is so ceaseless."[24] Ibn Ezra, however, frequently insists that "to know God, to understand His greatness, requires not only the mind but the heart and all the senses." This motif resounds in many of his religious poems. One begins:

Every form you see gives testimony: there is none beside Him. Every sound your ear hears sings His praise. Every odor you smell tells of His work, and everything you taste reveals the mystery of His greatness. Your hands are faithful witnesses to touch His great wonders, and your mind that thinks and reflects has its origin from Him.[25]

19. Patterned after a work bearing the same name by the Arabic philosopher Avicenna. Avicenna's work is available in a Hebrew translation published by David Kaufmann in *Kovetz Al Yad*, II (1886).
20. Printed in *Kerem Ḥemed*, IV, 1–5.
21. Naḥman Krochmal attempted to present Ibn Ezra's philosophical ideas in systematic form in "Ḥochmat Ha-Misken" in his *Moreh Nevuchei Ha-Zeman.*
22. For a discussion of Ibn Gabirol's influence on Ibn Ezra see D. Rosin, *MGWJ*, 1898, p. 29. In his commentary on the Torah Ibn Ezra also incidentally quotes Ibn Gabirol as a Bible exegete in several places.
23. Introduction to his commentary on Ecclesiastes.
24. *Kerem Ḥemed*, IV, 6.
25. *Diwan*, p. 44. Cf. Ibn Ezra's hymn "Azkir Ketzat Ha-Noraot," which is found in the *Maḥzor Montpellier;* reprinted in *Literaturblatt des Orients*, 1845, p. 282.

Ibn Ezra's religious poems[26] lack the flight of true poetry, the quality of genuine inspiration. They are not permeated with the flame of inner enthusiasm but shine with the calm light of noble, proud intellect and glisten with the radiance of philosophical reflection. Ibn Ezra, however, did not write religious poems only. Like his famous predecessors, the "three great stars," he also lamented the dismal fate of his exiled people in numerous elegies. "Israel lives benighted and wasted in exile and in poverty. Under Ishmael's hand we became a prey and a scorn; fleeing thence to Edom, we could not live there either."[27] In touching verses Ibn Ezra mourns the destruction of many Jewish communities in the fourth decade of the twelfth century when the fanatical Almohades established their rule in Spain. "God's punishment has come over you, O Spain," the poet laments, "and I cannot bewail the magnitude of your disaster."[28]

"In the books of the prophets," says Ibn Ezra in one of his national poems,

I sought and searched. Isaiah's words resounded in my ear, those words that announce the tidings of speedy salvation. But one generation follows another, and God's chosen people still languish in chains. A thousand years have already passed, and the distress grows ever greater! In their sufferings the people cry: "Wilt Thou still help us? Redeem us, then, as swiftly as possible! Hast Thou forgotten us? Then let us know it."

"Come now, Daniel, you delightful one," the poet further demands, "before your great and deep wisdom all mysteries are revealed, and what is concealed from others lies open before you. With my broken heart I ask you to declare whether 'the end' will come and your prophecy be fulfilled." The answer is stern and hard: "Do not ask! That which is deeply veiled may not be revealed."[29]

At times notes of reproof and admonition are also heard in Ibn Ezra's poems. "How foolish," he complains, "is the people of

26. To Ibn Ezra's religious poetry belongs also a unique group of didactic poems in the form of debates—a debate between Summer and Winter, between the Beasts and Man, between Bread and Wine, Festival and Sabbath, etc. The conclusion of all of these debates is that everything was created to praise God and His great works.
27. *Diwan*, p. 63. Ibn Ezra's *Diwan* was discovered only in modern times and published in 1886 by J. Egers. Many of Ibn Ezra's poems were also published by D. Rosin in the *Jahresberichten* of the Jewish Theological Seminary of Breslau (1884–95). In 1894–95 a collection of poems by Ibn Ezra under the editorship of David Kahana appeared. (In this collection several pieces that were not written by Ibn Ezra are printed.)
28. Egers, *Diwan*, pp. 68–69; D. Kahana, *op. cit.*, pp. 140–43.
29. Egers, *Diwan*, p. 99.

poverty and oppression; we live in double exile and yet constantly carry on controversies." In many poems Ibn Ezra laments his own bitter fate. Especially moving are two elegies in which he mourns the premature death of his only son, Isaac.[30] Saturated with sorrow are the verses the wanderer composed in his old age far from home: "There is a people which in days of sadness clothes itself in white rather than in black. I imitate this people in my old age; in memory of my youthful, long gone years I have decked my cheeks with white." "Heavier than lead are my troubles," the poet laments,

yet they have swum through entire seas and not drowned. Rivers of tears have my eyes shed, yet the flame that has devoured my heart is not extinguished. My powers are vanished and my soul is like ashes. Even those who have been sorely tried and much afflicted bear witness: generations have not seen sufferings like mine.[31]

In this homeless wanderer, however, glimmered a humorous spark which all the woes he experienced could not extinguish. Ibn Ezra wrote not only many wine and wedding songs, witty epigrams, and chess poems[32] but also humorous songs in which he mocks himself, the eternal ne'er-do-well. To be sure, under the laughter hidden tears are at times discernible. Sarcastically he relates how he must knock at the door of rich and arrogant patrons. "If I come early in the morning, the great man has gone out. If I come in the evening, he has just gone to bed. Now he is in his coach, now asleep. Woe to the poor man born without luck."[33] He has a cloak full of holes, but this is really a great advantage: "one can sift through it," says the poet, "either wheat or barley. . . . If one spreads it out at night like a tent, the stars appear through the holes and shine in the darkness."

In another poem he describes how luckless he has been all his life. "I have always tried to be a success, but nothing came of it. I was born under an unlucky star. If I were to deal in shrouds, no one would ever die. If my merchandise were candles, the sun would surely never set until I died."

30. The poet Alḥarizi relates in his *Taḥkemoni* that Ibn Ezra's talented son converted to Islam. This information, however, appears to be false. A manuscript (located in Aleppo) has been discovered with several poems by Isaac Ibn Ezra. In one of these, which begins with the line "Bi hazeman ḥitzei nedod shalaḥ," the poet complains that someone, out of enmity, slandered him with the false rumor that he had denied the faith of his fathers (H. Brody, *Shaar Ha-Shir*, pp. 159–60).

31. *Diwan*, p. 12.

32. Ibn Ezra was a skillful chess player. In D. Kahana's edition three chess poems are printed (pp. 152–60). There is some doubt, however, whether all three were actually written by Ibn Ezra.

33. Kahana, *op. cit.*, p. 10.

Ibn Ezra's sufferings did not, however, sadden his soul, and when his long life journey was drawing to a close he gratefully sang a paean on his death bed to the eternal source of life:

Joyfully my soul rises to its redeemer and protector. He has granted me happiness far greater than I deserve. In His great mercy He has revealed to me His marvelous ways. He has granted me long life to still my thirst for knowledge. Though my body and my flesh be destroyed, God is my help and my protector.

Abraham Ibn Ezra enriched medieval poetry with new elements. He introduced into it the humoresque, the light satire and lampoon. Typical is his poem about the flies that pester his life. His lampoons attacking misers, dice players, and communities which did not welcome him, the wandering poet, with sufficient cordiality are full of gall. His characterization of peoples according to the songs they sing is very witty: "The Arabs always sing about love and passion. Rome's songs celebrate the battlefield and vengeance. Full of profound thought and rich in knowledge are the songs of Greece. The peoples of India compose riddles and fables. And the Jews sing songs of praise and glory to God Almighty."

Ibn Ezra continued his literary activity to the final moments of his life. His last work, *Safah Berurah* (on Hebrew grammar), remained unfinished. With proud self-consciousness he declares in the introduction to this work: "Abraham, the son of Meir, will not be forgotten in future generations, and every understanding heart that thirsts after knowledge will remember his work." This hope was wondrously fulfilled. His free thought, and the garment of mystery and allusion with which he clothed his ideas, attracted to themselves like a magnet acute minds of later centuries. On his commentaries, especially his commentary on the Pentateuch, scores of new commentaries were written.[34] And for many centuries, until modern times, his name together with Maimonides' was inscribed "in all understanding hearts that thirst for knowledge."

But it was not only Ibn Ezra the free thinker and clever investigator, but also Ibn Ezra the mystic, astrologer, and devotee of diviners and soothsayers, who obtained in later generations many ardent followers. Among the mystics of the Kabbalah, in the eyes of those "wise in mysteries," this remarkable figure of Toledo was also a great authority, a man endowed with the holy spirit.

34. The well-known seventeenth-century scholar Joseph Solomon Delmedigo relates that he saw in Constantinople twenty-four commentaries on Ibn Ezra's commentary (*Melo Chofnajim*, p. 20).

CHAPTER EIGHT

The Satirical Romance in
Hebrew Literature

HE new motifs that Abraham Ibn Ezra introduced into Hebrew poetry soon found a brilliant representative in the person of the gifted and witty poet Jehudah ben Solomon Alḥarizi. The time and place of Alḥarizi's birth have not been established. It is merely conjectured that he was born around the year 1165 in the vicinity of Barcelona in Spain. He received a well-rounded education, and from his youth on throughout his days led the life of a wanderer. He visited southern France quite frequently, lived in Marseilles, Lunel, and other cities of Provence where, under the influence of Ibn Ezra's activity, interest in the Judeo-Arabic culture of neighboring Spain was strong. Interest in Maimonides' work became especially pronounced at that time in Provence, and the communities of Marseilles and Lunel corresponded with the great philosopher. Equipped with a thorough knowledge of Arabic and an outstanding stylist, Alḥarizi was much in demand by the communities of Provence as a translator who could familiarize them with the wealth of Judeo-Arabic scientific literature. The community of Marseilles commissioned him to write a Hebrew translation of Maimonides' Arabic commentary on the Mishnah, and in Lunel,[1] at the request of Jonathan ben David, a zealous disciple of Maimonides, Alḥarizi translated his *Guide for the Perplexed*.[2] In 1205 Alḥarizi returned to Spain, but not for long. Soon he undertook a long journey. He travelled in Egypt, Palestine, and Syria, and spent time in Baghdad, Alexandria, and Damascus where, it appears, he made the acquaintance of the major Karaite poet of the Middle Ages, Moses Darai, who also led a wanderer's life.

Ibn Ezra, as we have noted, was a roaming scholar. Jehudah Alḥarizi is the typical itinerant poet who earned a livelihood from his clever songs and epigrams. This source of livelihood was not, however, an especially secure one, and in the course of his wanderings the poet suffered greatly and lived in dire poverty. Evidence of this is provided in his well-known poem written in Ibn Ezra's style: "Were my tears to flow according to the measure of my sufferings, no dry place for a man to place his foot would be found in the whole world; yet the hope still lives in me that not only after the flood in Noah's time but for my tears, also, the rainbow will appear."

Alḥarizi was supported through aid given by wealthy patrons. But in the lands of the East, in the relatively undeveloped culture prevailing there, Jewish patrons were not greatly interested in poetry, especially in secular poetry. Regretfully Alḥarizi notes that the Golden Age of Hebrew poetry, when in the blessed land of the West, in cultured Spain, highly educated and sensitive connoisseurs of poetry and art lived, is now past. "For the fathers of song," the poet suggests,

for Solomon, Moses, and Jehudah,[3] their sun shone in the land of the West. In their generation they found many generous men who richly rewarded the pearls of their songs with fine gold. But I have come too late. There are no longer any patrons with charitable hearts; their sun has long since set. These poets lived on the banks of blessed rivers, but I must languish in the wilderness.[4]

In his old age Alḥarizi returned to his homeland and died there around 1225.

The major part of Alḥarizi's creative work is closely bound up with the name of the famous Arabic poet Abu Mohammed al-

1. In medieval Hebrew literature the city of Lunel bears the name Jericho.
2. The Latin translation of Maimonides' *Guide for the Perplexed* was made from Alḥarizi's Hebrew translation. On the virtues and defects of Alḥarizi's translation, see D. Kaufmann, *Gesammelte Schriften*, II, 163–66.
3. Solomon Ibn Gabirol, Moses Ibn Ezra, and Jehudah Halevi.
4. *Taḥkemoni*, p. 454 (the Warsaw edition).

Ḥariri of Basra (1054–1122), who raised to the peak of perfection the unique Arabic form of poetry known as the *makama*. The rise of this form is associated with the fact that, among the Arabs, the ripest fruit in the realm of poetry, namely drama, is lacking. Identical causes brought it about that among both the Arabs and the Jews the art of the theater, which flourished among the Greeks in antiquity as well as in medieval Christian Europe, did not develop.[5] As among the Greeks, so among the Christian peoples theatrical presentations were closely connected with the religious cult. Among the Greeks they were associated with the festival honoring the god Dionysus; in medieval Europe the cradle of theatrical art stood in the church, and the clergy fathered it. The theatrical presentations of the Middle Ages (the mysteries and miracle plays) developed out of the Catholic cult. The Christian populace, which at that time was still at a rather low level of culture and had not yet entirely forgotten its former idol worship, had to be familiarized by the clergy with the elements of the faith and the story of Jesus' life in a unique way. The text of the gospel was not read or told, but presented in images and pageantry. Not through the word, through abstract concepts and ideas, was the simple, unlettered multitude taught the substance of the Christian faith, but through clear, concrete forms that could be seen with the eyes and touched with the hands.

Quite different were conditions among the Arabs. Nomadic Bedouins, free children of the trackless deserts, they were not rooted in a specific plot of ground with its *baal*, its lord and master, whom one must appease with sacrifices and serve with the various ceremonies of an established cult. Theirs was the God of the vast distances, of the stormy sands, the God of the hot, burning winds that move over the boundless wastes, the unique and incomprehensible God who has no image or form and hovers over everything like the burning breath of the endless desert. The overheated Oriental imagination of these Bedouins did not require concrete forms and images; the word itself—not to be grasped, flowing, moving, trembling with life—caught their rich imagination with tremendous power and was at once embodied in living images, in colorful theatrical "representations."

In this way there arose among the Arabs a unique type of poetry which no European people possesses, namely, the *makama*. *Makama* literally means a marketplace where people come together to while away the time, listen to the news, and discuss communal affairs. The

5. We discuss this at greater length in our work *Ocherki Po Istorii Yevreyskovo Teatpa.*

·⸱[*165*]⸱·

same word is used to designate a type of poetry occupying an intermediate place between epic and drama, a kind of novel-drama in which two persons who carry on a dialogue appear: the chief person or hero, who relates his deeds, exploits, and pranks, and the narrator, a kind of oracular voice asking questions and making observations whereby the whole recital, as well as the behavior of the chief person, becomes clearer and livelier.

Every episode in the hero's colorful life is portrayed in a separate *makama*. The *makama* style is an altogether unique one. The dialogue is carried on in rhymed prose. The sentences are short, full of life and movement, rich in rhythmic sounds. Into the body of the recital are woven smaller and larger poems with rhymed verses in which the essence of the narrative is briefly summarized.[6]

Ḥariri's clever *makama*s with their chief person, Ibn Said, were extremely popular not only among the Arabs but also among the Jews in Spain. As early as the middle of the twelfth century a Jewish poet named Solomon Tzakbel composed an interesting *makama* after Ḥariri's model. Until modern times the only known source mentioning the poet Tzakbel was Alḥarizi, who recounts in the third *makama* of his *Taḥkemoni* that this poet composed a beautiful *makama* which begins with the words *Neum Asher ben Yehudah*, "the speech of Asher ben Jehudah." The *makama* itself was believed to have been lost, but many years ago J. H. Schorr discovered in an old manuscript a *makama*, under the heading *Taḥkemoni*, which begins with these words: "the speech of Asher ben Jehudah." Schorr promptly published it, indicating that it is undoubtedly Tzakbel's lost *makama*.[7] However, the author of these lines happened to find in an old manuscript of Harkavy's collection the same *makama*, but without the heading *Taḥkemoni*, in which it is explicitly stated that its author is Abu Job ben Sahal.[8]

6. For a fuller discussion see Kämpf, *Nichtandalusische Poesie andalusischer Dichter*, I, xvi–xvii.

7. *He-Ḥalutz*, III, 154–58. Kämpf (*Nichtandalusische Poesie*, pp. 195–96) at that time expressed his doubts whether this *makama* is actually the same one that Alḥarizi mentions. Steinschneider (*Hebräischen Übersetzungen*, p. 851) noted that in the *makama* a couple of verses of Jehudah Halevi's are quoted, and from this drew the conclusion that its author lived not earlier than the middle of the twelfth century. H. Brody went even further (*ZHB*, 1900, pp. 56–58) and wished to show that the *makama* was composed *after* Alḥarizi's *Taḥkemoni*. This theory, however, is very ill-grounded, for when one compares the *makama* "Neum Asher" with the twentieth *makama* in the *Taḥkemoni* it is much easier to believe that Alḥarizi here imitated another's original and did not himself serve as a model.

8. Only now does Alḥarizi's identification of the author of the *makama* "Neum Asher ben Yehudah" remain quite inexplicable. Either one must believe that Solomon Tzakbel wrote a different *makama* which begins

In any case, this *makama* is very interesting in form. It is distinguished from Alḥarizi's *makama*s by the fact that in it the second person is lacking. The narration is conducted in the name of the chief person, Asher ben Jehudah. The entire *makama* bears a clearly Oriental character. The hero relates how he spent the years of his youth in travelling and wandering about, eagerly pursuing new impressions and experiences.[9] When he returned home, his comrades welcomed him joyfully and spent several successive days with him in the fields in drinking bouts. The young hero, quite tipsy, walks with unsteady steps by a palace in which there is a harem. From it the song of a young woman is heard. Enchanted, our hero remains standing on the spot. The woman, however, does not appear, but suddenly at his feet falls a beautiful apple with a declaration of love in lovely and delicate verses. The hero proceeds with the apple in his hands, but he cannot forget the sweet voice of the woman; it still sounds in his ears and calls to him imploringly. The voice draws him back to the place where he picked up the apple, and there he sings a passionate song of love to the unknown beauty. But he receives no reply. This only spurs our hero on. His declarations of love become ever stormier, but the beauty still refuses to show herself. Troubled, he falls asleep. Soon, however, a company of maidens awaken him with the announcement that they have come as messengers of his beloved, who is deeply moved by his love and sends him a love letter. Then the maidens conduct him into a magnificent palace. From all sides wondrously beautiful melodies are heard, sung by young maidservants to the accompaniment of the most delicate musical instruments. Richly dressed maidens come to meet our hero and welcome him in the friendliest way. Suddenly, a soldier with a naked sword in hand rushes in with great clamor. Angrily he falls on our hero, intending to kill him because he has entered the women's quarters, something strictly forbidden to outside persons. Our hero is in deathly fright, but at this point he becomes aware that the angry warrior is a young woman in disguise, his beloved's best friend. The beloved has sent her to entertain him. Soon the beloved herself appears, but with her face covered by a veil. The hero is eager to see the radiant countenance of the object of his desire; he tears off the veil—and before him is the laughing face of one of his guild friends who had been

---

with the same words, or possibly that in Alḥarizi's text a whole sentence has accidentally fallen out after the words "he also studied the art of poetry and received . . ." and the following sentence, in which the *makama* "Neum Asher ben Yehudah" is mentioned, refers to another author, not Solomon Tzakbel.

9. The beginning of the *makama* in our manuscript is more complete than in the text published in *He-Ḥalutz*.

with him in the vineyards! The whole affair was a prank on the part of his comrades. They wanted to play a joke on their friend, who had a great weakness for romantic happenings.

The first Jewish *makama* poet was soon forgotten, however. He was obscured by the more gifted and clever Jehudah Alḥarizi. Several patrons, who admired Alḥarizi's talent, proposed to him that he translate Hariri's famous *makama*s into Hebrew. Alḥarizi readily agreed. A definite affinity between his talent and that of the Arabic *makama* poet is clearly discernible. Alḥarizi succeeded splendidly in overcoming all the difficulties of the Arabic original. His translation, entitled *Maḥberot Itiel,*[10] is truly a masterpiece. The translator understood the art of pouring the wine of poetry from one vessel to another in such a way that it would not lose its aroma in the process. The ease with which Alḥarizi renders the unique beauty of the Arabic original in Hebrew dress is astonishing. It suffices to read through the two poems celebrating the power of golden ducats (third *makama*) or the controversy among the poets (twenty-third *makama*) to obtain a clear conception of Alḥarizi's peerless rhyming art.

In his later years Alḥarizi regretted that he had expended so much effort on introducing the Arabic poet into Hebrew literature. In the introduction to his *Taḥkemoni* he complains, "I was compelled to tend foreign vineyards, and my own I neglected." He felt, he relates, that he had the obligation to revive the Hebrew language, "in order that all nations should see that there is no other language comparable to it."

In sadness mixed with scorn he speaks of the cultured Jews of his day who are so enchanted by the beauty of the Arabic language but entirely neglect their own. "They always complain that our language is poor, undeveloped, and insufficiently supple. But they do not understand that it is not the language that is at fault but themselves, who do not know the language of the Bible and how to make use of its wealth and beauty."[11]

That Alḥarizi himself understood how to employ the wealth and

10. *Maḥberot Itiel* has not come down to us in its complete form. There is only one manuscript of this work (in the library of Oxford University) and this manuscript contains only twenty-six out of fifty *makama*s. The remaining twenty-four were lost. The manuscript was published in 1872 by the Englishman Thomas Chenery.
11. *Taḥkemoni*, 10. It is highly probable that these words are aimed especially at Jehudah Ibn Tibbon, who complained in the introduction to his translation of Baḥya Ibn Pakuda's *Ḥovot Ha-Levavot* of the poverty of the Hebrew language in comparison with Arabic. At that time Jehudah Ibn Tibbon was already dead, but Alḥarizi was very angry with his son Samuel Ibn Tibbon, who had sharply attacked his translation of Maimonides' *Guide for the Perplexed.*

beauty of Hebrew was clearly demonstrated not only in his translation of Ḥariri but also in a poetic work of his own which appeared shortly after *Maḥberot Itiel*. In this work, the poem *Anak*,
consisting of 257 verses,[12] it is difficult to recognize the gay and
clever translator of *makamas*. Alḥarizi wrote his poem in southern
France before his journey to Palestine. Like a pious pilgrim setting
out to "the holy places" to offer prayer and purify himself of sin,
our poet was in a penitent mood. The entire work bears a serious
and didactic character.

"Let not yourself be dazzled," the poet admonishes, "by the joys
of the world. They quickly vanish, like the silver clouds at dawn.
As the lightening across the heavens, so do beauty and desire pass."
"The world is the sea, and on his little ship man is borne, driven by
time; toward him hastens, with wide open mouth, Leviathan—
death."[13] "How foolish is man with his prideful glory. Today he
stands at the zenith of splendor and power; tomorrow he lies trodden in the dust. He before whom but yesterday the world trembled
is today carried on wooden boards. Today princes are radiant in
the loveliest palaces; tomorrow they rot in dark graves."[14] "Now
man is decked out in velvet and silk, and his couch is of ivory;
tomorrow he lies buried under thorns." "Forget not, O man, that
the earth is your mother and soon you must return to her bosom."
"Forget not righteousness and justice! Remember, every moment is
counted, and life is brief. Let not the daughters of foolish pride
lead your hearts astray; choose the modest children of justice and
lovingkindness."[15] "Forget not that only he who removes himself
from worldly desires will enjoy eternal life."[16]

The poet turns humbly to God and confesses his sins. His only
hope is passionate, ardent prayer. This purifies man and cleanses
his sins. "Raise, O understanding child, your prayer to God; both
day and night supplicate Him; then will you be accepted and find
grace in His sight." "How happy are those who sacrifice themselves
for the sake of God's name; sweeter than the song of harps does
their name and praise resound." "I too, my God, am prepared to
drink to the last drop the cup of suffering for Thy holy word."

Not in the *Anak*, however, was Alḥarizi's talent revealed in all
its splendor. Nor was it with this poem that he acquired renown and
inscribed his name in the history of Hebrew literature. We have

12. Written, like Moses Ibn Ezra's *Tarshish*, in the *Tajnis* form. The *Anak*
    was first printed by H. Brody in *Zikkaron Le-Avraham*, 1908, pp.
    309–56.
13. Verses 133 and 149.
14. Verses 30, 43, and 167.
15. Verse 174.
16. Verses 123 and 131.

noted that Alḥarizi considered himself, as Solomon Ibn Gabirol had in his day, the savior of the Hebrew language. He could not, the poet says of himself, look on and see "how Hagar gives birth to beautiful children while Sarah remains barren." He therefore decided to become the champion of the language of the Bible, to show that one could write in it with the same facility as in Arabic on any theme whatever, not merely on divine matters, on sacred and exalted subjects, but also on profane and common ones, not only to give instruction, but also to joke, laugh, mock, and to entertain people. To this end he composed (in the period from 1214 to 1218) his famous collection of fifty *makama*s, entitled *Taḥkemoni*, after the pattern of Ḥariri's *makama*s.

This work, whose purpose, according to the author's own statement, was "to amuse and entertain tired people," justly occupies an honored place in the history of Hebrew literature. In the *Taḥkemoni* the Hebrew muse abandons the upper worlds, the heavenly realms, and descends with a mischievous smile on her lips into the noisy regions of ordinary life. Hebrew ceases to be the instrument only of exalted ideas and sentiments, of fervent praises and prayers, and becomes the instrument of profane, everyday subjects as well. The "holy" language of Sabbath and festival is transformed into a simple "weekday" language. The poet lets both the hero of his romance, Ḥeber the Kenite, and the friend who relates Ḥeber's deeds and exploits, Heman the Ezrahite, wander from place to place. They are everywhere—in modestly hidden sanctuaries, in noisy marketplaces, in every street and back alley. They encounter all kinds of people and creatures. And everything is in rapid motion; as in a kaleidoscope, everything reveals itself swiftly before the reader's eye in the most vivid colors and the most unexpected groupings.

Because of this the style of the *Taḥkemoni* is also extremely varied. Now the poet is solemn; he gives ethical instruction, preaches about morality (in the second *makama*), composes prayers and praises for the glory of the Creator (in the fifteenth *makama*). On the ruins of Jerusalem he laments the fate of Zion (*Makama* 28 and the song "Shalom Le-Ir Shalem" in the last *makama*). At the graves of the prophet Ezekiel and Ezra the Scribe he recites elegies (*Makama*s 35 and 50). He reports a religious debate between the pious "believer" and the "heretic" (*Makama* 17). He celebrates in enthusiastic songs the great Hebrew poets of Spain (*Makama*s 3 and 18). Then suddenly the serious poet vanishes, and in his place appears the waggish prankster and maker of jokes. Laughingly he tells a comical story about a farmer and a rooster (*Makama* 10), about the deeds of a charlatan doctor (*Makama* 30), about a foolishly arrogant merchant (*Makama* 34), about the bizarre behavior of a fool in love (*Makama* 48), and about the pranks of seven beauties (*Makama* 20). Alḥarizi is lavish with clever riddles and silly questions (*Makama*s 36 and 44), with lusty anecdotes (*Makama* 35), with epigrams and caustic sayings (*Makama*s 37 and 48). An extraordinary dialectician, he loves to describe long, heated debates in which each party attempts to demonstrate that there is none greater than he in the world: Day wrangles with Night (*Makama* 39), Man with Woman (*Makama* 40), Land with Sea (*Makama* 43), Generosity with Miserliness (*Makama* 42), the Sword with the Pen (*Makama* 40).

A child of the blessed Southland, the poet is in love with nature, beauty, and the joy of life. He celebrates the splendor of the Spanish fields, the beauty of the fragrant trees under whose shade the youths disport themselves in song and dance (*Makama* 49). Enthusiastically he describes how greatly infatuated he is with the charming daughters of Eve and with the false, intoxicating daughters of the vine:

I have entrusted myself to the daughter of the vine and she, like a serpent, has shown her falseness. I have declared my love to her, and she repays me with treachery and deceit. My mind, my soul has she hidden with herself. I warmed her with love under my heart, and she leaps up and beats my head.[17]

Not long, however, does the poet complain about the treacherous daughter of the vine:

Beloved friend, in the shade of the fragrant fields, under the wreaths of laurel and roses, let us drink and be merry. No one can resist the magic of the daughter of the vine, and the older she grows in years the younger and more impudent becomes the laughter to which she gives birth. God reckons a thousand years but a day, and a year but a moment; how I should love to live through a whole year of His and uninterruptedly drink the intoxicating cup.[18]

Characteristic of our poet is the fact that in the debate among the soul, the body, the mind, and the evil inclination (*yetzer ha-ra*), the last turns to the soul and says, "Rejoice before you must leave your habitation! Enjoy the cup of life before you must depart from the world. Over all creatures has God poured out His grace and blessing. Quickly take your portion, too."[19]

Alḥarizi's most original feature is his humor. The genre that

17. *Taḥkemoni*, pp. 401–2.
18. *Ibid.*, p. 427.
19. *Ibid.*, p. 142.

Abraham Ibn Ezra sought to introduce into Hebrew literature attained, in Alḥarizi, a high degree of perfection. His witty poems about the flea and the ant (*Makama* 4) and about the ugly woman (*Makama* 6) are genuine works of art in this realm.[20] Alḥarizi is infatuated with the comical; he is a master of clever wordplay and a bubbling spring of laughter. Not infrequently, however, his laughter becomes acid and caustic, and the puns are transformed into arrow-sharp lampoons and bitter epigrams.[21] Especially rich in these is the last, the fiftieth *makama*. The poet's satire attacks the hypocritically pious, the "painted vultures,"[22] the morally depraved, the spiritually empty,[23] and, more than all others, the tight-fisted. All who looked contemptuously on the wandering poet and refused to aid him in time of need he exposed to shame with his biting lampoons.[24] Especially severely and mercilessly does he take revenge on one miser, a doctor of Damascus. The lampoon in which the unlucky physician is so ruthlessly judged ends with the following lines:

Long did miserliness wander over the earth until she found her sweet rest in his heart. Were the Red Sea touched by his heart, its waters would at once dry up; the richest wells would be congealed into stone. Were blessed Mount Hermon touched by his foot, it would become more desolate than the accursed peaks of Gilboa. His tread burns up all the grasses and growing things, his breath kills everything that sprouts and lives.[25]

Alḥarizi, the wandering singer, the joker and master of cheerful stories and anecdotes, speaks with reverence and enthusiasm of the exalted role and significance of the gifted poet. Proudly he speaks also of himself, of the great power with which the Muse endowed him. "Through my praise," the poet declares, "the lowly are exalted; my word shatters the powerful and proud."[26] "When my mighty song sounds, it makes the whole generation tremble."[27] As Heine declared in his day that against the poet's strict judgment, no God, no redeemer, can be of any avail,[28] so the medieval singer

20. These poems have been translated into several European languages. Kämpf translated a considerable part of the *Taḥkemoni* into German.
21. See, for example, the 46th *makama*.
22. *Taḥkemoni*, p. 412.
23. *Ibid.*, p. 429.
24. *Ibid.*, pp. 396, 397, 398, 399, 400, 401, 406, 453, and 456.
25. *Ibid.*, p. 360.
26. *Ibid.*, p. 236.
27. *Ibid.*, p. 424.
28. See the last verses of Heine's poem "Deutschland."

Alḥarizi was certain that with his poems he made men immortal. One of his *makama*s ends with these words: "Their names I brought into my book; my iron pen has inscribed them for eternity, that later generations might know their deeds which I have written down."[29]

An intellectual aristocrat, our poet proudly declares: "Let your song be heard only by wise and understanding people, not by fools —they will spatter it with mockery. Spread not your precious pearls before dogs—they will trample it with their feet."[30]

In Alḥarizi's *makama*s poets frequently appear who, in the medieval style, conduct competitions with songs and poems. Each tries to overcome the others and show that he is the supreme master of the poetic art. One of these declares, "The source of my songs is hidden in my heart . . . the hidden treasures of words and the ice-cold spears of thought I forge together in the flame of my soul."[31]

Alḥarizi himself, however, cannot say this of all of his poems. One finds in his work numerous verses and poems that were not "forged in the flame of his soul" and which were given birth not by "the source hidden in the heart" but simply by the desire to amuse others, to demonstrate skill in versifying, to dazzle the reader with clever playfulness. Among these artificial pieces are the verses in which every line is constructed of three different languages—Hebrew, Aramaic, and Arabic (*Makama* 11), or those that are set up according to the order of the alphabet (*Makama* 33), etc.

As a poet, Alḥarizi doubtless cannot be compared to the "three great stars" of the earlier period. He himself frequently insisted that he was merely an epigone who appeared at the time when the sun of Hebrew poetry was already inclining toward its setting. Nevertheless, his significance is certainly no lesser than that of the great poets as far as creating and perfecting poetic forms and enriching the language are concerned. Under Alḥarizi's gifted pen the unique form of mosaic, the so-called *musiv* style which played such a large role in Hebrew literature, reached the peak of perfection.

In evaluating the historical role of the *musiv* style in Hebrew literature one must bear in mind that the ancient Greeks often employed quotations from Homer's work in order to obtain surprising effects and ingenious plays on words. In the same manner the Arabs employed the *musiv* style. They wove into their works entire verses of the Koran that really had no relationship to the subject,

29. *Taḥkemoni*, p. 369.
30. *Ibid.*, p. 449.
31. *Ibid.*, p. 162.

but by transposing or exchanging a word, at times merely by altering the stress of a word, they gave the sentence an entirely unexpected and, not infrequently, comical meaning.

As the Arabs made use of the Koran, so the Jews employed the Bible. It would, however, be erroneous to think that the Jews simply imitated the Arabs. Franz Delitzsch understood that in Hebrew literature the *musiv* style was not merely a clever plaything, as among the Arabs, but a major instrument of creation.[32] Philologists of modern times have expressed the obvious truth that language is not merely a kind of cipher of a pure sign-character, not simply a means of expressing thought. Rather, as the Italian critic Benedetto Croce noted, "only through the power of the word are man's feelings and impressions raised out of the dark realm of the human psyche to the bright domain of the clear, conscious spirit."[33]

"Our generation first made the discovery," writes the Russian scholar Potebnya,

that languages can be employed as signs that express thought only because they are themselves the instruments with the aid of which the primordial, the pre-linguistic, elements of thought are worked over and *newly created*. In this respect, therefore, languages may be considered the means that *create* [not merely express — I.Z.] thought. . . . Language may be compared to human vision: the least alteration in the structure of the eye produces altogether different images and sensations. . . . In similar fashion, every detail, every minute particularity in the structure of a language, creates, entirely without our consciousness or will, new groupings in the elements out of which thought is constructed.[34]

However, when we consider languages as separate, distinct systems of modes of thought, we must remember that the word is not always the faithful agent that reworks our feelings and sensations into the object of our knowledge and understanding. Speech is simply not capable of transmitting perfectly to another person our not thought itself but the image, the shadow of thought." Words are symbols and images with which a person wishes to affect another, to elicit in him certain thoughts and moods. But man never

32. Delitzsch, *Zur Geschichte der jüdischen Poesie*, p. 165: "The Jewish *musiv* is not a plaything. It is a national peculiarity of the stylist. A whole nation does not play; its style is the reflection of its life, the expression of its character."
33. Croce, *Aesthetic* (1920).
34. A. Potebnya, *Yazik I Narodnost* (*Vyestn. Yevropi*, IX [1895], 11–12).

succeeds in attaining this goal perfectly. The "new world" which man wishes to create, to use Potebnya's expression, "with the aid of the word" never satisfies him, never *can* satisfy him, for "how ineffective and powerless is the word!"

These "word sorrows," this incapacity of speech to transmit perfectly to another person a man's thoughts and feelings, increase tremendously when the speech is not a living one and when, in the same person, different systems of thought modes compete with each other, i.e., when different realms of the person's spiritual and intellectual life are associated with different languages. The Hebrew poets not only had to overcome the rigid bands of Arabic meter but also, together with all other true artists, to endure "word sorrows," dissatisfaction with the "dumbness" and colorlessness of the verbal image. The major difficulty, however, lay in the fact that the language in which the medieval Jewish poets wrote was not their mother tongue, not the language of the school and daily life. It was not in Hebrew that they saw their dreams; their mothers did not sing them to sleep in it in infancy. Yet, the Hebrew language for our medieval poets was by no means a dead language. It was still the language of the Bible, which continued to live in the consciousness of the people and remained always the basic foundation of the national culture and world outlook. Biblical images and expressions, Biblical laws and statutes, Biblical stories and narratives, were alive and dominated the consciousness of the people. Biblical characters and their deeds belonged not merely to the historical past; they were living, real persons in whose environment every Jew lived and whose air every Jew breathed from childhood on. Father Abraham and mother Rachel, the sons of Jacob and the daughters of Zelaphad, even Og the king of Bashan and Balak—all these well-known personalities were one's own. Their deeds and words were a part of the Jewish way of life; the Jewish schoolchild saw them even in his dreams.

Hence, the medieval Jewish poets very skillfully employed in their creative efforts the wealth of Biblical symbols, images, expression, legends, and proverbs that lived in the consciousness of the people. With a brief Biblical sentence or expression, with a mere allusion to a Biblical personality or story—in short, with the most economical means—the writer could often obtain the most brilliant effects, eliciting in the reader unforgettably clear images, colorful and sharp impressions. And economy of means, the secret of condensation and brevity, is the criterion of genuine art.

Jehudah Halevi, for example, desires to express his sorrow that his friend, the cultured and gifted poet Moses Ibn Ezra, is compelled to be a wanderer in a strange and barbaric land. This feeling he renders magnificently in beautiful Biblical symbols: "What has the dew of Hermon to do on Gilboa?" This setting of the dew of Mount Hermon, blessed by God, against Mount Gilboa, the mountain cursed by King David, on which the first Israelite king Saul, together with his son and warriors, perished so tragically, elicits in the reader raised on the Bible a striking image that remains inscribed in his memory. When the same poet wishes to give a picture of how he wept with bloody tears, he declares that the "waves of Dimon washed over him." The Jewish reader recalls quite well the Biblical sentence: "For the waters of Dimon shall be filled with blood" (Isaiah 15:9).

Solomon Ibn Gabirol complains of the "versifiers" who sully the pure goddess of song with their crude hands, and longs for a mighty figure to come and expel the band of talentless persons from the temple of poetry. This he expresses in a verse in which he prays that the new Phinehas ben Eleazar may come speedily. And the mention of this Biblical name is at once transformed in the mind of the Jewish reader into a clear, colorful image: this was the man who, with spear in hand, fought against those who wished to draw the newly liberated Israelites into the swamp of immorality and to forget, in the embraces of the daughters of Moab, the pillar of fire which pointed the way to the Promised Land. When the same poet complains of his friend Jekutiel that the latter has forgotten him, he calls his friend Avi-Zanoah. The reader versed in the Bible appreciates this apt play on words. Avi-Zanoah means not only "the father of forgetting"; the reader also recalls from the Bible that Judah's descendant Jekutiel had a son named Zanoah (I Chronicles 4:18). We could quote such examples by the hundreds. The more gifted the poet was, the more ingeniously did he employ the *musiv* style. Biblical phrases, names, and metaphors were transformed by his artistry into symbols, with whose aid he elicited clear images and concepts.[35]

35. But what in the true artist was a brilliant instrument of creation became a stumbling block for writers not gifted with the poetic spirit. The latter would pair Biblical verses and fragments mechanically, but were incapable of forging them together into a harmoniously complete entity. Instead of economy in material, the complete opposite was attained: a flood of words; tedious and burdensome rhetoric; in place of vivid colors and images, glittering but worthless fragments, unnecessary and extraneous dross that spoils and obscures the thought and content. All these negative sides of the *musiv* style appeared with special clarity only in the later period of decline and regression. The acute Joseph Solomon Delmedigo, who lived in the seventeenth century, gives a dreary picture of the corruption of style in his day in the introduction to his *Novlot Hochmah*.

The *musiv* style obtained new and unique forms in Alḥarizi. With no less ingenuity than the Arabic poet Ḥariri, who masterfully constructed imaginative portraits out of verses of the Koran, Alḥarizi employed in the rhymed prose of his *makamas* the treasures of the Bible. Exalted and inspired Biblical expressions obtain, in the cheerful poet, a double and, very often, highly humorous meaning. The clever similes, the frivolous leap from the noble and solemn to the simple and everyday, the mocking smile veiled in the classical garment sanctified by ancient tradition, cannot be rendered in any translation. Alḥarizi's *makamas* must be read in the original for one properly to appreciate his mastery in this genre.

In evaluating Alḥarizi's significance, one must consider another aspect of his literary activity. Alḥarizi was not only a poet but also a literary critic. In the third, eighteenth, and also partly in the forty-sixth *makama*, he provides an interesting historical-critical characterization of the Hebrew poetry of the Spanish-Arabic period up to his time. The generation in which he himself lives, Alḥarizi calls "the generation of epigones":

Since Solomon Ibn Gabirol left the world and Moses Ibn Ezra, Jehudah Halevi, and Abraham Ibn Ezra died, the well of poetry has dried up, inspiration has disappeared, and God's spirit no longer manifests itself. None of their successors can compare with them. We backward ones, like beggars, gather the crumbs and refuse that have fallen from their table. We hasten day and night over the ways trodden by them, but we cannot equal them.[36]

Alḥarizi also makes an interesting attempt to specify the basic principles of the art of poetry writing. The art consists, in his view, of seven principles. First of all, the poet must avoid words that are difficult to understand or do not sound beautiful, and hold strictly to the principles of meter and grammar. The poet ought also to place great emphasis on the theme and substance of the poem and, above everything else, polish each verse. He must also not be in haste to publish his poems. He should be as severe as possible toward his own creations and ruthlessly remove everything that is weak and unsuccessful. Out of fifty verses he should leave thirty; out of seventy, forty. "Then will his song be delicate and pure, like a beautiful bride."[37]

36. *Taḥkemoni*, p. 182.
37. *Ibid.*, pp. 183–84. Characteristic also is the passage in Alḥarizi's *Musarei Ha-Pilosofim* in which peculiarities of style are discussed. At the court of King Penisus four scholars came together—one from Greece, the second from India, the third from Rome, and the last from Persia. To the king's question, What is the essence of style?, the Greek answered:

Contemporaneously with Alḥarizi arose two other poets whose talent has a certain affinity to that of the author of the *Taḥkemoni*. They introduced into Hebrew literature the unique form of the so-called satirical romance, whose style is similar to that of the *makama*. With one of these two poets, Jehudah ben Isaac Shabbetai of Barcelona, Alḥarizi was personally acquainted and he praises him in his *Taḥkemoni*[38] as "master of the elegant style." The other was a poet known simply as Isaac.

Of Shabbetai's life virtually nothing is known. We know only, and this thanks to the poet himself,[39] the year of his birth and when his two poetic works were produced. One of the works, a didactic poem entitled *Milḥemet Ha-Hochmah Veha-Osher*, which Shabbetai dedicated to the patron Todros Ha-Levi, was written in the year 1214.[40] Its poetic value is very slight. The subject and content are clumsy and crude. There is also little originality in the moral of the work, namely, that wisdom and wealth ought to live together amicably because they cannot get along without one another.

Far more successful is Shabbetai's satirical romance *Minḥat Yehudah Sone Ha-Nashim*, which he completed in 1208 and dedicated to his patron and protector, the Jewish official Abraham Alfachar, who occupied an important post at the court of the Castilian king Alfonso VII. This work is written in rhymed prose interspersed with short poems, following the pattern of the *makama*. In the introduction, which has no relationship to the substance of the romance, the author relates in satirical fashion how in a certain country there grew up a "foolish, ignorant generation" which declared war on all the sciences and persecuted its wise men and scholars.

The romance itself relates how to a very wise and pious old man, Taḥkemoni, a divine figure appeared a number of times in a dream. This figure commanded him to tell the world that the source of all

---

The main thing in style is proportion and proper choice of expressions. The Persian said: The most important thing in style is the secret of measure, understanding when to abbreviate and when to expatiate. The Indian declared that good style demands above all clear expressions and poetically beautiful similes. The Roman said: The most precious thing in style is simplicity, and the worst is superfluous words.

38. Page 351.
39. In the introduction to *Minḥat Yehudah Sone Ha-Nashim*, according to the version which S. Z. Halberstam published (*Ginzei Nistarot*, III, 82–85), the author indicates that he completed this work in 1208, in the fortieth year of his life. Thus he was born in 1168. He died after 1225.
40. Printed for the first time in Constantinople, together with Shabbetai's second work, in 1543; reprinted in Frankfort in 1718, and also in 1884 at the end of the Warsaw edition of *Ben Ha-Melech Veha-Nazir*.

misfortunes and sorrows is woman. On his deathbed the old man begged his only son Zerah to avoid the company of women all his life:

Cursed is he who brings a woman into his house. Every trouble has a remedy, every misfortune a limit, but a married man is lost forever. No one can help him any more. . . . Remember then, my son, if you see a woman northward, quickly turn your face to the south. If you hear her voice in some gathering, leave the crowd as quickly as possible. If a woman takes hold of your garment, run away naked from her.

Zerah decided to fulfill the injunction of his father. With three of his faithful companions he set out for a strange but blessed land where myrtles and oleander trees always bloom. There Zerah successfully propagandized among the young men the idea that they should have nothing to do with women and flee from marriage as from a demon. A great stir was aroused among the female population of the land, and an assembly of women was convened. All came, old and young, beautiful and ugly. These took counsel together on how to remove the great trouble. One very clever old woman, Kozbi, devised a remedy. She undertook to capture Zerah's heart with the beauty of the loveliest maiden in the realm, Ayalah. And Zerah fell into the net the old witch set for him. In the declaration of love of Ayalah and Zerah the hot, passionate breath of the Southland is discernible. How Zerah's feeling of love grows ever stronger is artistically portrayed by the author. Forgotten by Zerah is his father's testament, and he begs Ayalah to marry him. The wedding is described in a humorous way—how the groom, intoxicated by love, pays no attention to the ambiguous text of the marriage contract and does not notice that, veiled under the canopy, a terribly ugly and malicious woman, Rizpah bat Ayah,[41] has been substituted for the beauteous Ayalah.

Only in the morning does Zerah, in deathly fright, learn how cruelly he has been deceived. And his wife, this affliction, tells him with satanic laughter that henceforth she is the mistress and he, miserable wretch, her servant. In a scene filled with crude but vivid colors Rizpah bat Ayah explains how she will make certain that her husband will be sated with troubles and sufferings all his days. The unfortunate Zerah begs help from his friends. Here the author himself intervenes. He comforts Zerah by telling him that he, the poet, is no more fortunate: "My fate is also yours. Through the marriage ceremony we have both made ourselves miserable. O

41. This Biblical name is here deliberately given. Its meaning is "the coal-black daughter of the hawk."

Zeraḥ, woe to both of us! Let us together weep and lament! Terrible is our common fate; both of us have been sold as bondmen to women!"

To help Zeraḥ out of his plight his friends decide to convene an assembly and propose that Zeraḥ divorce Rizpah bat Ayah. But many women also come to the assembly and insist that Zeraḥ remain with her all his life. It is then agreed that the king himself be consulted and his judgment accepted. All come to the king, and each side brings forward its arguments. Suddenly, the author himself intervenes and interrupts the romance in a completely unexpected way. The poet steps forth in his own person before the king with the following declaration: "I swear by God, who has exalted your throne and lifted your praise to the skies, that Taḥkemoni never lived, Zeraḥ never took Rizpah bat Ayah to wife, and all the other characters never existed. All were created by my dream. The poet's imagination gave birth to them."[42]

Two years after *Minḥat Yehudah Sone Ha-Nashim* appeared, an unknown young poet named Isaac decided it was necessary "to champion the honor of women" and to this end wrote in 1210, in opposition to the work of Shabbetai "the enemy of women," an apologetic romance entitled *Ezrat Nashim*.[43] "This work," declares the author, "will rejoice all persons in love who walk arm in arm in the fragrant fields under the shade of myrtle and lemon trees." The literary value of the work is very meager. The story is childishly naive, the technique clumsy, and the style diffuse and tedious. One point, however, is worth underscoring because it has a certain cultural-historical significance. *Ezrat Nashim* is dedicated to the same Jewish patron to whom Jehudah Shabbetai several years later dedicated his *Milḥemet Ha-Hochmah Veha-Osher*. It is generally difficult to find a medieval poetic work of secular content which does not contain, immediately after the title page, a poem of praise in honor of a Jewish "prince," who is endowed by the poem with all virtues and declared the savior of science and art. This is a very comprehensible phenomenon when one takes into

---

42. In 1225 Shabbetai wrote a "postscript" to his work in which he complains that someone has committed plagiarism and passed off several poems of *Minḥat Yehudah* as his own. Shabbetai also wrote a prose work, a historical chronicle. This work had a rather odd fate. The only manuscript copy fell into the hands of several inhabitants of Saragossa in the author's lifetime. For some reason, the work displeased them and they burned the manuscript. The deeply insulted author expressed his anger at these five residents of Saragossa in a caustic lampoon, *Divrei He-Alah Veha-Niddui* (published by I. Davidson in *Ha-Eshkol*, VI, 165–75).
43. Published by Halberstam in *Ginzei Nistarot*.

consideration the condition of the medieval book market and the circumstances under which literary works at that time found circulation. Before the invention of printing and the method of producing cheap paper out of rags, books were extremely expensive. Only a very wealthy man could permit himself such a luxury as purchasing a book.[44] Given such a severely limited circle of readers, a poet or scholar, if he himself was not wealthy, could devote himself to literary pursuits only if he was supported by a patron. The medieval Christian singers and poets—the troubadours, jongleurs, and minnesingers—derived their livelihood from declaiming and singing their songs in the palaces of the princes and nobles. The situation among the Jews was similar. When Solomon Ibn Gabirol, for example, praises the philanthropist Samuel Ha-Nagid, he emphasizes that it is thanks to the latter's kindness that his purse is filled with money.

Our Jewish "troubadour," the wandering poet Alḥarizi, as we know, derived a living from the fact that various Jewish officials and patrons supported him and paid him with gold coin for his clever verses and improvisations. Abraham Ibn Ezra also lived from such support, and most of his works were written at the commission of his patrons or pupils. In the later parts of our work we shall have occasion to speak at more length of the cultural role of Jewish patrons.[45] In his *Ezrat Nashim* the young "helper of women" addresses his songs:

Tell all the bright tidings: my work will rejoice all girlish hearts and the women will dance in a singing circle. . . . O my songs, hasten; fly to the gracious lord! Under his shelter seek help and support. Broad is his heart and generous. There you will find prepared the table and the chair and the gleaming candelabrum. Faithfully serve him like slaves; he will protect and aid you.

More important than Jehudah Shabbetai—not to speak of his opponent, the author of *Ezrat Nashim*—is the composer of another satirical romance, also a contemporary of Alḥarizi's, Joseph ben Meir Zabara of Barcelona. Zabara received a well-rounded education.[46] Besides rabbinic subjects, he studied various languages and sciences, especially medicine. Apparently the healing art was the

44. Of the scarcity of books in the Middle Ages we shall speak at greater length in Part Two of our work.
45. We shall also speak in Part Two about the institute of copyists of manuscripts and, along with this, about readers in that time.
46. One of his teachers was the well-known scholar Joseph Kimḥi (see *Otzar Neḥmad*, I, 105-6).

source of his livelihood.[47] His two little works, *Marot Ha-Sheten* and *Battei Ha-Nefesh*,[48] provide evidence of his extensive medical knowledge. The latter work has a special interest because in it the poet succeeded in overcoming certain technical difficulties and finding a definite term in Hebrew for each limb and organ of man's body, as well as describing their significance and function in flowing verses.

As may be conjectured from the introduction to Zabara's chief work, a good friend of his persuaded him to undertake a long journey with him. Apparently this journey gave him much grief, but he is also indebted to it for his major work, the satirical-didactic romance *Sefer Shaashuim*.[49] This book is also dedicated to a Jewish patron, a townsman of Zabara's, Sheshet ben Benveniste,[50] who occupied an important position with the king of Aragon. Alḥarizi praises him as "lord above all lords, whose name is celebrated in the east and in the west."

The *Sefer Shaashuim* consists of thirteen *makamas*. In these, two major persons figure, the author himself and his companion, the satan or demon Enan ben Arnan. The author wanders about with his frightful comrade, the disguised demon, from land to land, and the reader is informed about everything that happened to them on the way. But it is not the story itself that is most important in the *Sefer Shaashuim*. Thanks to its unique structure, Zabara's work occupies an honored place in the history of the development of poetic forms in Hebrew literature. We have seen in Shabbetai's *Minḥat Yehudah Sone Ha-Nashim* the surprising trick that is played by the author: in the middle of the narrative the poet himself suddenly intervenes, and he appears again at the end and all at once interrupts the story. The author of the *Sefer Shaashuim* follows a different way. He weaves the confused texture of his romance according to the pattern so admired in the Oriental countries, especially among the Arabs, in which a tangle of various little stories is surrounded by one major story. The unifying factor in Zabara's work is the meeting of the author with the demon and the description of what occurred to them. Only then does the author begin to spin his imaginative web of tales, parables, and witticisms.

47. In the introduction to his *Sefer Shaashuim* Zabara writes about his medical practice.
48. Published by Israel Davidson in 1914.
49. First printed in Constantinople in 1577; reprinted in 1886. We have used the critical edition of Davidson (1914). Besides the works mentioned, Zabara also wrote some liturgical poems (see H. Brody, *Shaar Ha-Shir*, pp. 170–88).
50. We shall have occasion to speak further of Sheshet ben Benveniste in Part Two.

All these follow each other like links of a chain. This colorful folkloristic material was gathered by the author from the most varied sources—ancient Hebrew, Greek, Arabic, and Indian. Especially interesting in this respect are *Makama*s two, three, five, six and twelve.

The second *makama* is a story about a clever fox and a deceived leopard. In it numerous fables and anecdotes about the mendaciousness of the fox and the silliness and wickedness of women follow one another. The tale of the frivolous widow given here became especially popular in later Jewish as well as European literature.[51] Somewhere in a distant land, this tale relates, it was the custom that the body of a hanged criminal could not be removed from the gallows for nine days. A watch was posted during this period to guard the body, so that the relatives and friends of the hanged man would not steal it from the gallows at night. One night a guard who was watching a gallows heard a great lamentation not far away. He walked toward it and saw a young woman lying on a fresh grave and weeping bitterly. This was a widow, lamenting her beloved husband. The same thing happened the next night. The guard began to console the widow, and within an hour she was making all kinds of coquetries. As they came a little later arm in arm to the gallows, the guard saw that the body of the hanged man had disappeared. He decided that he must immediately flee, for otherwise he would be severely punished for his negligence. The woman calmed him and proposed that he exhume her husband from his grave and hang him on the gallows instead of the condemned man. The guard refused; he could not take such a grievous sin upon himself. The widow then herself exhumed her husband. When the guard saw the body, he realized that it would not do because the condemned man was hairless with a large bald pate, while the exhumed man had a great deal of hair. "That doesn't matter," the widow calmly said, and plucked out from her dead husband's body all the hairs of his head, one by one. The corpse was then hanged on the gallows, and the romantic pair shortly afterward married.[52]

The substance and moral of the *makama* about the fox and the leopard is in complete antithesis to this tale. The leopard perishes because he refuses to heed the advice of his mate, the wise and thoughtful leopardess. The fox succeeds with his cunning stories in persuading his neighbor, the leopard, to leave his residence to-

---

51. See *Tosafot* to the Talmudic tractate *Kiddushin* 80 b; *Maaseh-Buch*, p. 108 (in the Wilmersdorf edition).
52. It is hard to believe that this is a simple retelling of the story, so popular in the Graeco-Roman world, of the widow of Ephesus. The story is undoubtedly much older. On this, see E. Grisebach, *Die treulose Witwe, eine chinesische Novelle.*

gether with his whole household, despite the fact that the mistress of the household strongly urges him not to let himself be led astray by the fox. And here is how it ends:

The leopard family left its home. In front walked the deceitful fox, who had promised to show the way leading into the beautiful country. They came to their goal. The land was full of rivers, springs, and swiftly flowing waters. The fox tenderly bids farewell to the leopard family, and joyfully turns around. His clever plan has succeeded; he has outwitted the leopard. "Finally," he says, "I have gotten rid of my burdensome neighbors; now their house with the whole neighborhood is under my rule." . . . And there, in the blessed land where the leopards built their new home, the season of rains and floods soon began. All the rivers and streams quickly overflowed their banks. Before long, in the middle of the night, while the leopard family was fast asleep, the angry waves, with great noise and tumult, suddenly rushed in. "Woe is me," the leopard cried in deathly fear. "Woe to him who follows the treacherous counsel of the fox and is deaf to his wife's faithful words." And the cold, angry waves covered him.

In the third *makama* a lovely little story stemming from India[53] about how a clever peasant girl artfully interprets the dream of a king and the latter marries her is told. From Indian sources also comes the story of the princess with the rose in the eighth *makama*. In the fifth *makama* a group of tales about a wise judge are braided together. One of these, the story of Jacob of Cordova and the false nobleman, appears in different versions in later European literature —in the collection *Gesta Romanorum*, in the Italian Boccaccio, and in numerous other sources. In the sixth *makama* we find an interesting version of the well-known story of Tobit. Zabara relates how the pious Tobit violates the cruel prohibition against burying the dead, then how he becomes blind, and how his son sets out on a long journey and meets the prophet Elijah. In the seventh *makama*, both major persons, the author and his companion, stop for the night with a very wise old man, who entertains them with anecdotes and clever sayings. Many of these anecdotes and sayings are encountered in later European literature, e.g., in *Gesta Romanorum*. In the next to the last *makama* we again have a story "hostile to women" which tells of a wicked woman at whose barbaric contrivances Satan himself is astonished.[54]

53. See Davidson, in his introduction to the *Sefer Shaashuim*, pp. 53–54. The Indian source is here given.
54. The tale that Zabara presents about the wise king and the silly woman who is willing to kill her husband is found in the *Meshalim Shel Shelomo Ha-Melech* (*Bet Ha-Midrash*, IV, 146–48) and in Rabbenu Nissim's *Ḥibbur Yafeh* (pp. 14–15 in the 1746 edition).

CHAPTER NINE

Epics, Romances, and Fables

OSEPH ZABARA's *Sefer Sha-ashuim* leads us into a new realm, the imaginative labyrinth of folklore, in which the fruits of folk wisdom and the flowers of folk dreams wander from land to land, exchange their dress, are enriched with new elements, and then serve as a fresh source for further folk creativity. The poet of the *Sefer Shaashuim* was very much taken with the custom that was so popular in the lands of India and among the Arabs, to entertain and amuse and, therewith, also instruct and give ethical counsel—all with the aid of light anecdotes and tales. This work, which is strongly influenced by Arabic, Indian, and Greek sources, serves as the clearest demonstration of the importance of the mediating role of the Jews in the field of European folklore. Themselves an eastern people, familiar with the Arabic and Greek sources which included many Oriental and Indian legends, parables, and tales, the Jews in the Middle Ages were the mediators between the worlds of the East and the West. They, perhaps more than all others, brought it about that the West became acquainted with many Oriental motifs, with the wealth of Indian and Persian-Greek legends and tales.[1] In that dark era, when the cultural riches of earlier generations lay buried and forgotten, the Jews were almost the only ones who faithfully guarded the legends, fables, and romances of the classical eastern world. Thanks to them, a significant part of these riches penetrated into Christian European literature by way of Arabia and Spain.

As early as the eleventh century, a baptized Jew, Moses the Spaniard (his Christian name was Peter Alfonsi), the court physi-

1. See Theodor Benfey, *Pantchatantra* (1859), p. 25.

cian of the Castilian king Alfonso VI, composed in Latin a collection of thirty-three stories entitled *Disciplina clericalis*.[2] "Whoever," says Moritz Steinschneider, "wishes to chart the path over which the Oriental tales migrated to Europe must take account of Alfonsi's *Disciplina* as of one of the major milestones marking this way." All historians of culture underscore the great influence exercised by Alfonsi's work on the development of the European novella.[3] In the Middle Ages and afterwards, a series of similar works which have a definite significance for medieval folklore also appeared in Hebrew. We shall dwell on only a few of the most important of them.

An altogether unique place among these is occupied by a work which until modern times was one of the favorite entertainment books of Jewish youth. This book is entitled *Sefer Ha-Yashar* and is a kind of Jewish "hero epic" embracing the ancient period from the creation of the world to the exodus from Egypt.[4] Who the author of this work was has remained unknown. In the introduction it is related in a very legendary manner that the *Sefer Ha-Yashar* derives from ancient times. The Egyptian king Ptolemy, who reigned after Alexander of Macedon, commanded his scholars to collect for him the books of laws and histories of all the nations of the world. When they turned to the Jews, these were unwilling to hand over the sacred Torah to idolaters. Therefore, instead of the Law of Moses, they gave the king's emissaries only the *Sefer Ha-Yashar*. When Titus captured Jerusalem, one of his generals found in a cave a pious old man who sat alone, absorbed in ancient parchment scrolls. The Roman warrior was delighted with the old man and his wisdom and took him along, together with all his scrolls and books. Their friendship became so close that the Roman would not part with the old man even when he had to set out with his army to war. Finally the general had a house built in Spain in the neighborhood of Seville, and there the old man spent his last years with his beloved books. In this old man's library, the introduction

2. The second and third chapters of this collection were translated into Hebrew in the Middle Ages and published under the title *Sefer Ḥanoch* in Constantinople in 1516 (together with "Divrei Ha-Yamim Shel Mosheh Rabbenu" and other writings).
3. See, e.g., G. Depping, *Les Juifs dans le moyen age* (1845), pp. 98–99.
4. Only the last few pages touch on the later period, from the Exodus to the time of the Judges. The book has also been reworked into Yiddish under the title *Tam Ve-Yashar*. On the title page it is said: "Because the deeds which God, blessed be He, performed from the creation of the world until Joshua brought the people of Israel into Palestine are related in this book, we have translated it from the holy language into Judeo-German so that all might know these marvellous and miraculous things."

indicates, the *Sefer Ha-Yashar*, which also bears the name *Toledot Adam*, was found.

This legend leads to the conjecture that the *Sefer Ha-Yashar* does, in fact, derive from Spain. To this added testimony is given by the numerous Arabic names occurring in it.[5] The anonymous author was an ingenious compiler and an excellent stylist. However, he did not always know the secret of weight and measure. Biblical narratives are often woven together by him with legends and stories from the Talmud and later Jewish sources up to the *Josippon*, of which we will speak at more length in a later part of our work.[6] But thereby the author not infrequently obtains lovely effects: for example, when he relates how Joseph was sold by his brothers as a slave to the Midianites and weeps at the tomb of his mother Rachel, who consoles her beloved child from the grave.

The author does not, however, confine himself to Jewish sources. It is worth noting that he possessed a certain amount of accurate and, for that time, extremely rare information about the ancient lands of the East. He tells, for instance, how the king of Ethiopia, Ciconis, in order to preserve for eternity his great deeds and wars, commanded that they be inscribed on stones. The author also relates that the petty kings of Canaan were under the sovereignty of the king of Egypt and that when a powerful enemy attacked them they would request military aid from the Pharaoh. He was familiar also with the stories and legends of the European peoples and utilized them in his work. We find in it, for instance, the well-known legend of the rape of the Sabine women; the author adds that "Abraham the son of Terah was then ninety-nine years old." The legend of the Centaur is also related. In the Hebrew epic, however, the Centaur is overcome by a Biblical hero, the mighty Zophah, the grandson of Esau. In the story of the ten sons of Jacob and their wars, which are portrayed at length in the *Sefer Ha-Yashar*,[7] it is easy to detect the influence of the old Romance ballads and songs celebrating the deeds of the famous knights. Even the patriarch Jacob is depicted as a great hero and man of war, rushing with unsheathed sword into the camps of the enemy, who flee from

5. Zunz conjectures that the *Sefer Ha-Yashar* was composed in the second half of the twelfth century.
6. On the way in which the author of the *Sefer Ha-Yashar* employed Jewish sources, see Zunz, *Gottesdienstlichen Vorträge*, pp. 163–65 (second edition).
7. The description of the heroic deeds of Jacob's sons occupies the central place in the *Sefer Ha-Yashar*. This explains why among most of the older sources (for example, Naḥmanides) the work bears the title *Midrash Benei Yaakov*.

him in dread. The duel between Judah and the prince Jashub is described in detail, following the order of medieval knightly tournaments. The story of how Simeon, surrounded on all sides by a host of enemy warriors, utters a terrible cry which reaches the ears of Judah, who hastens immediately to the aid of his brother, is strongly reminiscent of the poem about the medieval hero Roland, who, when surrounded by the enemy's battalions, sounds his horn with his last powers so that the desperate tones are heard by Charlemagne. Even the well-known Talmudic legend about the miraculous staff of Moses obtains in the *Sefer Ha-Yashar* a European coloration. According to the version of the *Sefer Ha-Yashar*, this staff, after many adventures, came into the hands of the Midianite priest Jethro. The latter planted it in his garden and declared that whoever could tear it out of the earth would be given his beautiful daughter Zipporah to wife. Many great heroes attempted to overcome the miraculous staff, but it would not move from its place until Moses arrived. With one hand he wrested it out of the earth, and the lovely daughter of Midian became his spouse.

In the version of some of the legends the influence of Christian sources is discernible, for example, in the description of how Satan tries to tempt Abraham and Isaac on the way to the sacrifice on Mount Moriah. The temptations of Satan are, to be sure, also described in some of the Hebrew Midrashim,[8] but there they bear a different coloration. In the *Sefer Ha-Yashar* certain expressions, e.g., Abraham's indignant cries at Satan, "Get thee behind us!" and "The Lord rebuke thee, Satan," remind one of similar passages in the Gospels. However, in places, especially where the conversation between Satan and Sarah is recounted, the author tries to give a more "Jewish" form to the narrative.

It is very possible that it was precisely because the author of the *Sefer Ha-Yashar* made such extensive use of foreign sources that the rabbis of the Middle Ages looked with a certain suspicion on this work and for a long time did not allow it to be printed. Only in the year 1625, after the text had passed the test of a very strict censorship on the part of the well-known scholar Leo de Modena, who discarded numerous passages, was the *Sefer Ha-Yashar* published, and this without the approval of the local rabbis, in Venice.[9]

8. See, e.g., the *Yalkut Shimeoni* (Polonnoye edition, 1805), p. 24.
9. Leo de Modena tells of this himself in his *Ari Nohem:* "And this is the *Sefer Ha-Yashar* that was printed here in Venice some twenty years ago without my knowledge and the knowledge of the sages, even though I removed from it the strange and false things" (p. 60). The nineteenth-century American author and communal leader Mordecai Manuel Noah published an English translation of the *Sefer Ha-Yashar* under the title *The Book of Jasher*.

An extremely interesting picture of the metamorphoses and changes which a literary work or legend undergoes when it migrates from one people to another is given by a didactic romance which derives from India and is known in the Greek reworking under the title *Barlaam and Josaphat* and in the Slavic and western European reworkings as *Varlaam and Josaphat*. The narrative substance of the original, which tells of the greatness and holiness of the Buddha, receives in the Greek version[10] a completely Christian dress. To the prince Josaphat comes the hermit Barlaam and persuades him with his pious words and wise parables that the Christian faith is the only true one. This fascinating work, which made itself at home in all medieval European literatures and became one of the most popular books of ethical instruction, sustained many transformations in the course of its wanderings, often changing its form according to the era or the condition of the prevalent culture and religious conceptions.

The Hebrew version of this work was produced in the first decades of the thirteenth century by the poet Abraham ben Samuel Ibn Ḥasdai of Barcelona.[11] Ibn Ḥasdai translated a great deal from Arabic into Hebrew. Especially well known is his translation of the work of the Arabic theologian Al-Ghazali, entitled *Moznei Tzedek*,[12] but he acquired renown with his Hebrew translation of the Indian romance, which he entitled *Ben Ha-Melech Veha-Nazir*.[13] Modern scholars[14] have demonstrated that Ibn Ḥasdai employed the Arabic version of the Indian romance, and that the Arabic text was written not according to the Christian-Greek *Barlaam and Josaphat*[15] but according to an older translation of the Buddha romance in the Persian Pahlavi dialect.[16]

10. Composed by a Christian Ethiopian named John around 1090.
11. In the second part of our work we shall have occasion to speak of the role that Ibn Ḥasdai played in the controversy between the followers of Maimonides and their opponents.
12. Published by Goldenthal in Leipzig in 1839.
13. Published for the first time in Constantinople in 1518. We have had occasion to compare this first edition with the very old parchment manuscript of the *Ben Ha-Melech Veha-Nazir* in the Firkovich Collection and are persuaded, as a result, that the printed text of the work is, unfortunately, very erroneous.
14. F. Homel, *Die älteste arabische Varlaams Version* (1887); N. Weisslowitz, *Prinz und Derwisch* (1890).
15. For a bibliography on this, see Steinschneider, *Hebräischen Übersetzungen*, pp. 865–67.
16. Weisslowitz, *op. cit.*, pp. 19 and 25 ff. The Arabic text was discovered by Homel in an old manuscript in 1890 (Weisslowitz, pp. 132, 134, and 135). Steinschneider and Liebrecht do not agree with Weisslowitz. They conclude that the Arabic version was composed according to the Greek-Christian text.

Ibn Ḥasdai's Hebrew version bears an altogether different coloration than the Christian-Greek. *Ben Ha-Melech Veha-Nazir* relates the story of a prince with a great hunger for knowledge whose father raised him in a palace on an isolated island. The king wanted the troubles and sorrows of the world hidden from his son and the twin brothers, sorrow and death, unknown to him. This ignorance, however, could not satisfy the young prince with his probing and searching spirit. Finally the ignorance was torn away, and, as through a rent curtain, the melancholy truth appeared. A certain hermit visited the palace, came to the prince in his private room, and revealed to him the great sorrow of the world. He explained how sad and vain human life is, how overflowing with suffering man's days are. He urged the prince to reject the desires of the world and to think day and night only of God and His power. The prince was greatly moved. With tears in his eyes, he bade farewell to the holy man. Now he knew the fate that awaited him: to be God's agent, the prophet of His word.

The numerous parables, stories, and legends with which *Ben Ha-Melech Veha-Nazir* is filled were taken by Ibn Ḥasdai not only from the Arabic text but also from Jewish sources, especially from the Talmudic Aggadah. The book is written in *makama* style; the rhymed prose is interwoven with short poems. Only the last three chapters (33–35), in which the nature of the human soul is discussed, are written in ordinary prose. In these, however, Ibn Ḥasdai did not make use of the Arabic text of the romance but of various philosophical works of his era.

In Ibn Ḥasdai's work there is no longer any trace of that lusty and carefree tone which dominates the romances of Alḥarizi and Zabara. A soft veil of tender sadness hovers over *Ben Ha-Melech Veha-Nazir*. The breath of the enchanted land on the banks of the Ganges is felt in its pages. To be sure, Ibn Ḥasdai finds that "happy is the young man who spends his youthful years in joy; in his old age also his heart will be filled with joy."[17] In the eighteenth *makama*, in which the experiences of a young man in love are depicted in lovely features, are verses that celebrate the enchantment of feminine beauty. "Why, O my beloved," complains the lover, "do you hide yourself from me behind closed gates. Your locks of hair, those black serpents that lurk around your rosy cheeks, are your guards, and the spears of your glances wound more deeply than Joab's sword which pierced Abner's heart."[18] "My lovely one," complains the lover further, "mocks my love. She avoids my steps

17. *Ben Ha-Melech Veha-Nazir* (Amsterdam edition, 1766), p. 33.
18. *Ibid.*, p. 69.
19. *Ibid.*, p. 70.

so that I shall not see her, and cruelly robs my eyes of sleep so that even in dreams I should not behold her face."[19]

These earthly, desirous melodies are, however, soon stifled in Ibn Ḥasdai by melancholy, ascetic chords. "Remember, my brother," he admonishes, "better to kiss the edge of the sword than to give burning kisses with avid lips; better to fall into the hands of murderers and robbers than to be caught in the net of desire."[20] "Let not woman's beauty dazzle your eye; the wine of love must not excite your heart. The lovely face of a woman is like light at evening time; it burns the wings of whatever its brightness enchants."[21]

One must not pursue joys and pleasures; these only lead astray and blind the eyes, like "a beautiful red apple with a worm in its core."[22] In artistic verses the poet describes how vain are the joys of earth with all their splendor and beauty.

The earth beguiles and dazzles with the glory of her splendid colors. With all her valleys and mountains, her colorful meadows and blooming fields, it calls to you, "Come hither, enjoy my gifts. I will clothe you in velvet and brocade. The richest banquets, the sparkling cup, await your lips. In the fragrant shade of odorous trees you may rest in sweet dreams." O, do not believe it. As quickly as smoke all passes away! What glistens and charms today like the moon's tender, silver rays is consumed tomorrow by corruption and worms. The enchanting palaces of today are tomorrow exchanged for the narrow prison of dark graves.[23]

In verses reminiscent of Solomon Ibn Gabirol the poet speaks of the darkness of the endless night: "Tell me, beloved friends, do you know how the brightness of day looks? I have long since forgotten its appearance."[24] Everything is ephemeral, everything passes away like a dream, and of all the riches of the world only the covering of the grave remains.[25] Narrow is the prison of life; it deserves only mockery and contempt. Death alone is to be praised; it opens the gates leading to eternal life.[26] Enthusiastically the poet sings a paean to death: "Do not weep, my beloved, on the day of my death! Sweeter than the best spices is to me the dust

20. *Ibid.*, p. 71.
21. *Ibid.*, p. 103.
22. *Ibid.*, p. 43.
23. *Ibid.*, p. 16.
24. *Ibid.*, p. 26.
25. *Ibid.*, p. 65.
26. *Ibid.*, Makama 20 *et al.*

that will cover my grave. Like a swallow in a net has my soul languished in its captivity. Now the net is broken and the captive set free."[27] "Sing praises to death, my friends; if men knew how sweet it is, they would bow down before it like faithful servants."[28]

"Great is the joy of the soul," the poet repeats, "when it leaves its dwelling on earth."[29] The only true goal in the world is to purify the soul, to bring it to the peak of perfection, and to serve God with good deeds. Homilies such as these are woven together with parables, stories, and proverbs from the Talmud and Midrashim, as well as foreign sources, mainly the Indian-Arabic text. From an ancient Midrash is certainly taken the story of the man with three friends.[30] The beloved friend about whom the man was concerned day and night abandoned him as soon as misfortune overtook him, and it was precisely the third friend of whom the man thought least who did not forsake him and aided him in his extremity. The first friend is the riches of the world about which a man is anxious his whole life through; the second is his family; the third is his good deeds. A clear Indian coloration suffuses the tale of the gardener and the talking bird which ends with the moral: "Do not trouble yourself, my son, about what you have lost; do not desire what you cannot attain; do not believe in what cannot be."[31]

Ibn Ḥasdai, who doubtless was not only the translator but also the author of all the poems that appear in *Ben Ha-Melech Veha-Nazir*, possessed the gift of the true lyricist. An especially powerful impression is made by the poems in which sorrowful notes are heard. Says the poet in one of the first songs,

Three things grieve me greatly, and the fourth tears my heart to pieces: when the mighty wings of the eagle are cut down and flies spread their wings over his head; when the horns of the ox are broken and timorous little lambs push him about; and when the sick lion must be humbly silent before the little foxes which only yesterday trembled before his shadow. But more terrible than all these is when the man of righteousness and justice is trodden underfoot by vile clods and arrogant barbarians.

"Is your heart embittered and the burden of life heavy? Take the wanderer's staff in hand; in exile you will find your comfort.

27. *Ibid.*, p. 30.
28. *Ibid.*
29. *Ibid., Makama* 34.
30. *Ibid., Makama* 11.
31. *Ibid., Makama* 21, p. 79. On the Indian source see Weisslowitz, *op. cit.*, pp. 112–13.

Were it a curse to be a wanderer, how would Abraham have received from God the command, 'Go, leave your father's house!'?"[32]

In later generations, when Jewish life in Europe became ever darker and a veil of sorrow enveloped the ghetto, Ibn Ḥasdai's *Ben Ha-Melech Veha-Nazir*, with its heartfelt, elegiac tone, became one of the favorite books among Jews. As early as the fifteenth century it was translated into "Judeo-German,"[33] and in later times several other translations appeared.

Of greater cultural-historical significance than Ibn Ḥasdai's *Ben Ha-Melech Veha-Nazir* is the Hebrew translation of Bidhâpati's Indian collection of parables and fables, *Kalilah Ve-Dimnah*, which had a very large influence on European folklore. This remarkable treasury of Indian popular wisdom was obtained by the Christian peoples of Europe from the Arabs through the mediation of the Jews. On the circumstances under which the Arabic text of *Kalilah Ve-Dimnah* arose, we find in Abraham Ibn Ezra[34] the following legend:

The famous caliph Al-Tzapaḥ learned that in India the various sciences had attained a very high level. The caliph commanded that a scholar be found who understood both the language of the Indians [Sanskrit] and Arabic, and that he be asked to translate some of the Indian scientific works into Arabic. The caliph was told that the Indians have a very important book on statecraft, on how the king should govern his land and people. This work is written in the form of fables concerning beasts and birds, and the number of the fables is very great. The title of this book which is so popular in India is *Kalilah Ve-Dimnah* i.e., the lion and the ox,[35] of which the first chapter speaks. . . . The caliph then invited a learned Jew who understood both languages and charged him to translate this work. . . . When the caliph finally read *Kalilah Ve-Dimnah*, he was enchanted and expressed the desire to become familiar with other works of the sages of India as well.

It is now difficult to determine whence, in twelfth-century Spain,[36] the story arose that this book, which was so popular among the Arabs, was translated by a Jew. It is clear, however, that Ibn Ezra's report is no more than a legend without any kernel of truth,

32. *Ben Ha-Melech Veha-Nazir*, p. 69.
33. This "Old-Yiddish" translation has remained in manuscript, but considerable fragments were published by M. Erik in his *Wegen Alt-Yiddishen Roman un Novella* and W. Staerk in *Landau-Buch*.
34. In the introduction to his Hebrew translation of the astronomical tables of Mohammed Ibn Almanti (in David Kahana's edition, II, 107).
35. Ibn Ezra's explanation is incorrect. Kalilah and Dimnah are the names of two jackals.
36. Ibn Ezra wrote his introduction in 1161.

and that it was not through the Jews that the Arabs became familiar with *Kalilah Ve-Dimnah*. Ibn Ezra, however, is correct when he characterizes it as a book on the art of statecraft. This work, which was composed in thirteen chapters by the Buddha's followers, is a very unique "lawbook" and guide for kings and princes. Not through abstract principles and rules, but through fables and anecdotes in which beasts and birds play the role of men, does it teach how a king ought to conduct himself with his subordinates. In time, when on the banks of the Ganges the religious sect of the Brahmins prevailed, this work of the Buddha's sages received an altogether different appearance. Bitter enemies of the Buddhists, the Brahmins avenged themselves on the spiritual child of their rivals. They left of *Kalilah Ve-Dimnah* only the first five chapters and added to these many new tales and fables from the most varied sources. In this way, the lawbook divided into thirteen chapters was transformed into a book of fables of five chapters, *Pantchatantra* (five books), and the complete text of *Kalilah Ve-Dimnah* was eventually lost. But before the Brahmins mutilated *Kalilah Ve-Dimnah* and transformed it into *Pantchatantra*, a scholarly Persian physician named Barzau brought with him from India to Persia many manuscripts, among them the text of *Kalilah Ve-Dimnah*, and translated it into the cultural language of the Persians at that time, the Pahlavi dialect.[37]

Barzau wrote a long introduction which was later translated into Arabic and Hebrew. The introduction is characteristic of this highly educated and liberal man. "I set myself the task," declares Barzau,

of becoming familiar with the most varied peoples, of investigating thoroughly their customs and ways of life. I soon became persuaded that every people has its own language, its own laws and religious views. Every nation praises and admires the doctrine which it has inherited from its fathers, and every people attempts to show that only its faith and beliefs are true and that others are vain and false. Every people wishes to annihilate all other peoples. One persecutes the other, oppresses and reviles the other's faith. . . . Great is the hatred of one people for another, and the warfare flames like an infernal fire. I then

37. When this physician lived has not been definitely established. In the Hebrew translation it is indicated that Barzau was court physician to a Persian king who reigned from 531 to 579 C.E. F. Homel believes that Barzau also brought with him from India the Buddha romance and translated it into Persian and that this translation served as the model for *Ben Ha-Melech Veha-Nazir*. Homel conjectures that Barzau lived in the fourth century (see the supplement to Weisslowitz, *op. cit.*, pp. 149, 168, and 178).

decided to turn to the sages of each people and have them familiarize me with their religion and their laws. I said to them: "Explain to me the foundations of your faith. Tell me who your God and protector is. I wish to fathom the truth." All gave their replies. However, I soon became convinced that each praises only his own faith and mocks all others. Each recognizes only his own, and the foreign has no value whatsoever for him. I did not find a single one, either among those of little understanding or among the wisest, who really told me the truth. Not one of them persuaded me, for I believe only in what I have myself investigated and proved.[38]

In the same introduction Barzau tells the remarkable and profound story which gained entry into all the European literatures and so enchanted the brilliant Russian writer Leo Tolstoy. A man runs away in deathly terror from a lion and falls into a deep pit. He manages to take hold of two branches growing out of the walls of the pit. As he tries to support himself with both feet on the branches, he sees that below him, on the floor of the pit, lurks a terrible serpent with open mouth ready to swallow him. Trembling, the man clings to the branches. But suddenly he notices that the branches, his only support, are being greedily eaten up by the teeth of two mice, one white, the other black. Ever thinner become the little branches. It will not be long before their stalk is completely eaten through, and the miserable man will then fall into the abyss, straight into the mouth of the serpent. Filled with cold despair is the man, but he observes that near one of the branches some bees have built their nests and filled them with honey. The man at once forgets everything and, hanging over the dreadful abyss, greedily begins to lick the honey.[39]

The deep pit, Barzau explains, is our earthly world and the branches, man's life, which is constantly consumed by the two mice, day and night. The serpent with open mouth is death which lurks for man, and the honey is the petty joys and pleasures for the sake of which man forgets everything else in the world.

Barzau's Pahlavi translation of *Kalilah Ve-Dimnah* was eventually lost, but before this happened the work was rendered into Arabic in the reign of the caliph Al-Manzur (754–75).[40] This trans-

38. We quote according to the Hebrew translation of Jacob ben Eleazar.
39. This story is also found in *Even Bohan* of Kalonymos ben Kalonymos (1865 edition), pp. 93–94, and in other later Jewish and Arabic sources.
40. Several hundred years earlier *Kalilah Ve-Dimnah* was translated from Pahlavi into Syrian. A substantial part of this translation was discovered only in 1870. The scholar Bickell published it (1876) with a German translation and a very valuable introduction by Theodor Benfey.

lation, which was disseminated in various versions, became extremely popular among both the Arabs and the Jews who lived in their midst, and in the first half of the thirteenth century, at the commission of the Jewish physician and patron Benveniste, it was rendered into Hebrew by the poet and philologist Jacob ben Eleazar.

Jacob ben Eleazar acquired renown for his work on Hebrew phonetics, *Pardes Rimmonei Ha-Ḥochmah*, and his philological handbook, *Sefer Ha-Shalem*, which in time disappeared. A talented poet and master of the *musiv* style,[41] he splendidly fulfilled his translating task. The entire work is rendered into lovely rhymed prose.[42] The two poems and the introduction preceding the translation testify that the translator appreciated the unique beauty of the Indian work. He asserts that *Kalilah Ve-Dimnah* is the "lawbook" of the Indians, and that under this apparently childish garment of fables and parables the profoundest wisdom is concealed. With his poetic sensitivity Jacob ben Eleazar realized that out of this remarkable book gaze the eyes of an old, wise child, eyes in which the dreaming soul of the mysterious land of the Ganges burns with magical rays.

The translator declares:

This book was rendered into Hebrew by Jacob ben Eleazar. It was created in ancient days by the great sages of India. This work is their most precious treasure. It is their Torah, their prophet, their guiding star. In it are told stories of beasts, fishes in the sea and birds that ascend to the heavens. The old understand the wisdom hidden in it. Children laugh, and think these are merely lovely stories. When the child matures, he will know how to appreciate the depth of wisdom of this book, how beautiful are its pearls and wise its words.

The Arabic version which Jacob ben Eleazar employed consisted of fourteen chapters.[43] Each chapter begins with a question which King Dislam asks the "friend of wisdom" (philosopher) Sendebar, who replies with tales and parables.[44] Every story has a

41. Jacob ben Eleazar also wrote original poems. Several of these were published by H. Brody in *Shaar Ha-Shir*.
42. The translator emphasizes that the translation is not literal, for he believes that if one wishes a translation to be beautiful in the literary sense he must take strict account of the unique qualities of the language into which he is translating.
43. Excluding the introduction of the Persian translator.
44. For example, the first chapter begins as follows: "And Dislam, the king of India, said to Sendebar who was a lover of the wisdoms of the land of India, 'Let us have parables told between two pure-hearted, faithful friends.'"

particular moral lesson. When, for example, the Indian "lawbook" wishes to express the fundamental ethical principle set forth by the Talmud in the well-known dictum, "What is hateful to thee, that do not to thy neighbor," it relates the story of a lioness whom a hunter robbed of her two cubs, flaying their skins. The mother was in great anguish but her neighbor, a bear, explained to her, "This is your recompense for the fact that you devoured the children of others to still your hunger." The lioness had to admit that the judgment was just: "What you do not like, that do not to another." Into the parables and fables are frequently woven profound ethical maxims and sayings. In the eighth chapter, for example, which discusses the sorrows and misfortunes that hatred and enmity bring man, we find this sentence: "To despise and bear hatred, this is a great sorrow and a deep woe."

The Hebrew translator hoped that his rendering, "the child to which he gave birth," would have "eternal life." His hope, however, was not realized. The largest part of his work was eventually lost. Only the first two and a half chapters and the introduction survived. And it was not Jacob ben Eleazar's superb translation which had the privilege of playing a significant cultural role but another, far less successful one. Around the year 1250 a second Hebrew translation of *Kalilah Ve-Dimnah* appeared. The name of the translator has remained unknown. Some scholars have called the translator Joel, but this is no more than a conjecture.[45] The version of the Arabic text which the anonymous translator employed was almost the same as that which Jacob ben Eleazar had in hand, except that at the end there were two additional chapters which apparently were lacking in the text of the first translator. As a stylist the anonymous translator is considerably inferior to his predecessor. He rendered the entire work in prose, and in places the style is awkward and crude. But it was this unsuccessful work which became the source of all the European translations and reworkings of *Kalilah Ve-Dimnah*. A baptized Jew, John of Capua, employed it in his Latin translation, to which he gave the title *Directorium Vitae Humanae.* This translation was the source of the Spanish,[46] German, Dutch, Italian, and English versions. The source of the Slavic versions of *Kalilah Ve-Dimnah* was the Greek text which was translated from Arabic around the year 1081 by the baptized Jew Simeon Seth, a court physician of the emperor of Byzantium.

45. See Steinschneider, *op. cit.,* pp. 875–76.
46. There is another, older Spanish translation of *Kalilah Ve-Dimnah* which also derives from Jewish translators who were engaged in literary activity at the court of the Castilian king Alfonso.

With each people this collection of Indian fables obtained another coloration and took on a unique form. Each milieu placed its own stamp on it, and thus it gradually became an organic part of the local folklore. Historians of culture and ethnographers have discovered that a significant segment of the most popular folk tales of Europe derive from the Indian "lawbook," *Kalilah Ve-Dimnah.*

In still another respect the second Hebrew translation was more fortunate than its older and superior counterpart. Its text suffered very little from the ravages of time. Only the introduction and the first one and a half chapters were lost. The remainder of the text has come down to us in full and was published, together with the chapters which survived of Jacob ben Eleazar's translation, by Joseph Dérenbourg.[47]

Closely related to *Kalilah Ve-Dimnah* is another work that derives from India, *Mishlei Sendebar.* Apparently this book went through the same metamorphoses as *Kalilah Ve-Dimnah.* From the Indian original it was translated into the Pahlavi dialect, thereafter into Arabic, and only then was the Hebrew version produced from the Arabic.[48] When and where the Hebrew text first appeared has not been established. It is merely conjectured that its birthplace was Arabic Spain.[49]

The work is constructed according to the complex Oriental form, exemplified in Joseph Zabara's *Sefer Shaashuim,* of surrounding numerous little stories with one major story. To a childless Indian king, Bibor,[50] a son was born in his old age. The wisest of the king's seven sages,[51] Sendebar, brought him up. As the result of a libelous charge made by one of the king's young wives, the prince was condemned to death. The judgment was to be executed within seven days. To save the innocent young prince, one of the seven sages comes each day and attempts with all kinds of tales and parables to persuade the king that, in the name of justice, he ought immediately to annul his decree. Each story is concluded by the sage with the admonition: "Destroy not your only son for the sake of your wife; let yourself not be led astray, for the deceitfulness

47. Dérenbourg, *Deux versions hebraïques du livre Kalilah et Dimnah* (1881).
48. For bibliographical details see Steinschneider, *op. cit.,* pp. 887–88.
49. The work was first printed in Constantinople in 1516 in a collection of various legendary stories (*Kibbutz Sippurim Shonim*) such as "Divrei Ha-Yamim Shel Mosheh Rabbenu," "Petirat Aharon," "Tuvi ben Tuviel," etc. We have employed this extremely rare edition, as well as an old manuscript found in the Leningrad National Library in the Firkovich Collection.
50. In the printed text the king is called Kibor, in the manuscript Bibor.
51. Aristotle figures among the seven sages.

of women is boundless." As soon as the sage departs, the king's young wife comes and endeavors on her part to persuade him, also with stories and parables, that the prince must be punished. For seven consecutive days the struggle goes on. The stories extend like links of a chain until the sages finally succeed in demonstrating the woman's treachery and the prince is saved.

Several of the tales are strongly reminiscent of Boccaccio's *Decameron*, e.g., the comical narrative about the jealous old man who intends to go on a long journey. He hires a young maidservant to look after his wife, so that she will behave herself properly and not disgrace him. The old man does not realize that the servant girl whom he has left as a guardian is a young man in disguise—in fact, his frivolous wife's lover. When he calmly departs, the lovers rejoice and laugh at the deluded husband.

The anonymous Hebrew reworker of *Mishlei Sendebar* undoubtedly had considerable literary talent. His language is sharp and clear. He appreciates the secret of brevity. Everything is in proper measure, without superfluous words and free of inconsequential details that do not belong to the subject and can only weaken its impression.[52] In places in the Hebrew translation, the influence of Jewish sources is discernible, e.g., in the story of King David and his son Amnon. Especially characteristic in this respect is the end of the work. In all the European versions of *Mishlei Sendebar*, the young wife who made the false accusation against the innocent prince is condemned to strict punishment.[53] In the Hebrew text, however, the prince begs his father to forgive her, and when the king reminds the sage Sendebar that, according to their agreement, he has the right to demand a reward consisting of anything he wishes, the sage answers: "My request is that what you yourself do not like, you do not to another, and that you love your people as yourself." With this the book ends.

Kalilah Ve-Dimnah and *Mishlei Sendebar* clearly demonstrate how popular among the Jews of that time were foreign books of stories and fables. This fondness for foreign tales portraying the life of strange peoples and lands called forth dissatisfaction in certain Jewish circles. They saw in it a sign of excessive self-deprecation before the alien environment and its culture, something which might produce a weakening of the national self-consciousness. In

52. These virtues appear most clearly when one compares the Hebrew *Mishlei Sendebar* with the very diffuse Greek reworking (see *Literaturblatt des Orients*, 1842, p. 753). There is also a Hebrew translation of this quite unsuccessful Greek reworking under the title *Ḥayyei Irstu ben Doklitonus Melech Roma*.
53. See Steinschneider, *op. cit.*, p. 892.

this respect the fable poet Isaac ben Solomon Ibn Sahulah is extremely interesting.

For the few details known to us of Ibn Sahulah's life we are indebted to his own works. Born in 1244[54] in Spain in Guadalajara and raised in Burgos,[55] he thereafter led a wandering life and earned his living from the practice of medicine.[56]

"I saw," he complains,

that many of our people run after foreign models. They are dazzled by Greek philosophy and are charmed by Arabic fables and various foreign tales. What is strange pleases them most. So I said to them bitterly, "You children of the holy stock, you who stem from the source of eternal light! You have become like gypsies. Your own treasures you cast into the dust, and chase after foreign playthings and worthless trifles. . . . Behold, I will now create something new. I will take these fables, parables and tales for which you are so eager, stories about beasts of the field and birds of the deserts, and will wrap them, not in foreign garments, and weave them together, not with sayings and maxims of foreign sages—Ishmaelites, Edomites, Moabites and Arabs—but with the words of our Torah, with the divine parables of our prophets, and with the wise riddles and allusions of our Talmudic sages." . . . And in order that my *Meshal Ha-Kadmoni* should please the children also and be loved by them, and that they should eagerly read my stories, I have adorned them with beautiful pictures and illustrations.

All the old printed editions of Ibn Sahulah's work, as well as several manuscripts, are, in fact, decorated with numerous illustrations. The splendid Venice edition[57] has seventy-nine lovely pictures and drawings. In most of the pictures, however, it is easy to discern precisely that against which Ibn Sahulah considered it necessary to struggle, namely, the influence of "foreign models." Many pictures waft the breath of the Italian Renaissance. Several even bear a Christian coloration, e.g., the twenty-second picture

54. In the introduction to *Meshal Ha-Kadmoni* the author indicates that he wrote this work in the year 1281 when he was thirty-seven years old.

55. See his introduction to the commentary on the Song of Songs, *Kovetz Al Yad* (1891).

56. Ibn Sahulah complains very frequently of his wandering life in *Meshal Ha-Kadmoni* and in his commentary on the Song of Songs. He also speaks of his medical practice in *Meshal Ha-Kadmoni*, p. 63.

57. The year of this edition is not indicated. The well-known bibliographer S. Wiener conjectures that it appeared around 1550. Benjacob, in his *Otzar Ha-Sefarim*, and Eleazar Schulman, in *Sefat Yehudit-Ashkenazit*, p. 157, also point out that a certain Gershon Wiener in 1693 issued a Yiddish translation of *Meshal Ha-Kadmoni*. Unfortunately we could not obtain this translation anywhere.

portraying the knight kneeling before the priest. The text itself which ought, in the author's view, to provide something "altogether new" is also not entirely free from the influence of the "Ishmaelites" and "Arabs." First of all, the form: *Meshal Ha-Kadmoni* is written in typical Arabic *makama* style. The entire work, which is divided into five "gates" or chapters, has the form of a dialogue between the author and a certain *makshan* (a raiser of difficult questions). Following the pattern of similar Arabic and Indian works, the discussion in *Meshal Ha-Kadmoni* is also conducted not with theoretical inquiries and logical arguments but with tales and parables. Just as in *Kalilah Ve-Dimnah, Mishlei Sendebar,* and similar works, the chief persons of the *Meshal Ha-Kadmoni* also raise time and again the simpleminded question, "And how was the thing?" Immediately thereafter a story or parable with birds and beasts follows as reply.

On the other hand, the moral or conclusion which accompanies the tales and fables bears in Ibn Sahulah a completely Jewish aspect. All the characters, whether beasts or birds, appearing in *Meshal Ha-Kadmoni* are thoroughly proficient in Biblical and Aggadic literature. The deer, for example, in Ibn Sahulah is a Jewish deer, a great expert in Talmud. The rooster spouts verses from the Bible, the rabbit is proficient in rabbinic codes and books of ethics. He points out that of the three kinds of love the most important is the love of the Creator for His creatures.[58] Even the wild bird of prey, the hawk, splits hairs in the laws of damages like a clever student in a Talmudic academy.[59] In general, the beasts and birds in Ibn Sahulah have nine measures of speech, and their long disputations produce a tedious impression on the reader.

It must, however, be admitted that the author of *Meshal Ha-Kadmoni* sometimes displays genuine humor. The scene, for instance, in which the rooster describes how righteous he is, how delicately and modestly he conducts himself with his wives,[60] is excellent. Filled with sarcasm is the description of how a common workman and a scribe travel together. "You are, after all, so learned and wise; why then are you so poor?," the worker asks the scribe. The scribe answers, "Our sages placed upon scribes and teachers of children so many fasts and obligations to work at the lowest payment, in order that they might never become rich from their work. And, indeed, concerning them the Gemara has said, 'Poverty and affliction are seemly for Israel.'"

58. *Meshal Ha-Kadmoni*, p. 39.
59. *Ibid.*, pp. 27–28.
60. *Ibid.*, p. 27.

In *Meshal Ha-Kadmoni* are also scattered numerous details that have a certain ethnographic interest, inasmuch as they provide some notion of the contemporary way of life and depict the manners and mores of that era. Among the sinful people who "have no share in the world to come," for example, our author includes not only heretics, informers, and apostates, but overly strict communal officials (*parnassim*) who cast fear on the community and butchers who are constantly drunk on wine. In *Meshal Ha-Kadmoni* a clear portrait of the condition of education and scientific knowledge in that period is also given. The author constructs his work according to the same "chain form" as the *Sefer Shaashuim* and *Mishlei Sendebar*, but his tales and parables often overflow with scientific speeches and practical information. The four-footed and two-winged characters of *Meshal Ha-Kadmoni* not infrequently carry on long, learned debates and, in this way, the author presents in clear form very (for that time) extensive information about the various sciences, such as philosophy, cosmography, astronomy, geography, etc. Some of the details are highly interesting, for example, the explanation that differences in languages are the result of climatic conditions,[61] or the description of how the human eye is constructed.[62]

Among the various branches of science Isaac Ibn Sahulah mentions astrology, which occupied an important place in medieval life. Here he touches on a motif which figured prominently in the battle of ideas[63] that erupted in Jewish intellectual circles at that time. The long-footed stork appears in *Meshal Ha-Kadmoni* as a convinced fatalist denying the reality of free will. He is persuaded that the stars and planets rule the destiny of man, who, with all his will, cannot in the slightest way alter his fate, which is predetermined through the movements of the celestial luminaries. Man, with the aid of the profound science called astrology, can only learn the art of reading the mysterious signs in the heavens and, through the motions of the planets, unveil the secret of the future and predict the fate and end of each man.[64] This fatalist theory is strongly opposed by the frog, in whose name the author expresses his own views. Astrological dreams, declares the frog, are child's play and old wives' tales deriving from India and Babylonia. They are pure swindlery and barbaric ignorance. Let those people who believe in magic and other such follies occupy themselves with

61. *Ibid.*, pp. 30–33.
62. *Ibid.*, p. 45.
63. We shall have occasion to speak at length of this struggle in the later parts of our work.
64. *Meshal Ha-Kadmoni*, p. 53.

astrology, but Jews may not do so. They may not violate the prohibition "You shall not use enchantments nor observe times" (Le-
viticus 19:26). A godly man may not devote himself to magic and
fortune tellers. He must rely on the Creator and His grace, as is
said in the Torah: "The Lord your God shall you fear."

Isaac Ibn Sahulah's work, together with *Mishlei Sendebar* and
Kalilah Ve-Dimnah, belongs to a field of literature which from
ancient times was very popular among Jews. Parables and fables of
the life of beasts were greatly admired even in the period of the
sages of the Talmud. Some of these, e.g., Rabbi Meir, were masters
of "fox fables." *Kalilah Ve-Dimnah*, however, bears a definitely
foreign impress. And Isaac Ibn Sahulah, who battled for national
forms, had too slight a notion of the secret of brevity; his fables
are burdened with extraneous elements that have no relationship
to the story. What Sahulah did not manage to do, i.e., become a
national Jewish fable poet, was achieved by his more gifted contemporary, Berechyah ben Natronai Ha-Nakdan, one of the most
talented fable poets of medieval Europe.

The details of Berechyah's life have remained completely unknown to later generations. After long debates and the investigations of various scholars,[65] it has still not been definitely established
when and where he lived and worked. It is merely conjectured that
he flourished in the middle of the thirteenth century. A man of
philosophical education and extensive knowledge, Berechyah translated several scientific works into Hebrew. The most important of
these is his translation of Adelard of Bath's Latin "nature questions"
(*Quaestiones Naturales*), to which he gave the Hebrew title *Dodi
Ve-Nechdi*. He acquired his reputation, however, with his famous
work *Mishlei Shualim*, a collection of one hundred seven fables.[66]

Berechyah drew his fables from various sources, from Bidhâpati's
and Aesop's ancient collections, from medieval Christian fable
poets, and from the Talmud and Midrashim. Some of them he
created himself. In complete contrast with Ibn Sahulah, Berechyah
is extremely chary of words. His parables are written in lovely
rhymed prose with brief and sharp expressions. Every sentence is

65. See Carmoly, *La France Israelite*, pp. 21–39; Renan-Neubauer, *Les Rab-
bins français*, pp. 490–500; Jacobs, *Fables of Aesop*, p. 174; Jacobs,
Jewish Encyclopedia, III, 53–55; Steinschneider, *op. cit.*, pp. 958–62;
Steinschneider, *Letterbode*, VIII, 25–35. See also Herman Gollancz'
introduction to Berechyah's two philosophical-ethical works, *Sefer Ha-
Hibbur* and *Sefer Ha-Matzref* (first published in 1902).

66. In the first Mantua edition (1557–59), of which we have made use,
another fable is given at the end. This begins with the words: "Hear
now the words of Rabbi Krespia Ha-Nakdan." It is doubtful whether
this fable was written by the author of *Mishlei Shualim*.

in proper place. Each fable is preceded by a two-line verse in which its essence is summarized, and at the end the moral lesson is also given in verse. Not infrequently several other didactic lines follow the moral in the tales of *Mishlei Shualim*.⁶⁷

To give the reader some notion of Berechyah's manner and style, we here present paraphrases of three of his parables:

I A Parable of a Cedar Tree and a Thorn

Let the rich man not exult in his wealth,
It will not be his forever.

A cedar of Lebanon whose crown reached to the heavens was extremely proud of his gigantic growth and thick, powerful branches. Among all the trees, he was unique; in all the forests there was none comparable to him. Suddenly he noticed beneath him a thornbush humping up with its dwarfish parts. "You petty growth," the cedar indignantly cried out; "how dare you stand near me, the king of the forest? All the trees bow down before me, the loveliest birds nest in my branches, and you dwarf, with your ugly thorns, who can desire you, to whom can you be of any use?" Calmly and quietly the thorn replied: "Why this boasting, why this great anger? Yes, you are great and powerful, but I advise you, be careful. Soon comes the day of wrath, and your pride and greatness will fall! Your crown and beauty will lie in the dust. Your mighty trunk, your gigantic branches, will be sawed into boards and masts. And I—I will survive you. No ax will be raised over me, and calmly I will look on and see your pride go under."

> Very often a man exults in his wealth or beauty,
> And looks with contempt on his poor brothers.
> But his wealth quickly passes away,
> His might and greatness are broken,
> And the strong man lies in the dust
> Before him who is humble and poor.

II A Fable Concerning an Ox, a Lion, and a He-Goat

He who is persecuted and cast down
Trembles constantly before afflictions and plagues.

An ox once met a lion on his way and fled from him. In deathly terror he heard the lion's angry roars behind him. Crawling barely alive into a cave, he sought safety there. Suddenly in a corner he saw a he-goat. The ox trembled mightily and could not stand on his feet. Astonished,

67. In 1561 a Christian scholar, M. Hanel, issued a Latin translation of *Mishlei Shualim* together with the original.

the he-goat asks, "Why do you tremble so? We are, after all, like brothers, raised from childhood on in the same flock." "Ah," answers the other, "all animals now appear to me like wild leopards and lions. Yesterday, I would not have been afraid of, nor hidden from, anyone. Today the lion attacked me, and I tremble before every shadow."

> He who is persecuted and cast down
> Trembles constantly before afflictions and plagues.
> In every corner, in every nook,
> He senses only danger and terror,
> For in everyone he sees deathly hostility.
> He always thinks he will be discovered by his enemy;
> Before every rustling leaf he runs away in fright.

III A Parable of Two Deer

> If the fool is quiet and speaks no word,
> He is believed wise and his place is among sages.

Near a pond in an open field two deer stand. One tells the other a quiet secret. A stranger would not have understood a word. A man passes by and, in surprise, asks the deer, "Why such stillness? You both stand quite alone and may express your thoughts aloud; no one will overhear your secret." "No," they reply, "we are not telling any secrets. We simply have no strength. Our minds are weakened, and we are glad to do nothing."

> When fools are silent and do not raise their voices,
> They are considered wise; all praise and laud them.
> If the fool reveals what he thinks and believes,
> He is mocked and laughed at by all.

With Berechyah's *Mishlei Shualim* we leave Spanish-Arabic territory. As we have noted, it has not been definitely established where Berechyah lived. Joseph Jacobs, the scholarly investigator of fable literature in the Middle Ages, attempted to prove that the author of *Mishlei Shualim* was born in England.[68] Many other investigators, however, do not agree, and we consider more correct the suggestion that he lived in Provence, whose Jews were under the strong intellectual influence of their brethren in neighboring Spain.

We leave Spanish soil only temporarily, but we depart at the moment of an important transitional period, when Jewish culture

68. See *Jewish Encyclopedia*, III, 53.

in Spain was at a crossroads and a new page in its history had just begun. In the person of Maimonides Jewish philosophical thought in Spain reached its zenith. His younger contemporary, Jehudah Alḥarizi, was the last Jewish poet of stature in the Iberian peninsula. The first signs of intellectual decline, which was closely connected with the general crisis that Arabic culture then experienced, appeared in Spanish Jewry. The fanatical caliphs of the Almohade dynasty were mortal enemies of free inquiry and science, and the caliphs Al-Manzur and his son Al-Mamun were particularly noted for their zealotry. They severely persecuted the thinkers who lived in Spain at that time and, at their command, the works of earlier philosophers were burned. In the Islamic mosques Aristotle, Al-Farabi, and Avicenna were put under the ban, and the religious leaders in their sermons endeavored to show that the ideas and systems of these thinkers were nothing but heresy.

As a result of the persecutions of the Almohades, many Jewish families fled from southern Spain and settled in Provence and in northern Spain, which was Christian. In the first half of the thirteenth century, however, the most powerful kingdom of Christian Spain, Castile, managed to score one victory after another over the Arabs of southern Spain. In 1236 Ferdinand III captured the oldest center of Arabic civilization in Spain, Cordova, and with this broke the power of the Almohades. After Cordova, the cities of Jaén and Seville and the greater part of Andalusia soon fell. With this a new period in the history of Jewish culture in Spain began, a period that was significantly influenced by a lower civilization than the Arabic, namely, the Christian Castilian. In the cultural life of the Spanish Jews new tendencies appeared, and it was the name of Maimonides that became the banner around which a bitter war of ideas erupted that lasted for generations and had a vast influence on the further development of Jewish culture.

In order to appreciate clearly and understand correctly the historical causes and effects of this struggle, however, we must first become familiar with the culture and literary creativity of the Jewish communities in the neighboring Christian lands of western Europe.

BIBLIOGRAPHICAL NOTES

The Arabic-Spanish Period

CHAPTER ONE

FROM IBN SHAPRUT TO IBN GABIROL

On the history and culture of the Jews in Spain, see H. Graetz, *Geschichte der Juden* (Leipzig, 1853–76); S. W. Baron, *A Social and Religious History of the Jews*, rev. ed. (Philadelphia, 1952–); S. Katz, *The Jews in the Visigothic and Frankish Kingdoms of Spain and Gaul* (Cambridge, 1937); M. Güdemann, *Das jüdsiche Unterrichtswesen während der spanisch-arabischen Epoche* (Vienna, 1873); Y. Baer, *Die Juden im christlichen Spanien*, 2 vols. (Berlin, 1929–36) (English translation, *The Jews in Christian Spain*, 2 vols. [Philadelphia, 1960, 1966]); and A. Neuman, *The Jews in Spain, Their Social, Political and Cultural Life During the Middle Ages*, 2 vols. (Philadelphia, 1942).

On the early liturgical poets Jannai and Kallir, see *Piyyutei Yannai*, ed. M. Zulay (Berlin, 1938); *Maḥzor Yannai*, ed. I Davidson (New York, 1919); and S. J. Rapoport, *Toledot Eleazer Ha-Kallir*, 2nd ed. (Warsaw, 1912).

On rhyme and meter in the Hebrew poetry of Spain see M. Hartmann, *Die hebräische Verskunst* (Berlin, 1894); B. Halper, "The Scansion of Medieval Hebrew Poetry," *JQR*, n.s., IV (1913–14), 153–224; A. Mirsky, "Teḥilato Shel He-Ḥaruz," *Moznayim*, VI (1958), 450–58; and N. Allony, *Torat Ha-Mishkalim Shel Dunash, Yehudah Ha-Levi, Ve-Avraham Ibn Ezra* (Jerusalem, 1951).

On Hebrew poetry in Spain generally see M. Sachs, *Die religiöse Poesie der Juden in Spanien*, 2nd ed. (Berlin, 1901); A. Geiger, *Jüdische Dichtungen der spanischen und italienischen Schule* (Leipzig, 1856); J. M. Millás Vallicrosa, *La poesía sagrada hebraicoespañola* (Madrid, 1948); idem, *Literatura hebraicoespañola* (Barcelona, 1967); S. Spiegel, "On Medieval Hebrew Poetry," in *The Jews: Their History, Culture, and Religion*, ed. L. Finkelstein, Vol. II (Philadelphia, 1949); J. Schirmann, "The Function of the Hebrew Poet in Medieval Spain," *Jewish Social Studies*, XVI (1954), 235–52; idem, "L'Amour spirituel dans la poésie hébraïque médiévale," in *Les Lettres romanes* (Louvain, 1961); *idem, Ha-Shirah Ha-Ivrit Be-Sefarad Ube-Provans,* 3 vols. (Jerusalem, 1956); I. Davidson, *Otzar Ha-Shirah Veha-Piyyut: Thesaurus of Medieval Hebrew Poetry,* 4 vols. (New York, 1924–33).

On the development of Hebrew grammar and lexicography generally, see H. Hirschfeld, *A Literary History of Hebrew Grammarians and Lexicographers* (London, 1926).

On Menaḥem Ibn Saruk, see S. Gross, *Menaḥem ben Saruk* (Breslau, 1872); D. Kahana, "Rabbi Menaḥem ben Saruk," *Ha-Shiloaḥ,* XVII (1907), 129–39, 425–31; M. Landau, *Beiträge zum Chazarenproblem* (Breslau, 1938).

On Dunash ben Labrat, see D. Kahana, *Dunash ben Labrat: Kovetz Shirov* (Warsaw, 1894); N. Allony, *Dunash ben Labrat: Shirim* (Jerusalem, 1947); M. Wilensky, "Dunasch ben Labrat," in *Encyclopedia Judaica,* Vol. VI (Berlin, 1931).

On Jehudah Ḥayyuj, see B. Drachman, *Die Stellung und Bedeutung des Jehudah Ibn Chajjug in der Geschichte der hebräischen Grammatik* (Breslau, 1884).

On Jonah Ibn Jannaḥ, see his *Kitab al Tanḳiḥ (Sefer Ha-Rikmah),* a critical edition, with the translation of Jehudah Ibn Tibbon, ed. M. Wilensky (Berlin, 1929–30); and W. Bacher, *Leben und Werke des Abulwalid Ibn Ganach* (Leipzig, 1885).

For Samuel Ha-Nagid's poetry, see *Rabbi Shemuel Ha-Nagid: Diwan,* a critical edition by A. M. Habermann (Tel Aviv, 1946–47); *Diwan of Shemuel Hannaghid,* ed. with introduction and notes by D. S. Sassoon (Oxford, 1934); his *Ben Mishlei,* a critical edition by S. Abramson (Tel Aviv, 1948); his *Ben Kohelet,* a critical edition by S. Abramson, (Tel Aviv, 1953). On Samuel's life and work, see J. Schirmann, "Shemuel Ha-Nagid Ke-Meshorer," *Kenesset,* II (1937), 393–416; J. Schirmann, "Samuel Hannagid, the Man, the Soldier, the Politician," *Jewish Social Studies,* XIII (1951), 99–126; S. M. Stern, "Le-Toledot Rabbi Shemuel Ha-Nagid," *Tziyyon,* XV (1950), 135–45; and Y. Levin, "Le-Ḥeker Ben Mishlei Shel Rabbi Shemuel Ha-Nagid," *Tarbitz,* XXIX (1960), 146–61.

CHAPTER TWO

SOLOMON IBN GABIROL

A fine annotated edition of Ibn Gabirol's poems was published by H. N. Bialik and J. H. Ravnitzki under the title *Shirei Shelomo ben Yehudah Ibn Gabirol* in three volumes (Berlin-Tel Aviv, 1924–32). A critical edition of his *Anak*, with a translation into German, was published by A. Neumark under the title *Ibn Gabirols Anak* (Leipzig, 1936). A good sampling of his hymns and liturgical poems, with English translations in verse by Israel Zangwill, appears in *Selected Religious Poems of Solomon Ibn Gabirol* (Philadelphia, 1932). The Hebrew texts of the poems in this volume were critically edited by Israel Davidson, who also supplied a valuable introduction.

Ibn Gabirol's *Tikkun Middot Ha-Nefesh* was translated into English under the title *The Improvement of the Moral Qualities* by Stephen S. Wise (New York, 1901). The translator also included an essay on the place of Ibn Gabirol in the development of Jewish ethics. *Mivhar Ha-Peninim* (as Jehudah Ibn Tibbon called his Hebrew translation of the Arabic text) was translated into English by B. H. Ascher (London, 1859) under the title *Choice of Pearls: A Collection of Ethical Sentences, Maxims, Etc.* On the question of Ibn Gabirol's authorship of *Mivhar Ha-Peninim*, see A. Marx, "Gabirol's Authorship of the Choice of Pearls and the Two Versions of Joseph Kimhi's *Shekel Hakodesh*," *Hebrew Union College Annual*, IV (1927), 433–48.

The Latin translation of Ibn Gabirol's *Mekor Hayyim*, entitled *Avencebrolis Fons Vitae*, was edited by G. Baeumker (Münster, 1892–95). Jacob Bluwstein's Hebrew translation of the Latin text was published in Jerusalem, 1926, with an introduction by Joseph Klausner.

On Ibn Gabirol as a poet, see A. Geiger, *Salomo Ibn Gabirol und seine Dichtungen* (Leipzig, 1867); M. Sachs, *Die religiöse Poesie der Juden in Spanien*, 2nd ed. (Berlin, 1901); Senior Sachs, *Cantiques de Solomon Ibn Gabirol* (Paris, 1868); D. Yellin, "Shelomo Ibn Gabirol: Ha-Ish Veha-Meshorer" and "Shelomo Ibn Gabirol Be-Tor Paytan," in his *Ketavim Nivharim*, Vol. II (Jerusalem, 1939); and J. M. Millás Vallicrosa, *Shelomó Ibn Gabirol como poeta y filósofo* (Madrid-Barcelona, 1945).

On Ibn Gabirol's philosophy, see M. Bieler, *Der göttliche Wille (Logosbegriff) bei Gabirol* (Würzburg, 1933); K. Dreyer, *Die religiöse Gedankenwelt des Salomo Ibn Gabirol* (Leipzig, 1929); Jacob Guttman, *Die Philosophie des Salomo Ibn Gabirol* (Göttingen, 1889); Julius Guttmann, *Philosophies of Judaism* (Philadelphia, 1964); A. Heschel, "Das Wesen der Dinge nach der Lehre Gabirols," *Hebrew Union College Annual*, XIV (1939); I. Husik, *A History of Medieval Jewish Philosophy* (Philadelphia, 1916);

D. Kaufmann, *Studien über Salomon Ibn Gabirol* (Budapest, 1899); D. Rosin, "The Ethics of Solomon Ibn Gabirol," *JQR*, 1891, pp. 159–81; M. Wittmann, *Zur Stellung Avencebrols (Ibn Gebirols) im Entwicklungsgang der arabischen Philosophie* (Münster, 1905); and J. Wijnhoven, "The Mysticism of Solomon Ibn Gabirol," *Journal of Religion*, XLV (1965), 137–52.

CHAPTER THREE

MOSES IBN EZRA

Moses Ibn Ezra's poems were edited by H. N. Bialik and J. H. Ravnitski, with notes by D. Yellin, 2 vols. (Tel Aviv, 1929). An edition of his secular poems, *Shirei Ha-Ḥol*, was published by H. Brody (Berlin-Jerusalem, 1935–42), and of his religious poems, *Shirei Kodesh*, by S. Bernstein (Tel Aviv, 1957). Ibn Ezra's *Kitab al-Muḥaḍara wal-Mudhakarah* was translated into Hebrew, with introduction and notes, by B. Halper under the title *Shirat Yisrael* (Leipzig, 1924). A good sampling of his poetry, translated into English by S. Solis-Cohen from texts critically edited and annotated by H. Brody, is to be found in *Selected Poems of Moses Ibn Ezra* (Philadelphia, 1934).

On Ibn Ezra's life and his poetry, see L. Dukes, *Moses ben Esra aus Granada* (Altona, 1839); S. Kämpf, *Nichtandalusische Poesie andalusischer Dichter* (Berlin, 1858); M. Sachs, *Die religiöse Poesie der Juden in Spanien*, 2nd ed. (Berlin, 1901); H. Brody, "Moses Ibn Ezra: Incidents in His Life," *JQR*, n.s., XXIV (1934), 309–20; and A. Diez Macho, *Mose ibn Ezra como poeta y preceptista* (Madrid-Barcelona, 1953).

CHAPTER FOUR

JEHUDAH HALEVI THE POET

A complete critical edition of Jehudah Halevi's *diwan* was published by H. Brody in four volumes (Berlin, 1894–1930) under the title *Diwan des Abul-Hasan Jehuda Ha-Levi*. An incomplete collection of his poems was issued, with introduction and notes, by A. E. Harkavy, *Rabbi Yehudah Ha-Levi* (Warsaw, 1893–95). *Selected Poems of Jehudah Halevi*, translated into English by Nina Salaman (Philadelphia, 1924), contains a fine sampling of his songs of Zion, love and bridal songs, poems of friendship, and devotional poems. Some of Halevi's poems were translated into German by Franz Rosenzweig in his *Jehuda Halevi: Zweiundneunzig Hymnen und Gedichte* (Berlin, 1926).

On the life and work of the poet, see J. Schirmann, "Hayyei Yehudah Ha-Levi," *Tarbitz*, IX (1938), 35–54, 219–40, 284–305; S. D. Goitein, "Ha-Parashah Ha-Aharonah Be-Hayyei Rabbenu Yehudah Ha-Levi Le-Or Kitvei Ha-Genizah," *Tarbitz*, XXIV (1955), 21–47; *idem*, "Rabbi Yehudah Ha-Levi Be-Sefarad Le-Or Kitvei Ha-Genizah," *Tarbitz*, XXIV (1955), 134–49; *idem*, "The Biography of Rabbi Judah Ha-Levi in the Light of the Cairo Genizah Documents," *PAAJR*, XXVIII (1959), 41–56; S. S. Cohon, "Jehuda Halevi," *American Jewish Year Book*, XLIII (1941–42), 447–88; S. Baron, "Jehuda Halevi: An Answer to a Historic Challenge," *Jewish Social Studies*, III (1941), 243–72; J. M. Millás Vallicrosa, *Yehudá Ha-Leví como poeta y apologista* (Madrid, 1947); and R. Kayser, *The Life and Times of Jehudah Halevi* (New York, 1949).

CHAPTER FIVE

RELIGIOUS PHILOSOPHY FROM SAADIAH GAON TO MAIMONIDES

The literature on Philo is vast. A few of the most valuable and illuminating of modern studies are E. Bréhier, *Les Idées philosophiques et religieuses de Philon d'Alexandrie*, 2nd ed. (Paris, 1925); I. Heinemann, *Philo's griechische und jüdische Bildung* (Breslau, 1932); E. Stein, *Die allegorische Exegese des Philo aus Alexandrien* (Giessen, 1929); H. A. Wolfson, *Philo: Foundations of Religious Philosophy in Judaism, Christianity and Islam* (Cambridge, 1947); E. R. Goodenough, *An Introduction to Philo Judaeus* (New Haven, 1940); and S. Sandmel, *Philo's Place in Judaism* (Cincinnati, 1956).

On the Karaites, see L. Nemoy (ed.), *A Karaite Anthology* (New Haven, 1952); I. Markon, "Karäer," in *Encyclopedia Judaica*, IX (Berlin, 1932), 923–54; R. Mahler, *Ha-Karaim* (Merhaviah, 1949); and S. Poznanski, *The Karaite Literary Opponents of Saadia Gaon* (London, 1908). On Hiwi Ha-Balchi, see I. Davidson, *Saadia's Polemic Against Hiwi Al-Balkhi* (New York, 1915).

The Arabic text of Saadiah's *Sefer Ha-Emunot Veha-Deot*, entitled *Kitab al-Amanat wal I'tikadat*, was edited by S. Landauer

(Leiden, 1880). The work was translated into English by S. Rosenblatt under the title *The Book of Beliefs and Opinions* (New Haven, 1948). On Saadiah's thought, see Jacob Guttmann, *Die Religionsphilosophie des Saadia* (Göttingen, 1882); I. Efros, "Saadya's Theory of Knowledge," *JQR*, n.s., XXXIII (1942–43), 133–70; L. Finkelstein (ed.), *Rab Saadia Gaon* (New York, 1944); A. J. Heschel, "The Quest for Certainty in Saadia's Philosophy," *JQR*, n.s., XXXIII (1942–43), 213–64; H. Malter, *Saadia Gaon, His Life and Works* (Philadelphia, 1921); A. E. Neuman and S. Zeitlin (eds.), *Saadia Studies* (Philadelphia, 1943); D. Neumark, *Essays in Jewish Philosophy* (Cincinnati, 1929); E. I. J. Rosenthal (ed.), *Saadya Studies* (Manchester, 1943); *Saadia Anniversary Volume*, American Academy for Jewish Research (New York, 1943); M. Ventura, *La Philosophie de Saadia Gaon* (Paris, 1934); M. Zucker (ed.), *Saadiah Al Ha-Torah* (New York, 1961).

The original Arabic of Bahya Ibn Pakuda's *Hovot Ha-Levavot*, entitled *Kitab al-Hidaya ila Faraid al Kulub*, was edited by A. S. Yahuda (Leiden, 1912). Bahya's work was translated into English under the title *Duties of the Heart* by M. Hyamson (New York, 1925–47). On Bahya's thought, see D. H. Baneth, "The Common Theological Source of Bahya Ibn Pakuda and Ghazzali," in *Magnes Anniversary Volume* (Jerusalem, 1938); Julius Guttmann, *Philosophies of Judaism* (Philadelphia, 1964); I. Husik, *A History of Medieval Jewish Philosophy* (Philadelphia, 1916); D. Kaufmann, *Die Theologie des Bachja Ibn Pakuda* (Vienna, 1874); and G. Vajda, *La Théologie ascétique de Bahya Ibn Paquda* (Paris, 1947).

An edition of the original text of Jehudah Halevi's *Kuzari*, together with Jehudah Ibn Tibbon's Hebrew translation, was issued by Hartwig Hirschfeld (Leipzig, 1887). Hirschfeld also published an English translation of the *Kuzari* (London, 1905). A translation into French was published by M. Ventura under the title *Le Livre du Kuzari par Juda Hallevi* (Paris, 1932). On Halevi's philosophy, see E. Berger, *Das Problem der Erkenntnis in der Religionsphilosophie Jehuda Hallewis* (Berlin, 1916); I. Epstein, "Judah Halevi as Philosopher," *JQR*, n.s., XXV (1935); I. Efros, "Some Aspects of Judah Halevi's Mysticism," *PAAJR*, XI (1941); D. Kaufmann, "Jehudah Halevi," in *Gesammelte Schriften*, II (Frankfurt, 1910); D. Neumark, "Jehuda Hallevi's Philosophy in Its Principles," in his *Essays in Jewish Philosophy* (Cincinnati, 1929), pp. 219–300; L. Strauss, "The Law of Reason in the *Kuzari*," *PAAJR*, XIII (1943); and H. A. Wolfson, "Halevi and Maimonides on Prophecy," *JQR*, n.s., XXXII (1942), 345–70; XXXIII (1942), 49–82.

Joseph Ibn Zaddik's *Sefer Ha-Olam Ha-Katan* was edited by S. Horovitz (Breslau, 1903). On his thought, see M. Doctor, *Die Philosophie des Josef Ibn Zaddik* (Münster, 1895), and G. Vajda, "La Philosophie et la théologie de Joseph Ibn Zaddiq," in *Archives d'histoire doctrinale et litteraire du moyen âge* (1949).

Abraham Ibn Daud's philosophical work *Emunah Ramah* was edited in Hebrew and translated into German by S. Weil (Frankfurt-am-Main, 1852). His historical chronicle *Sefer Ha-Kabbalah* was edited by A. Neubauer in *Medieval Jewish Chronicles and Chronological Notes*, 2 vols. (Oxford, 1887). A new critical edition, with a translation into English and notes, was issued by G. D. Cohen (Philadelphia, 1967).

On Ibn Daud's philosophy, see Jacob Guttmann, *Die Religionsphilosophie des Abraham Ibn Daud* (Göttingen, 1879); Julius Guttmann, *Philosophies of Judaism* (Philadelphia, 1964); and I. Husik, *A History of Medieval Jewish Philosophy* (Philadelphia, 1916).

CHAPTER SIX

MAIMONIDES

A number of volumes of Maimonides' *Mishneh Torah* have been rendered into English by various translators under the general editorship of J. Obermann (New Haven, 1949 *et seq.*). The series is entitled *The Code of Maimonides*. On Maimonides as Talmudist and codifier, see L. Blau, *Das Gesetzbuch des Maimonides historisch betrachtet* (Leipzig, 1914); Ch. Tchernowitz, "Maimonides as Codifier," *Maimonides Octocentennial Series*, Pt. III (New York, 1935).

Maimonides' *Moreh Nevuchim* was translated into English by M. Friedlaender under the title *The Guide for the Perplexed*, 3 vols. (London, 1881–85). A one-volume edition of this translation, without notes, was also published (5th impression, London, 1928). A splendid new translation with introduction and notes by S. Pines, together with an introductory essay by L. Strauss, recently appeared (Chicago, 1963). The Arabic text of the original, *Dalalat al-Ha'irin*, was published, together with a French translation entitled *Le Guide des égarés*, in 3 vols. by S. Munk (Paris, 1856–66). A German translation, *Führer der Unschlüssigen*, was published by A. Weiss in 3 vols. (Leipzig, 1923–24).

The literature on Maimonides as a philosopher is immense, and only a few items can be listed here. A valuable older collection of essays on Maimonides' philosophy is to be found in W. Bacher, M. Brann, D. Simonsen, J. Guttmann (eds.), *Moses ben Maimon, sein Leben, seine Werke und sein Einfluss* (Leipzig, 1908–14), which contains, among others, the following important essays: P. Bloch, "Charakteristik und Inhaltsangabe des Moreh Nebuchim"; H. Cohen, "Characteristik der Ethik Maimonis"; Jacob Guttmann, "Der Einfluss der Maimonidischen Philosophie auf das christliche Abendland"; and Jacob Guttmann, "Die Beziehungen der Religionsphilosophie des Maimonides zu den Lehren seiner jüdischen Vorgänger."

Other significant essays and books on Maimonides include A. Altmann, "Das Verhältnis Maimunis zur jüdischen Mystik," *MGWJ*, LXXX (1936); W. Bacher, *Die Bibelexegese Moses Maimunis* (Budapest, 1896); F. Bamberger, *Das System des Maimonides: eine Analyse des More Nevuchim vom Gottesbegriffe aus* (Berlin, 1935); S. W. Baron (ed.), *Essays on Maimonides* (New York, 1941); idem, "The Historical Outlook of Maimonides," *PAAJR*, VI (1935), 5–113; J. Becker, *Mishnato Ha-Pilosofit Shel Ha-Rambam* (Tel Aviv, 1956); B. Z. Bokser, *The Legacy of Maimonides* (New York, 1950); Z. Diesendruck, "Maimonides' Lehre von der Prophetie," *Jewish Studies in Memory of Israel Abrahams* (New York, 1927); Z. Diesendruck, "Die Teleologie bei Maimonides," *Hebrew Union College Annual*, V (Cincinnati, 1928); I. Efros, *Philosophical Terms in the Moreh Nebukhim* (New York, 1924); I. Epstein (ed.), *Moses Maimonides: Anglo-Jewish Papers in Connection with the Eighth Centenary of His Birth* (London, 1935); Julius Guttmann, *Die religiösen Motive in der Philosophie des Maimonides, Entwicklungsstufen der jüdischen Religion* (Giessen, 1927); E. Hoffman, *Die Liebe zu Gott bei Mose ben Maimon, ein Beitrag zur Geschichte der Religionsphilosophie* (Breslau, 1937); E. S. Koplowitz, *Die Abhängigkeit Thomas von Aquin von R. Moses ben Maimon* (Würzburg, 1935); J. L. Maimon, *R. Moshe ben Maimon* (Jerusalem, 1960); D. Rosin, *Die Ethik des Maimonides* (Breslau, 1876); S. B. Scheyer, *Das psychologische System des Maimonides* (Frankfurt-am-Main, 1945); L. Strauss, "Maimonides Lehre von der Prophetie und ihren Quellen," *Le Monde Oriental*, XXVIII (1934); idem, *Philosophie und Gesetz: Beiträge zum Verständnis Maimunis und seiner Vorläufer* (Berlin, 1935); idem, *Persecution and the Art of Writing* (Glencoe, Ill., 1952); J. Teicher, "Observations critiques sur l'interpretation traditionelle de la doctrine des attributs negatifs chez

Maimonide," *REJ*, 99 (1935); H. A. Wolfson, "Maimonides on Negative Attributes," *Louis Ginzberg Jubilee Volume* (New York, 1945); *idem*, "Note on Maimonides' Classification of the Sciences," *JQR*, n.s., 26 (1936).

For biographies of Maimonides, see I. Abrahams and D. Yellin, *Maimonides* (Philadelphia, 1903); A. J. Heschel, *Maimonides: Eine Biographie* (Berlin, 1935); S. Zeitlin, *Maimonides: A Biography* (New York, 1935); and I. Münz, *Maimonides: The Story of His Life and Genius*, translated from the German, with an introduction, by H. T. Schnittkind (Boston, 1935).

CHAPTER SEVEN

ABRAHAM IBN EZRA

Some of Abraham Ibn Ezra's poems are contained in his *Diwan* which was edited by J. Egers in 1886. Many others are to be found, with a German translation, in D. Rosin, *Reime und Gedichte des Abraham Ibn Ezra* (Breslau, 1885–94). Fifty-one previously unpublished poems of Ibn Ezra were published by H. Brody in *Yediot Ha-Machon Le-Heker Ha-Shirah Ha-Ivrit*, VI (1945), 1–45. Some of his liturgical poems were published by N. Ben-Menahem in *Sinai*, XXI (1947) and XXV (1949).

On Ibn Ezra as a poet, see T. Lewin, *Avraham Ibn Ezra: Hayyav Ve-Shirato* (Jerusalem, 1969); M. Sachs, *Die religiöse Poesie der Juden in Spanien*, 2nd ed. (Berlin, 1901); K. Albrecht, "Studien zu den Dichtungen Abraham ben Ezras," *Zeitschrift der deutschen morgenländlichen Gesellschaft*, LVII (1903); D. Kahana, *Rabbi Avraham Ibn Ezra*, 2 vols. (Warsaw, 1894); and S. M. Stern, "The Muwashshahs of Abraham Ibn Ezra," in *Hispanic Studies in Honor of J. González-Llubera* (Oxford, 1959).

On Ibn Ezra as a Bible exegete and philologist, see W. Bacher, *Ibn Ezras Einleitung zum Pentateuchkommentar* (Vienna, 1876); *idem*, *Abraham Ibn Ezra als Grammatiker* (Strassburg, 1882); M. Friedlaender, *Essays on the Writings of Abraham Ibn Ezra* (London, 1877).

Ibn Ezra's philosophy is discussed by D. Rosin, "Die Religionsphilosophie Abraham Ibn Ezras," *MGWJ*, XLII (1898), XLIII (1899); G. Orschansky, *Abraham Ibn Ezra als Philosoph* (Breslau, 1900); Julius Guttmann, *Philosophies of Judaism* (Philadelphia, 1964); I. Husik, *A History of Medieval Jewish Philosophy* (Philadelphia, 1916); and S. Heller-Wilensky in *Tarbitz*, XXXII (1962–63), 227–95.

On Ibn Ezra's astrological notions, see R. Levy, *The Astrological Works of Abraham Ibn Ezra* (Baltimore, 1927). His astronomical work is discussed by J. M. Millás, "Avodato shel R. Avraham Ibn Ezra Be-Ḥochmat Ha-Techunah," *Tarbitz*, IX (1937–38), 306–22, and by A. Marx, "The Scientific Work of Some Outstanding Medieval Jewish Scholars," in *Essays and Studies in Memory of Linda R. Miller* (New York, 1938).

CHAPTER EIGHT

THE SATIRICAL ROMANCE IN HEBREW LITERATURE

A new edition of Alḥarizi's *Taḥkemoni* by Y. Toforovsky appeared in Tel Aviv in 1952. His *Maḥberot Itiel* was also published in a new edition by Y. Peretz (Tel Aviv, 1951). The introductory *makama* and the first fifteen "gates" of the *Taḥkemoni* were translated by V. Reichert in his *The Taḥkemoni of Judah Alḥarizi* (Jerusalem, 1965).

On Alḥarizi's work, see K. Albrecht, *Die im Tachkemoni vorkommenden Angaben über Harizis Leben, Studien und Reisen* (Göttingen, 1890); A. Levy, "Juda Al-Harizi," *REJ*, LIX (1910), Appendix, pp. vii–xxvi; J. Schirmann, *Die hebräische Übersetzung der Maqamen des Hariri* (Frankfurt-am-Main, 1930); *idem*, "Le-Ḥeker Mekorotav Shel Sefer Taḥkemoni Le-Yehudah Alḥarizi," *Tarbitz*, XXIII (1952), 198–202; *idem*, "Yehudah Alḥarizi Ha-Meshorer Veha-Mesapper," *Moznayim*, XI (1940), 101–15; and A. Percikowitsch, *Al-Harizi als Übersetzer der Makamen Al-Hariris* (Munich, 1932).

An edition of Solomon Tzakbel's *makama* "Neum Asher ben Yehudah" was published by J. Schirmann in *Yediot Ha-Machon Le-Ḥeker Ha-Shirah Ha-Ivrit*, II (1936), 152–62.

On the work of Jehudah Ibn Shabbetai and Isaac, see D. Kaufmann, *Gesammelte Schriften*, III, 470–77 (Frankfurt-am-Main, 1915); I. Davidson, *Parody in Jewish Literature* (New York, 1907); and H. Gross, *Die Satire in der jüdischen Literatur* (1908).

Joseph ben Meir Zabara's *Sefer Shaashuim* was edited, with introduction and notes, by I. Davidson (New York, 1914). A fine translation into English was published by Moses Hadas under the title *The Book of Delight*, with an introduction by Merriam Sherwood (New York, 1932). On Zabara's work, see I. Abrahams, *The Book of Delight and Other Papers* (Philadelphia, 1912); M. Steinschneider, "Joseph Ibn Sebara," in *Gesammelte Schriften*, I (1925), 162–71; and E. Baneth, "Bemerkungen zum Sefer Scha'aschuim," *MGWJ*, LIX (1915), 121–30 and 170–79.

CHAPTER NINE

EPICS, ROMANCES, AND FABLES

For Peter Alfonsi, see A. Hilka and W. Söderhjelm (eds.), *Die disciplina clericalis des Petrus Alfonsi* (Heidelberg, 1911), and J. Jacobs, *Jewish Ideals* (London, 1896).

An English translation of the *Sefer Ha-Yashar* was published (New York, 1840) under the title *The Book of Jasher* by Mordecai Manuel Noah, with a preface on the history of the book. For a discussion of its Jewish sources, see L. Zunz, *Die gottesdienstliche Vorträge der Juden*, 2nd ed., pp. 163–65.

An edition of Abraham Ibn Hasdai's *Ben Ha-Melech Veha-Nazir* was published by A. M. Habermann (Tel Aviv, 1952). On the original sources of this work, see N. Weisslowitz, *Prinz und Derwisch* (Munich, 1890); J. Jacobs, *Barlaam and Josaphat* (London, 1896); and H. Peri (Pflaum), *Der Barlaam-Legende* (Salamanca, 1959). For comprehensive bibliographies, see M. Steinschneider, *Hebräischen Übersetzungen* (1893), pp. 863–67, and V. Chauvin, *Bibliographie des ouvrages arabes*, III (Liège, 1892–1922).

On Jacob ben Eleazar and *Kalilah Ve-Dimnah* see J. Dérenbourg, *Deux versions hebraïques du livre Kalilah et Dimnah* (Paris, 1881), and M. Steinschneider, "Zu Kalila we-Dimna," *Zeitschrift der deutschen morgenländlichen Gesellschaft*, XXVII (1873), 553–65. See also C. Brockelmann, "Kalila wa-Dimna," in *Encyclopedia of Islam*, III (London, 1927). For Jacob ben Eleazar's poetry, see J. Schirmann, "Sippurei Ha-Ahavah Shel Yaakov Ben Eleazar," in *Yediot Ha-Machon Le-Heker Ha-Shirah Ha-Ivrit*, V (1939), 209–66, and "Les Contes rimés de Jacob ben Eleazar de Tolède," in *Le Mémorial E. Lévi-Provençal* (Paris, 1961).

A new edition of *Mishlei Sendebar* was published by A. M. Habermann (Tel Aviv, 1946). An English translation by M. Epstein appears in his *Tales of Sendebar* (Philadelphia, 1967).

Isaac Ibn Sahulah's *Meshal Ha-Kadmoni* was published by Y. Toforovsky in a new edition (Tel Aviv, 1953). On Ibn Sahulah, see S. M. Stern, "Rationalists and Kabbalists in Medieval Allegory," *Journal of Jewish Studies,* VI (1955), 73–86.

A new edition of Berechyah Ha-Nakdan's *Mishlei Shualim* was published by A. M. Habermann (Jerusalem, 1946). An English translation by M. Hadas under the title *Fables of a Jewish Aesop* appeared recently (New York, 1967). Berechyah's *Dodi Ve-Nechdi* (his Hebrew translation of Adelard of Bath's *Quaestiones Naturales*) was edited, with an English translation, by H. Gollancz (London, 1920). Gollancz also edited, and translated into English, Berechyah's ethical treatises, *Sefer Ha-Ḥibbur* and *Sefer Ha-Matzref* (London, 1902).

Glossary of Hebrew Terms

Aggadah (or **Haggadah**): The non-legal part of the post-Biblical Oral Torah, consisting of narratives, legends, parables, allegories, poems, prayers, theological and philosophical reflections, etc. Much of the Talmud is aggadic, and the Midrash literature, developed over a period of more than a millennium, consists almost entirely of Aggadah.

Amora (pl. **Amoraim**): The title given to the Jewish scholars of Palestine and especially of Babylonia in the third to the sixth centuries whose work and thought is recorded in the Gemara of the Talmud.

dayyan: A judge in a rabbinical court who is competent to decide on cases involving monetary matters and civil law as well as questions of a religious or ritual character.

Gaon (pl. **Geonim**): The spiritual and intellectual leaders of Babylonian Jewry in the post-Talmudic period, from the sixth through the eleventh centuries C.E. The head of each of the two major academies of Babylonia, at Sura and Pumbeditha, held the title Gaon. The Geonim had considerable secular power as well as religious authority, and their influence extended over virtually all of world Jewry during the larger part of the Geonic age. The title Gaon is occasionally applied in a general honorific sense to a very eminent Judaic scholar.

genizah: A depository for used and damaged sacred books, manuscripts, religious utensils, etc. The most widely known *genizah* was discovered in modern times in the synagogue of Fostat (Old Cairo), which was built in 882.

Hasidism: A religious and social movement established by Israel Baal Shem Tov (1700–61) in Volhynia and Podolia, based on the Kabbalah as expounded by Rabbi Isaac Luria. Hasidism stressed the omnipresence of God and encouraged religious ecstasy, joyfulness, and humility.

Haskalah: The movement for disseminating modern European culture among Jews from about 1750 to 1880. It advocated the modernization of Judaism, the westernization of traditional Jewish education, and the revival of the Hebrew language.

Kabbalah: The mystical religious tradition in Judaism. This tradition is described at length throughout the present *History*.

Kaddish: The best-known doxology in the Jewish liturgy. Originally recited at the conclusion of an exposition of the Aggadah in a house of study, it eventually became the special prayer for mourners.

maamad (pl. *maamadot*): A complete set of *pityyutim* for the Day of Atonement (see *piyyut*).

maskil (pl. *maskilim*): An adherent of Haskalah (see above).

Midrash (pl. **Midrashim**): The discovery of new meanings besides literal ones in the Bible. The term is also used to designate collections of such Scriptural exposition. The best-known of the Midrashim are the Midrash Rabbah, Tanhuma, Pesikta De-Rav Kahana, Pesikta Rabbati, and Yalkut Shimeoni.

Mishnah: The legal codification containing the core of the post-Biblical Oral Torah, compiled and edited by Rabbi Judah Ha-Nasi at the beginning of the third century c.e.

Mitnagdim: The opponents of Hasidism. They obtained this title after the issuance of an excommunication against the adherents of the Hasidic movement by Elijah, the Gaon of Vilna, in 1772.

paytan: A liturgical poet (see *piyyut*).

pilpul: In Talmudic and rabbinic literature, a clarification of a difficult point. Later the term came to denote a sharp dialectical distinction or, more generally, a certain type of Talmudic study emphasizing dialectical distinctions and introduced into the Talmudic academies of Poland by Jacob Pollak in the sixteenth century. Pejoratively, the term means hairsplitting.

piyyut (pl. *piyyutim*): A Hebrew liturgical poem. The practice of writing such poems began in Palestine, probably around the fifth century c.e., and continued for centuries, enriching the Jewish Prayer Book. Perhaps the greatest of the medieval writers of *piyyutim* were Solomon Ibn Gabirol and Moses Ibn Ezra.

Sanhedrin: A Hebrew word of Greek origin designating, in rabbinic literature, the assembly of seventy-one ordained scholars which served both as the supreme court and the legislature of Judaism in the Talmudic age. The Sanhedrin disappeared before the end of the fourth century C.E.

sefirah (pl. *sefirot*): A technical term in Kabbalah, employed from the twelfth century on, to denote the ten potencies or emanations through which the Divine manifests itself.

selihah (pl. *selihot*): A special type of *piyyut* begging mercy and pardon for sin.

Shechinah: A term used to imply the presence of God in the world, in the midst of Israel, or with individuals. In contrast to the principle of divine transcendence, Shechinah represents the principle of divine immanence.

Index

Index

Index

Über die Metra und Versgedichte,
63n

Varlaam and Josaphat (*Baarlaam and Josaphat*), 189
Verhältnis Albert dem Grossen zu Moses Maimonides, Das, 150n
Voskhod, xi

Waxman, Meyer, x
Wegen Alt-Yiddishen Roman, 193n
Weinreich, Max, x
Weiss, Isaac Hirsch, x
Weisslowitz, N., 189n, 192n, 194n
Wiener, S., 200n
Wise, Stephen S., 54n
Wissenschaft des Judentums, ix, x, xiv

Yad Ha-Hazakah (*Mishneh Torah*), 134, 136–39
Yahuda, A. S., 116n
Yalkut Shimeoni, 188n
Yashar, Sefer Ha-, 186–88

Yellin, David, 27n, 28n
Yesod Ha-Mispar, 158n
Yesod Mora, 158n
Yevreyskaya Entsiklopedia, xii
Yevreyskaya Starina, xi
Yevreyski Mir, xi
Yiddishe Velt, Die, xii
Yuhasin (Abraham Zacuto), 108n

Zabara, Joseph ben Meir, 181–84, 190, 198
Zacuto, Abraham, 108
Zambri, Joseph, 62n
Zangwill, Israel, xix, 49n, 60n
Zifronovitz, A., 119n
Zinberg, Israel, xi–xix
Zohar, xvi, 10
Zunz, Leopold, ix, x, xiv, 75, 187
Zur Geschichte der jüdischen Poesie, 63n, 174n
Zur Geschichte und Literatur, x
Zur Kenntnis der neu-hebräischen religiösen Poesie, 53n

This book was set in eleven point Janson, it was composed, printed and bound by Kingsport Press, Kingsport, Tennessee, the paper is 'Lock Haven' Offset, manufactured by the Hammermill Paper Company. The design is by Edgar J. Frank. Initial design is by Edward F. Zink.